ROUTLEDGE LIBRARY EDITIONS:
TRADE UNIONS

Volume 10

ECONOMIC CRISIS, TRADE UNIONS AND THE STATE

ECONOMIC CRISIS, TRADE UNIONS AND THE STATE

Edited by
OTTO JACOBI, BOB JESSOP,
HANS KASTENDIEK and MARINO REGINI

Routledge
Taylor & Francis Group
LONDON AND NEW YORK

First published in 1986 by Croom Helm Ltd.

This edition first published in 2023
by Routledge
4 Park Square, Milton Park, Abingdon, Oxon OX14 4RN

and by Routledge
605 Third Avenue, New York, NY 10158

Routledge is an imprint of the Taylor & Francis Group, an informa business

British Library Cataloguing in Publication Data
A catalogue record for this book is available from the British Library

ISBN: 978-1-032-37553-3 (Set)
ISBN: 978-1-032-39321-6 (Volume 10) (hbk)
ISBN: 978-1-032-39332-2 (Volume 10) (pbk)
ISBN: 978-1-003-34924-2 (Volume 10) (ebk)

DOI: 10.4324/9781003349242

Publisher's Note
The publisher has gone to great lengths to ensure the quality of this reprint but points out that some imperfections in the original copies may be apparent.

Disclaimer
The publisher has made every effort to trace copyright holders and would welcome correspondence from those they have been unable to trace.

ECONOMIC CRISIS, TRADE UNIONS AND THE STATE

Edited by

Otto Jacobi, Bob Jessop, Hans Kastendiek and Marino Regini

CROOM HELM

London • Sydney • Dover, New Hampshire

Croom Helm Ltd, Provident House, Burrell Row,
Beckenham, Kent BR3 1AT

Croom Helm Australia Pty Ltd, Suite 4, 6th Floor,
64-76 Kippax Street, Surry Hills, NSW 2010, Australia

British Library Cataloguing in Publication Data

Economic crisis, trade unions and the state.
1. Industrial relations – Europe
I. Jacobi, Otto
331'.094 HD8376.5

ISBN 0-7099-1447-4

Croom Helm, 51 Washington Street, Dover,
New Hampshire 03820, USA

Library of Congress Cataloging in Publication Data
Main entry under title:

Economic crisis, trade unions, and the state.

Includes index.
1. Industrial relations–Great Britain–addresses, essays, lectures. 2. Industrial relations–Italy–addresses, essays, lectures. 3. Industrial relations–Germany (West)–addresses, essays, lectures.
4. Trade-unions–Europe–addresses, essays, lectures.
5. Europe–economic conditions–1945- –addresses, essays, lectures. I. Jacobi, Otto.
HD8391.E26 1986 331'.094 85-28055
ISBN 0-7099-1447-4

Printed and bound in Great Britain by
Biddles Ltd, Guildford and King's Lynn

CONTENTS

PREFACE

This volume, like a parallel one on "Technological Change, Rationalization and Industrial Relations", is a result of tri-national co-operation. Most of the contributions were originally presented at two conferences which we organised at Cambridge and at Torino in autumn 1983. There were several crucial preconditions for the - as we hope - successful outcome of both volumes. We thank the authors for their readiness to revise, in some cases rather substantially, their papers for publication; Bob Jessop and Marino Regini for their active share in editorial responsibility; Ingrid Zierold, who works with us in Frankfurt, for her assistance. Bob Jessop played the key role in preparing the whole volume for publication and revised some of the translations. We are also indebted to the Volkswagen Foundation for funding our present research project on the relationship between trade unions and the state in Great Britain, Italy and West Germany and for sponsoring the meetings at Cambridge and Torino. Additional subsidies were given by the German Research Council and by the Goethe-Institut at Torino.

Otto Jacobi and Hans Kastendiek

Institut fuer Sozialforschung
Frankfurt am Main, July 1984

ABBREVIATIONS

ACAS	Arbitration, Conciliation and Advisory Service
BAG	Bundesarbeitsgericht (Federal Labour Court)
BL	British Leyland
BSC	British Steel Corporation
CA	Concerted Action
CBI	Confederation of British Industry
CDU	Christlich-Demokratische Union
CGIL	Confederazione Generale Italiana di Lavoro
CIR	Commission on Industrial Relations
CISL	Confederazione Italiana Sindacati Liberi
CSU	Christlich-Soziale Union
DC	Democrazia Cristiana
DGB	Deutscher Gewerkschaftsbund
EETPU	Electrical, Electronic, Telecommunications and Plumbing Union
ESC	Economic and Social Council
FDP	Freie Deutsche Partei
GCHQ	General Communications Headquarters
GDP	Gross Domestic Product
KA	Konzertierte Aktion
KWS	Keynesian Welfare State
NCB	National Coal Board
NEDC	National Economic Development Council
NHS	National Health Service
OECD	Organisation for Economic Cooperation and Development
PCI	Partito Communista Italiano
PSI	Partito Socialista Italiano
SDP	Social Democratic Party
SPD	Sozialdemokratische Partei Deutschlands
TUC	Trade Union Congress
UIL	Unione Italiana del Lavoro
YTS	Youth Training Scheme

Introduction

CORPORATIST AND LIBERAL RESPONSES TO THE CRISIS OF POSTWAR CAPITALISM

Bob Jessop, Otto Jacobi, Hans Kastendiek

This volume is most directly concerned with the changing relations between trade unions and the state in the current economic crisis. The contributors do not restrict themselves to this issue, however, since it is closely connected to many other questions. Some of these questions concern the specificity of different national formations and conjunctures and are discussed more fully in the relevant parts of the present volume. Here we intend to examine the economic crises whose specific national character and political repercussions form the backdrop to the following essays. In general terms economic crisis as such has no immediate and unequivocal consequences for union-state relations. To argue otherwise would involve neglecting the complex mediations involved in the organisational forms and strategies of trade unions, various branches and agencies of the state, and other significant economic and political actors. It would mean neglecting the crucial role played by the <u>organisational</u> and <u>political</u> repercussions of economic crisis in providing the immediate stimulus for reshaping and reworking such relations. This is nowhere more obvious than in the changing significance of unemployment and inflation and the fact that governments today can be re-elected with record levels of unemployment: a politically unimaginable event in the years when the Keynesian welfare state was at its height. But many other examples could be cited.

This does not mean that economic crisis is completely irrelevant to the changing patterns of union-state relations. Above all the changing nature of the capital relation and the dominant pattern of accumulation impose significant constraints on these as on other social relations. But these constraints are often effective only <u>post hoc</u> and are mediated through learning experiences which depend in turn on economic and political strategies and the balance of economic and political forces. Thus, if we devote some attention to the crisis of postwar capitalism, it is to sketch a crucial parameter delimiting economic and political struggles over the most appropriate response to economic crisis. We deal first with the nature of the postwar boom and its political framework before the crisis first became widely evident in 1974-5. We then consider the current crisis and its principal features. Next we discuss two tendencies discernible in the various solutions to the crisis currently being sought and comment on their implications for union-state relations. Finally we locate the specific problems of the three countries considered in this volume in terms of their different situations in the global crisis <u>within</u> capitalism (we are not witnessing the global crisis <u>of</u> capitalism) and assess their implications for the relations between state and unions.

The Postwar Boom: Accumulation and Political Economy

One of the problems involved in considering union-state relations is to identify the general economic conjuncture in which they operate. We argue here that significant changes are required because the general context has changed. Although most of our contributors do not explicitly refer to this context, it is evident that one phase of capital accumulation is ending and the search for a new regime of accumulation is under way. Such an approach is often identified with long-wave analyses of capitalist development and we have some sympathy with these sorts of analysis - particularly those that adopt an institutional approach. In following this line of enquiry we are not arguing for an ineluctable and unilinear periodisation of capitalist development. But there is considerable historical evidence for distinct phases of economic performance, each with its own momentum, over the last century and a half. These phases of capitalist expansion do not follow an inexorable logic nor do they obey quasi-natural economic laws of motion. There is also considerable scope for variation in performance across different economies. But these phases are associated with a general set of institutions and policies not only at the international level but even at the national level. The movement from one phase to another can have various causes and is often precipitated by exogenous factors or accidental shocks. Nonetheless the basic vulnerability of a given phase with its distinctive regime of accumulation is often rooted in more significant endogenous factors (for a general survey of long-wave theories and an examination of different phases, see Maddison, 1982, pp. 94-5).

The dominant regime of accumulation in the capitalist world economy after 1945 involved the consolidation of Fordism in the accumulation process and the hegemony of the USA in the world economy.

Fordism can be characterised briefly as a pattern of capital accumulation based on mass production and mass consumption. In more detail it involves the following elements: the development of mass production based on moving assembly-line techniques and the expansion of semi-skilled labour at the expense of both skilled and unskilled labour; managerial concern with the organisation of the collective labour process in an enterprise rather than with the fragmented labour performed by the de-skilled individual worker (i.e., the dominance of Fordism over Taylorism); the liberalisation of trade and the transnationalisation of production; the much increased importance of the wage-relation (as opposed to, but certainly not to the exclusion of, domestic labour) in securing the reproduction of wage-labour; the correspondingly increased importance of the mass consumption of standardised commodities and/or the collective consumption of goods and services provided by the state in contrast with the consumption of individualised commodities and/or home-produced goods and services; and, finally, the increased importance of the state in securing the conditions for economic growth and the reproduction of wage-labour.

The postwar period has often been described as 'Keynesian'. But this label disguises as much as it illuminates. For it suggests that the primary characteristic of the postwar period was state intervention in the sphere of distribution (on the demand side) rather than the capitalist reorganisation of the labour process in the sphere of production (on the supply side). It also generalises the Keynesian practices of some governments to all metropolitan capitalist societies. Yet several leading economies did not adopt an explicitly Keynesian approach or did so at a late stage in the development of postwar capitalism (most notably the USA, France, Italy, West Germany, and Japan in contrast to Britain, Austria, and Scandinavia). On the other hand both the explicitly Keynesian and the non-Keynesian economies were all committed to a strategy of postwar reconstruction and economic expansion based on Fordism. Moreover, even where Keynesian techniques were pursued by government, any success they might have had (and it is by no means certain that such techniques were universally successful) was clearly related to the more general economic conjuncture provided by Fordism and US hegemony. In this sense the 'Keynesian' label can easily exaggerate the importance of Keynesian techniques in securing full employment even where Keynesianism was explicitly adopted. Finally this label emphasises the ideological framework of policy-making at the expense of the actual policy and institutional conditions which secured postwar growth. Thus we find many politicians and commentators ignoring the complex ensemble of conditions underpinning the postwar boom and arguing for a return to the Keynesian welfare state (hereafter the 'KWS') as a solution to current problems.

In contrast we prefer to see Keynesianism in the context of Fordism - as one among a range of techniques for securing economic expansion in the Fordist regime. Specifically it involves using budgetary policy to manipulate aggregate demand in the interests of full employment and stable economic growth within a generally favourable global economic conjuncture. How far individual governments committed themselves to full employment and/or adopted Keynesianism to this end depended on the institutional structures and balance of economic and political forces in particular societies (see, for example, Apple, 1983).

The second important factor in the postwar boom was the hegemony of the United States in the postwar world. This was based on its dominant position in terms of gold reserves, share in world industrial output, ability to provide essential capital goods during postwar reconstruction, and nuclear predominance. In arguing that the USA was hegemonic, however, we are not simply saying that the USA was dominant. Economic hegemony does not just involve the use of economic, military, and political power to promote the particular interests of the dominant nation. Instead it involves the exercise of economic <u>leadership</u> in such a way that not only are the <u>long-term</u> interests of the hegemonic nation served but also the more immediate interests of other nations; in turn this means that the hegemonic power must sometimes sacrifice its short-term interests so that it can help secure the cohesion and stability of the global system. It is in this sense that we can argue that there is currently a crisis of US hegemony in the world economy. For the United States is now using its undoubted economic, military, and political power primarily to defend its short-term interests at the expense of other national economies and global stability.

These twin features of the postwar boom phase had important implications for the economic role of the state and the political regime of accumulation. The state acquired responsibility for actively managing the national economy to secure the conditions for continued economic growth and mass consumption. It also had to ensure that its national economic policies were complementary to the global regime of accumulation. This responsibility was exercised through the use of fiscal, budgetary, and monetary policy to regulate the national economy (especially, but not exclusively, at the macro-level) and/or to influence the allocation of investment capital to productive purposes in order to supplement the logic of market competition and the decisions of banking capital. In turn this implied that the interests of capital and labour coincided at least in respect of maintaining aggregate demand and full employment since full employment is a major precondition for the maintenance of demand in the mass production-mass consumption system (cf. Przeworski, 1980).

This permitted (but did not necessarily ensure) the corresponding recognition of trade union rights of organisation and collective bargaining and the political acceptance of trade unions as more or less active social partners in economic and political management. In any event the development of economic growth and full employment transformed the bargaining power of trade unions even where they operated only within the framework of market forces and did not (or could not) reinforce their market power through direct political bargaining. Also linked to this pattern of class compromise was the possibility of building and extending a welfare state. This possibility reflected both the increased political acceptability of the demands of unions and/or labour parties and the scope which an expanding welfare system offered to socialise the reproduction of labour-power and to enhance the economic leverage of the state in managing the national economy.

It is in this sense that we can talk of the 'Keynesian welfare state' as a _theoretically typical_ feature of the period of the postwar boom. But this does not mean that it was _empirically universal_. Not all metropolitan capitalist societies actually developed a 'KWS' (some retained a dual economy without complete Fordism and/or developed only a social security state); nor does it mean that those societies which developed a 'KWS' restricted their governments and unions to the limited role envisaged in its initial liberal version based on contra-cyclical budgetary policy and an insurance-based welfare system. Indeed some commentators have suggested that there is an inherent dynamic to the KWS which leads to progressively greater and deeper state involvement (e.g.,

Martin, 1979). Differences in this respect were related to national variations in institutional structures politically as well as economically and/or to the changing balance of forces among capital, labour, and intermediate groupings. In turn these variations influenced the nature and timing of the economic crisis which currently affects the capitalist world.

Beyond Postwar Capitalism

It is well-known that the postwar boom began to falter in the late 'sixties and that the first oil price shock in 1973-4 precipitated the eventual collapse of the postwar regime of accumulation. At the time it was less evident what economic and political responses were appropriate and what new regime(s) of accumulation might follow both globally and on the national level. Indeed the response(s) are still crystallising (often on an *ad hoc*, trial and error basis) and the process of rebuilding a regime of accumulation still continues. Nonetheless certain basic parameters can be sketched with due regard for future uncertainties and national variations.

The most significant shifts since 1974-5 have been the growing consolidation of a 'post-Fordist' system of production and reorganisation of the international economic system in the wake of the crisis of US hegemony. The newly dominant labour process introduces electronics and the micro-chip into production and permits (without requiring) the polarisation of the labour force into unskilled manual workers and highly skilled workers with developed mental and/or supervisory roles. Internationally we can observe a move from fixed to floating exchange rates along with developing threats to freedom of trade and investment. Yet the internationalisation of production also continues apace and there are significant shifts in the international division of labour associated with the new pattern of production.

We can now identify two (by no means exhaustive) general conditions for a renewed upswing in accumulation. Firstly, there must be a favourable climate for a renewed cycle of investment, especially in the new technologies; and, secondly, there must be a new international economic order in which the USA alone or in combination (*pax trilateralis*?) re-establishes a hegemonic order. We are not concerned here with the second general condition. Moreover, owing to the brevity of this introduction, we cannot treat the first condition with the detail it deserves. But we can say that changing the balance of forces between capital and labour both economically and politically is particularly crucial and this in turn means attacking above all the concessions gained by the labour movement in organising the labour process and determining the size and nature of public expenditure and state economic involvement. It is in this context that the KWS is significant both symbolically and in terms of its real impact on the balance of forces in those countries where it has proved important. Thus the repertoire of responses typically includes an assault on the rights of unions in general and a retrenchment in the various components of the welfare state.

These conditions are reflected in the changing nature of state intervention in the economy. It is often remarked that the state was actively involved in constituting the conditions for the rise of capitalism, disengaged during the phase of liberal, competitive capitalism, and began to intervene again with the supposedly last and highest stage of monopoly capitalism. It is less often remarked that a similar periodicity of intervention characterises each of the different phases of capitalist development. Thus states were actively involved in creating the conditions for the postwar boom in the period of postwar reconstruction (which involved far more than simply Keynesian demand management and extended to the supply side and capital-labour relations more generally), disengaged somewhat in the hey-day of the postwar boom, and began to intervene more fully as the boom began to falter. Likewise states must now intervene once again on the supply-side to create the conditions for the next long wave of capital accumulation. This is evident even among supposedly liberal regimes as well as among the more etatist and/or corporatist regimes. In all cases it is essential to remove the principal obstacles to renewed accumulation as well as to secure the appropriate incentives to investment and economic restructuring.

This point is worth stressing because of two contrasting (but complementary) fallacies in discussing the state's role in the postwar boom and in the current conjuncture. Supporters of current government strategies in Britain and elsewhere sometimes suggest that a massively interventionist state has been cut back and that the state is now playing a more liberal, laissez-faire role. This argument confuses the state's *actual* role at the *end* of the postwar phase with its *projected* role at the *height* of the coming phase. Conversely critics of these strategies sometimes suggest that the state's role in the postwar boom involved little more than macro-level demand management and socialised welfare provision whereas the state's current role involves significant supply-side intervention and the rise of the strong state in conjunction with major welfare retrenchment. This comparison stresses the limited and benign role of the state at the height of the postwar boom and neglects its important supply-side functions during the earlier period of postwar reconstruction - functions analogous to those being undertaken during the present period of restructuring to consolidate a fresh phase of accumulation. In neither case is like being compared with like and state intervention is therefore misrepresented.

The End of the KWS?

What does this imply for the future of the KWS? The conditions in which it might reinforce capital accumulation have passed and the fully developed KWS is now widely recognised as an obstacle to renewed accumulation. In particular it is seen as a disincentive to investment and to work and thereby undermines both sides of the capital-labour relation. This leads to rejection of the commitment to full employment based on the high wage economy presupposed in the high and rising levels of mass consumption associated with Fordism. In part this rejection reflects the end of the economic conditions which produced the full employment conjuncture of the postwar period and in part it reflects changes in the political and ideological climate that accompanied it. Likewise, whereas the postwar KWS was oriented to universal welfare benefits with an optimum level of provision as the dominant mode of collective consumption in the field of social policy, the current period is characterised by selective welfare benefits, a move towards minimal levels of provision, and greater reliance on private or market provision.

This is not to argue that only one version of a future regime of accumulation is possible. Patterns of accumulation will vary with many factors, including an economy's position in the international division of labour, contrasting linkages between state and economy, and different national traditions. Thus, to take only the second factor for the moment, just as we can distinguish in very broad terms between liberal and statist approaches to managing the postwar regime of accumulation (contrast the USA and France, Britain and Japan), so there appear to be at least two different types of response to the current crisis: a neo-liberal and a neo-statist solution. The changing economic conjuncture means that these approaches differ significantly from the liberal and statist approaches found in the three successive periods of the postwar regime of accumulation. For the primary focus of these new approaches is how to secure the introduction of a post-Fordist labour process and to restructure the international economic order in the light of an already consolidated international division of labour.

For the purposes of this introduction we restrict ourselves to the implications of these changes for union-state relations in neo-liberal and neo-statist responses. Essentially we can say that the neo-liberal response involves a strong emphasis on the recommodification of labour-power, the privatisation of the public sector, and the deregulation of the private sector. This involves fundamental changes in the role of organised labour and the scope of the welfare state - shifting the balance of power in the labour market towards capital and establishing a social security state alongside expanding market and occupational welfare systems. The social basis of this regime of accumulation is certainly not found in organised labour as a whole but instead there is an effort to create a supporting class of small businessmen and other petty bourgeois strata and/or to transform privileged groups of workers into petty property- and/or capital-owners. State involvement in the economy does not cease (although the rhetoric of a politicised monetarism might suggest otherwise) but it is more often fiscal in nature and/or oriented towards encouraging market forces rather than counter acting them.

In contrast the neo-statist response involves further decommodification to compensate for the deficiencies of the market, an active structural policy to improve market forces, and regulation to limit the operation of market forces. This is compatible with political exchanges with organised labour either through a policy of mutual sacrifice (along the lines of Austro-Keynesianism with its 'kollektive Verelendung') and/or through a bifurcation of organised labour into high-waged, productive sectors and low-waged, marginal, or redundant workers. In the changed international economic conjuncture, a concern with inflation is typically necessary and qualifies any commitment to full employment. But monetarism is more technical than political and is only one of several counter-inflationary techniques in which organised labour could become involved (cf. Jessop, below).

In sketching these responses we have avoided precise predictions about the role of unions. For the current conjuncture is one in which international factors are crucial and unions cannot play a major role here. In addition the precise character of the labour movement, including parties as well as union organisation, has a crucial intervening role. The three country studies below illustrate this well.

Different National Responses

Although we have written about the global crisis of capitalism, national responses to this crisis are clearly no more universal than they were in the 1930s. The latter decade witnessed, inter alia, the New Deal in the States and National Socialism in Germany, National Government in Britain and Social Democracy in Sweden. Responses today include Reaganism and Thatcherism, Mitterrand's socialist austerity programme, attempts at a social contract or political exchanges in Italy, and the Modell Deutschland. If the range of responses in the thirties was facilitated by the crisis of international economic hegemony order and the resort to protectionism and autarky, it is worth noting even today that a complex international division of labour need not require all national economies to pursue the same economic and political strategy. Not only is it impossible for every national economy to be hegemonic or dominant; but equally important is the need for non-hegemonic societies to follow complementary strategies. Aglietta has demonstrated the complementarity within Europe of, for example, the high-growth, regular devaluation strategy of France and the low-growth, disinflation strategy in West Germany (cf. Aglietta, 1982). Similarly the relatively closed economy of Japan and the 'workshop states' of Hong Kong and Taiwan require that other economies be relatively open if their expansion is to continue. Which countries will be favourably and which unfavourably integrated into this pattern will depend not on some overall systemic need but on the changing modalities of economic and political struggle in specific countries (cf. Lipietz, 1984). It is in this context that the question of neo-liberal and neo-statist responses becomes particularly interesting.

We have identified the pattern in West Germany as a <u>virtuous circle</u>. This virtuous circle depends on its favourable position within the postwar international division of labour as well as its uniquely flexible dual system of union representation. West Germany has specialised in the technologically advanced capital goods sector and is strongly export-oriented. Indeed it tends to enjoy a high trade surplus in almost any conjuncture. But it does depend crucially on the continued expansion of the world market (especially for capital goods) to maintain profits and investment; it also depends on continuing technological innovation to achieve 'technological rents', to sustain more basic industries, and to finance its high-wage economy. The principal domestic threats to this virtuous circle come from union opposition to rationalisation and to wage restraint. In principle these threats can be contained through the pressures of international competition in the dynamic export sector and/or through strict control over aggregate demand (amounting to disinflation) reinforced by effective regulation of distributional conflicts in those sectors least affected by international competition. During the seventies the pattern of disinflation and high growth linked with social partnership was reinforced by the emergence of the Modell Deutschland strategy with its selective corporatism combined with continued strong controls over monetary and exchange rate policy. In this way the state oriented its policies towards an export-led strategy and the social and political costs were managed through selective corporatism and a strong state.

In Britain the problem is not one of relative over-industrialisation (of being a strong link, so to speak, in a weak chain) but of progressive de-industrialisation (of being a weak link even when the chain was strong). The dominance of the commercial and overseas financial interests of the City at the expense of domestic industry, the veto power of a fragmented trade union movement, a particularly strong commitment to the KWS, a finely balanced adversary system of party competition, and, more recently, the transformation of sterling from an international reserve into a petro-currency - these have produced 'stagflationary' tendencies which have reinforced the long-term relative decline in Britain's international industrial competitiveness. The exhaustion of both the corporatist and the liberal approaches to management of the 'KWS' and the crisis of the political system provided the conditions for the movement to the neo-liberal Thatcherite solution. Thatcherism is committed to breaking out of the impasse in British political economy and is as much concerned with reorganising the unions and the welfare state in this context as it is to recommodification, privatisation, deregulation, and, significantly, internationalisation. The underlying weakness and fragmentation of the union movement and the continuing crisis in the political system mean that Thatcherism enjoys a degree of decisional autonomy in government missing in both Germany and Italy. This provides it with extensive room for pursuing policies intended to lead out of the impasse - whether or not they do so remains to be seen.

Italy is characterised by a virulent circle in which the impasse appears to be continually reproduced rather than resolved. This has much to do with the regime of accumulation in Italy - characterised by Aglietta as a vicious circle of hyperinflation and devaluation. This has existed since the investment- and export-led economic miracle of the fifties and early sixties was broken by the hot autumn of 1969 and the first oil shock. Internationally price-competitive consumer goods still have an important role in Italy's industrial structure but overall the Italian economy is not specialised and its competitiveness depends on the continued flexibility of its labour-force due to sub-contracting, the informal economy, and a dual labour market. Since 1973 the prospects for growth have rested precariously on the ability of competitive currency depreciation to boost exports and to provide a space for productivity growth. Such increased productivity as has occurred derives largely from labour-intensive industries and investment in micro-electronics. However this strategy has been limited by the indexation of prices and wages (which are adversely affected by depreciation of the lira and the movement in public sector prices) and the increasing resort to public subsidies to industry and agriculture to preserve political support. The weak tax base and the bureaucratism of the Italian state give a further twist to inflationary pressures. It is in this context that the Italian union movement has been involved in political exchanges focused around the *scala mobile*, state political support for organised labour, and support for industry. As our contributors show, however, this political exchange has failed. The impasse remains.

CONCLUSIONS

In this introduction we have sketched the background to the global economic crisis of postwar capitalism and the attempts to secure the conditions for a renewed period of accumulation and prosperity. In particular we have emphasised the difficulties of reverting to the economic and political *status quo ante* in terms of full employment, social welfare, and union-state relations. We have also sketched the background to the different national responses to the global economic crisis. For it is the specific institutional and organisational features of different national systems which mediate the impact of the global crisis and condition the specific responses in union-state relations as in other matters. The case studies below provide fascinating evidence for the variability of national responses and their contribution to a possible global recovery.

REFERENCES

M. Aglietta, 1982: 'World Capitalism in the Eighties', New Left Review, 136

N. Apple, 1983: 'The Rise of Full Employment Capitalism', in S. Clegg et al., (eds.), The State, Class, and Recession, London and Canberra

A. Lipietz, 1984: 'Imperialism or the Beast of the Apocalypse', Capital and Class, 22

A. Maddison, 1982: Phases of Capitalist Development, Oxford

A. Martin, 1979: 'The Dynamic of a Keynesian Economy', in C. Crouch, (ed.), State and Economy in Contemporary Capitalism, London

A. Przeworski, 1980: 'Social Democracy as an Historical Phenomenon', New Left Review, 122

PART ONE

"The Current Crisis: cul-de-sac or Crossroads?"

Chapter 1

THE END OF THE KEYNESIAN CONSENSUS*

Elmar Altvater, Kurt Huebner, Michael Stanger

The crisis in the mid seventies did not fall from a clear sky. But that the "thunderstorm of the world market" would thunder so violently, that in the ensuing years one depression would produce another, has given rise to much surprise. At first no-one really wanted to believe that the crisis of 1974 did not simply involve an economic downswing, which would soon be superseded by a renewed upswing as in the long period of prosperity after World War II, and that it also marked the beginning of a fundamental structural upheaval in the whole world economy. But it has since become apparent that this crisis is not only an economic crisis but also affects society as a whole and has in every respect a political dimension. As in all struggles for the survival of the fittest it is the weakest forces who have come to grief: within a highly industrialised Western Europe whole regions have been hit by de-industrialisation in the last ten years, whole sectors of the Western European capitalist societies have been eradicated, traditional and highly valued skills of employees have been rendered superfluous, traditional values have been questioned, and political guidelines and concepts have proved outdated.

Why have the economic policies, concepts and formulae of the 50s and 60s not sufficed for solving the crisis of the 70s and 80s?

This question not only refers to the crisis of the economy but to the crisis of a model of economic policy which for a long period of time was valid in almost all highly advanced capitalist countries which had implemented it only with slight modifications and which has to be replaced now. The post-war pattern of economic policy during the long period of prosperity was inspired by Keynesian thought and was thus called "Keynesianism" so that this period could be termed a

"Keynesian era". Its particular forms varied from country to country but the general principle was identical. Here we only want to describe the basic principle to get a better understanding of the consequences of the end of the Keynesian consensus.

The concept of Keynesianism identifies a policy model which seemed to be able, for a comparatively long period of time, to reconcile the contradiction between capitalism and liberal democracy. This contradiction was noted by Marx and has been emphasized now and again by more recent critics of capitalism (e. g. Kalecki, 1943, whose thesis of a "political economic cycle" rests on this contradiction, or Gintis and Bowles, 1981). The poles of this contradiction can be described as the politico-economical structures and the historical forces of the mode of production on the one hand, and, on the other, the system of domination and participation in society (as an ensemble of economic relations and political and ideological agencies). But it cannot be taken for granted that those who are being exploited (in the most general sense) in the production process will consent to this situation. Thus, if they do consent to exploitation, this must be due to specific "mystifications" and, within ideological discourses, to appeals which justify this relationship as being both natural and just - thereby leaving no hope of ever transforming it (cf. the extensive literature on the consciousness of wage-earners, see also Laclau 1981). It is also important that the growth process proceeds smoothly and that capital accumulation be profitable because this is a pre-requisite for satisfying the culturally defined level of material needs.

The contradiction between capitalism and liberal democracy takes concrete form as an always precarious relationship between the accumulation of capital and the creation of a consensus. In the theoretical debate about the state these two moments have been established as functions of the state, whose fulfilment is often mutually contradictory. These two sides of this contradiction are located, however, on different levels of the structure of society. For the accumulation of capital as a historical force in the mode of production and consensus as a principle of the formation of society are, as far as they are seen as the functional aspects of state policies, determined in different ways. As long as the means of production and the accumulation process are domains of privatised decision-making by the owners of capital and are thus "depoliticised", all decisions concerning them can be oriented to the logic of private capital realisation. But their legitimation and thus every creation of consent depends on whether the accumulation of capital also provides for the interests and needs of those who do not participate in such private "de-politicised" decisions or only play a subordinate position in this process. Joan Robinson saw the first big crisis of economics as an academic discipline in the fact that, during the world-wide depression of the thirties, it had not been able to analyse theoretically the level of employment and was thus unable to put forward arguments for an economic policy. Keynes himself defined the problem as follows:

> When 9,000,000 men are employed out of 10,000,000 willing and able to work, there is no evidence that the labour of these 9,000,000 men is misdirected. The complaint against the present system is not that these 9,000,000 men ought to be employed on different tasks, but that tasks should be available for the remaining 1,000,000 men. It is in determining the volume, not the direction, of actual employment that the existing system has broken down. (Keynes 1936:379).

What matters is, therefore, developing methods of economic policy which can raise the level of employment politically - provided this has not already taken place as a result of decentralised, de-politicised decisions about the production and accumulation process. A solution to this problem, which could thus eliminate this apparent shortcoming of the system, could be seen in politicising the decisions concerning production and accumulation, that is, by at least partially nationalising investments and by partly nationalising the means of production.

There are quite a few who suggested this way out of the dilemma created by the crisis: the Communist Parties in the form of radical nationalisation but also, in the course of the crisis in those days, the trade unions and parts of Social Democracy though in the moderate form of an "economic democracy."

The policy model which is so closely associated with Keynes, however, takes another path; and it was this which was followed in the post war period by almost all developed capitalist countries. It is concerned with a political exchange, a compromise between the classes. On the one hand, this exchange implies the fundamental acceptance of private control over the means of production, that is, the de-politicisation of the sphere of production, and, on the other hand, the capacity of the state to intervene in the economic process, through affecting the spheres of circulation and realisation. Micro-economy and macro-economy thus follow different criteria accord to a motto which was coined by the SPD at its party conference in 1954 in Dortmund: "As much market as possible, as much planning as necessary." The state can only secure its intervention potential with means rooted in the sphere of circulation: the law and the money. As both media are not only limited in quantity but are also as contradictory as society itself - from which they are after all taken - the effect of interventions is basically restricted by the system. But nevertheless this limitation does not appear equally clear in each phase of development. For a long time - from the immediate post war period till the mid-seventies - permanent income increases and securing a high level of employment, compensated - as a sort of "exchange" (quid pro quo) - for the abandonment of the politicisation of the production process. A special form of "industrial relations" was thus emerging, centred around the state as a decisive factor which was regarded as an active interventionist state engaged in economic policy by stimulating growth according to a formula coined by Willy Brandt in 1970: "Without economic growth - no internal reforms and on the other hand: without internal reforms no economic growth."

To understand this formula one must add, however, that growth is ultimately shaped by the decisions of private enterprises and that reform policy is ultimately shaped by the decisions of the state. This compromise was supposed to lead, symbiotically, to a social optimum. Both sides - growth and private capital; reforms and the state - became interdependent. And, last but not least, this interdependence was supposed to be for the benefit of all.

This model is especially clear in Scandinavian capitalism (Amoroso 1980). More generally, since the thirties, there was little dispute that production decisions (and thus the accumulation process) should remain in the hands of capital. This had its price, however, since it was likewise agreed that the political field should be consensually determined by the organisations of the labour movement, that is, by Social Democracy. Another part of the "Keynesian policy model" becomes apparent here: if it is possible for the economic and political spheres to be shaped by a different logic in each case, then it is also possible for Social Democracy to be "in command" of state policy. One might even go further. For it is highly functional for the system that, whereas the capital accumulation is organised by private capital, the task of organising consent is carried out by a party rooted in the mass of the wage and salary earners. This consensus, however, cannot be had for nothing. The reforms mentioned by Brandt cost money, the settlement of the interests of the masses makes it necessary to expand the welfare state. At this point we come to a further part of the "Keynesian policy model": the Keynesian interventionist state can only function as a guarantee as long as it works as a social welfare state, that is, as long as it is transferring funds by means of secondary distribution in order to protect the individual against the risks which are a corollary of wage labour and in order to guarantee an adequate standard of living to those who are not yet (children, young trainees) or no longer (pensioners) or who are temporarily and through no fault of theirs (sick persons, victims of accidents) not integrated into the work process.

An increasing part of wage-earners' income thus becomes a social wage via the mediation of the state with its social budget.[1] For that reason the equilibrium of accumulation and consensus is also related to material preconditions, to the feasibility of a redistribution via the welfare state. On the other hand this possibility widens and narrows according to the growth of what can be redistributed. In this context the logic of this policy model presupposes that the preconditions of redistribution can be created again by an indirect, indicative stimulation of growth, that is, by Keynesian interventions, even if the decisions about the accumulation of capital (the investment decisions) still remain with private enterprises. This implies, however, at least two problems.

First there is no guarantee that the logic of the accumulation decisions and of the targets of the state are congruent and that they can remain like that over a longer period of time. The separation of the political and economic spheres would have to be superseded to overcome this fundamental shortcoming of state interventionism. Otherwise there is no alternative for the state but the hope that the private decision-makers are willing to co-operate and "play the game". But unfortunately, even without the conscious compliance of the private agents, there are instabilities inherent in the accumulation process of capital. In particular the profit-oriented accumulation process proceeds cyclically and displays a tendency for the rate of profit to fall. But we are only concerned here with the consequences for the Keynesian policy model. In this context we should note that the class structure of capitalism means that conflicts over the conditions for the reproduction of the labour-power cannot be avoided. Wage disputes, conflicts about working conditions and rights of control in the factory are part and parcel of the everyday life of capitalist production. The success which can be achieved in these conflicts by the workers is not simply determined by their militancy (cf. Przeworski 1980). What is surely significant is the fact that, in a phase of prosperity, hence of successful Keynesian interventionism, the chances for imposing workers interests are favourable. As elements of the welfare state these interests can also be secured to some extent as achievements safeguarded by the state. In this way the reproduction of labour no longer depends predominantly on the relative power of capital and worker on the labour market but is mediated by the state. Thus the commodity character of labour is modified and the wage partly becomes a "citizen wage". This tendency actually undermines one principle of capitalist development, namely, the free ("free" in its capitalist meaning) labour market. Indeed, by undermining the market regulation of the price of labour, capitalism loses part of its flexibility to respond to its crisis tendencies with strategies of lowering wages.

But a <u>second reason</u> for the decreased potential is possibly even more important for growth. From its inherent logic capital generates an increase of the so-called organic composition of capital with negative effects on profitability: the tendency to control the conditions of the production process and to gain advantages in the competition of capitals by increasing the productivity of work, leads to a displacement of human labour by dead labour.[2] The effect of this mechanism is that profitability is not only hard-pressed as a result of the direct collision of interests between capital and labour but also by the latent strategies of capital to substitute human labour by dead labour. For a Keynesian economic policy this has far-reaching consequences because investments which are stimulated with the intention of securing employment have to mobilise ever increasing masses of capital to create the same amount of jobs.

This effect is emphasised by the fact that, during the long phase of prosperity, concentrations of capital have emerged which can thwart the state's attempts to control the economy solely by their disposition of sums of money - which is also used as an instrument of intervention by the state. By now it is trite to note that, because of the big companies, especially the transnational companies, and - increasingly important - the internationalisation of the credit systems, the regulation of the growth process by the nation-state encounters almost unsolvable problems. This development can also be interpreted as the victory of value (and the law of value) over the political control of the states (over Keynesianism as a political principle). There are in principle only two ways out of this situation: either the neo-liberal alternative, to clear the road for the capitalist logic of value and realisation to become "economic necessities" - by strengthening the free play of market forces and by a minimal state - or the politicisation of the sphere of production by seizing the production and investment decisions.

Considering that growth thus tends to stagnate because of a long-term fall in profitability of capital and that at the same time the capacity for stimulating investments by means of Keynesian intervention is restricted, society moves towards a "zero-sum game". Only those resources can be mobilised which have been taken from somewhere else because growth is stagnant or shows a downward movement. This, however, undermines the welfare state as the most important moment of the Keynesian policy model. The theoretical foundations for this process are supplied by the neo-liberal and monetarist dogma, which explains the causes of the crisis as an excessive drain on the production apparatus by the "claims and interests of social groups", especially those of the trade unions. According to this doctrine it is therefore very important to reduce the 'overload' which overburdens the scarce resources as well as the capacities of the political administrative system and/or to reverse the pathological dynamics of positive feedbacks which have been generated by the welfare state in order to put an end to the self-generating positive rate of increase of the social budget.

In the first phase of the crisis it seemed as if the welfare state was only being restructured to accommodate it to the changed situation without introducing substantial changes in its volume and targets; more recently, however, a cut-back of key elements of the welfare state is under way. Quantitatively this cut-back is not so far-reaching that the so-called "social security net" would be completely rolled up. It is, however, a crucial point that the qualitative principle of social welfare and security, hence the prevailing basis of the political stability of society, is under attack.

This implies the dismantling of the Keynesian model of an equilibrium of accumulation and consensus as the basis of a specific compromise. On the surface - it is the inflation which has increased in speed since the mid-sixties and has thus upset the 'trade off' between unemployment and inflation which forms the basis of every Keynesian policy. The 'discomfort index' has now replaced the 'Phillips graph' to describe the economic situation of a country: since the mid-seventies inflation and unemployment have no longer been alternatives but have been added together to define the degree of discomfort. An artificial word - stagflation - has been widely adopted to describe the economic situation of the Western European countries since the 70s. In fact a new situation has emerged which can no longer be characterised in terms of unemployment rates, underemployment of capacity, numbers of bankruptcies, negative balances of payments, inflation rates, etc. It is the Keynesian policy model itself, as a complicated compromise structure based on dynamic growth, which has become unsettled. The specific achievement of this model in creating the material basis for reconciling the contradiction between capitalism and democracy is jeopardised (on the decline of the Keynesian class compromise, see Skidelsky 1979; Bordogna and Provasi 1981). Meanwhile there has been a growing understanding that new conceptions of politics - with regard to the targets as well as to the tools and strategies have to be developed. By directing the distribution of gratifications and sanctions, economic policy always discriminates positively and negatively and is therefore also social policy. But this also implies that a new concept of economic policy cannot be implemented simply on the basis of more or less intelligent elaborations. It can only be carried through as a result of disputes and conflicts which could well be ferocious. This also holds true, of course, for trade union concepts of an alternative economic policy. In this case - provided that the thesis of the failure of Keynesianism is really true - the two main options are: the neo-liberal monetarist solution or the wider politicisation of decisions concerning the production and accumulation process by nationalisation, control of investment and control of work.

The end of Keynesianism announces the second crisis of political economy: as in the thirties, the heart of the matter is the level of employment but the quality and distribution of work are also at stake. Whilst attempts were made to influence the quantity indirectly by manipulating the total level of demand (according to policy rules elaborated by Keynes), the quality of work can only be influenced in the production process and thus through measures which directly affect the private disposition of property. There is no doubt that this is not a question of a neutral realisation of alternative concepts of economic policy but a question of power - except when the control and direction of investments and production is imposed by an authoritarian state in the interest not of capital as a whole but of big and important fractions of capital. This latter form of planning is necessarily linked to "national efforts" which typically take the form of armament and mobilisation for war. German fascism is the most appalling example here. As a result of the failure of Keynesianism and of the decline of a monetarist policy which will never be able to keep its promises, we suspect that in "highly developed" capitalist countries (which therefore have also "highly developed" problem areas) forms of an authoritarian planning of the economy could be developed as a third paradigm of economic policy. This planning would occur not only on the macro but also on the meso - and with large companies even on the micro - level. Such a model could also again be conducive to a fatal resolution of the increasing contradiction between capitalism and democracy. It is therefore vital to develop alternatives to such a model. In his investigation of the changes of industrial relations in the countries of Western European capitalism Colin Crouch concluded that with the lasting crisis and especially with high or even rising mass unemployment the conflicts between labour and capital would necessarily come to a head:

> The struggles will be fundamental because the working class is strong in the factories and they will be political struggles because the working class plays an important role in relation to the state. (Crouch 1979, p. 181)

The author admits that the working classes in most of the countries were badly prepared for these conflicts. But this qualification does not change much of his basically optimistic view that capital could hardly succeed in manoeuvring the working class and the trade unions into a position of weakness. In the early 80s there are, however, hardly any signs in the Western European countries of a strong trade union taking the offensive even in the crisis or because of the crisis. At best the trade unions have succeeded in building up defensive lines to protect past achievements, at worst they have suffered defeats. This has meant not only permanent unemployment for the young, the old, women, and those who are not considered efficient enough; but also curtailments of the standard of living by reducing the individual wage and important achievements of the welfare state. It thus becomes clear that the power position emphasised by Crouch no longer exists when millions of workers outside the factories wait for a job and inevitably need a different basis of mobilisation beyond the factory to pursue their still largely individualised disputes.[3] Even the close relationship between trade unions and the state is at this point no guarantee for success and for politicising conflicts because the state, by invoking "economic necessities", is trying to depoliticise exactly these conflicts.

The dilemma of the trade unions is now apparent. On the one hand, a successful wage policy can no longer be negotiated under the collapsing roof of growth and full employment achieved by a Keynesian policy; on the other hand, it is unlikely that a policy expressing the interests of the working class can be put through without fierce conflicts. At the same time the conditions of the struggle have been changed because for the moment the trade unions have been weakened by the crisis. It is therefore no accident that for the present the conservative, neo-liberal, monetarist option gets the upper hand as a result of the decay of the Keynesian policy model. The crisis thus turns out to be a point where decisions about development strategies have to be taken. The renunciation of Keynesianism, the current implementation of monetarist restrictionist policies, and the austerity proscribed for public budgets (especially in the field of social expenditure) in most of the Western industrial countries show that this decision has already been taken.

The monetarist strategy of overcoming the crisis aims at restoring the profitability of capital which fell in the prosperity period of the last years. It is not confined to that, however, because this target apparently cannot be achieved with the traditional tools of Keynesian policy. This is why the above-mentioned compromise is being revoked. The creation of a consensus for the accumulation process of capital no longer takes place via the political representation of the employees and via an expansion of the social security system but according to the logic of the economic pressures of the market. The intention is to reduce the political mediation of the accumulation process under the pretext of debureaucratisation and a restriction of excessive public expenditure. There are indeed defects of the Keynesian model. But these are not invoked against its abuse but against its philosophy. The argument for a reduction of excessive and thus superfluous bureaucracy is therefore used to reduce just those rights of participation in the indirect management of production as well as the co-determination concerning production decisions which have in any case always been partial. This policy option therefore not only entails a deterioration of the employment situation and a reduction of incomes but also a cut-back of the welfare state and of the democratic rights of participation which Keynesianism required. All of this takes place in a climate of conservative-authoritarian tendencies which seems unfavourable for reforms. Pre-Keynesian formulae have been taken out again and have been rigorously implemented as economic policy. Whether described in a self-confident way as a "counter-revolution" by Milton Friedman or in a defamatory way as "revolutionary" by its defendants, the neo-liberal, monetarist policy concepts aim at undermining the consensus which had been the basis of successful Keynesian policy for decades. "Organised capitalism" which is the result of the historical process of "the masses entering the state" through their organisations (Maier 1975), of concentration processes in the economy and of increased public expenditure, is to be disorganised and replaced by the free play of market forces. Or seen from the other side: capitalism which is penetrated by the state on all levels ("durchstaatlichter Kapitalismus") is to become privatised again by reducing the public sphere. The attempts at capitalist planning - even if indirect or only general regulations for the production - are to be "de-regulated". Thus the objective is a reconstruction and strengthening of private markets and the cut-back of their politically controlled social commitments. Everything considered, this is a 'roll-back', in fact a counter-revolution, which deeply affects the trade unions.

But we have already pointed out that developing and putting through alternative concepts meets with a lot of difficulties. For the labour movement and especially for the trade unions the crisis is also a crucial point in their development and requires new political approaches. Past experiences of many years have shown that a return to the Keynesian concept of prosperity is not possible. Indeed a new phase of prosperity like that which occurred up to the mid 70s will remain a bad illusion. Thus a compromise between the classes which is safeguarded by the interventionist and welfare state can no longer have the same basis as before. The bridge which made the compromise feasible economically and politically has collapsed and there are now two alternatives: either the revival of the market forces at the expense of the

Keynesian structures of compromise including the welfare state and the possibilities for institutionalised participation in society will prove successful or else an offensive for the growing politicisation of the production and accumulation process can be started.

It is, however, rather obvious that this politicisation cannot be conceived as a radical, revolutionary seizure of power by taking command of the state and the economy. In the highly developed Western European countries there will be no return to the revolutionary strategies of the phase between the Russian Revolution and World War II. Alternatives for the development of society can only be formulated and promoted in a different way which might provide a "third road" between Keynesianism and Social Democracy on the one hand and the model of the Russian Revolution on the other. This is a road of "progressive reformism" which in the first instance counters the neo-liberal assault to drive back the influence of workers in state and economy in order to institutionalise the new post-Keynesian forms of politics. The historical point of reference for this kind of policy is the demand for "economic democracy" (Wirtschaftsdemokratie).

This strategy is in fact post-Keynesian in the sense that the specific exchange between economy (accumulation of capital) and politics (creation of consensus, democracy) is no longer accepted and consequently lays down a changed role for the state with regard to the planning of the economy. State intervention is no longer confined to the spheres of circulation and realisation by means of manipulating aggregate demand but it is equipped with expanded powers vis-à-vis the production process and thus towards the decision-makers of capital. This is a matter of gaining power - which will not be granted voluntarily - and it goes always beyond the mere re-attainment of full employment.

The historical experiences with claims for an "economic democracy" in the thirties show that a reformist strategy without an employment programme is as inadequate as an employment programme trying to pick up the threads of the phase before the crisis. For the current situation this implies that alternative strategies can neither implicitly nor explicitly assume that the Keynesian class compromise can still function.

The main difficulties arise from the fact that strategies have to be developed which make reforms look possible even in a phase of economic stagnation. The regaining of full employment is without doubt a central point of such a programme.

One has to ask, however, what full employment actually means: full employment at which individual working-times, in which production processes, under which forms of organisation, at which technological levels, in the production of which products for which markets, in which political power structures?

These questions introduce many complications into defining the direction of alternative strategies and generate much controversy. The answers to these questions within the Western European trade union movement today are neither uniform nor definitive.

NOTES

* This contribution is a revised version of our introduction to Altvater et. al. 1983

1. From this indisputable tendency Gintis and Bowles (1981) derived the thesis of a 'de-commodification' of labour, i. e. a reduction of its commodity character. The wage is then transformed from a renumeration for selling labour to an employer into a 'citizen wage'.

2. In a situation of capital-intensive technical progress the increase in work productivity is only possible with a growing capital intensity. A higher rate of increase in capital intensity than in work productivity results in a rise of the capital-output ratio. This can be compared with the organic composition of capital after the realisation process provided that not only the fixed constant capital (in machines, buildings etc.) but also the circulating constant capital (raw materials and supplies) is calculated. When capital stock K indicates constant capital c and the net production output Y the value product v + m then K/Y is an indicator for c/v+m. Cf. Okishio 1974 and Stamatis 1977.

3. The assumption of a powerful position in the plants is due to the experience of full employment over a long period of time and to an 'operaistic' ('workerist') interpretation of the relationship between capital and labour. Marx's category of a 'reserve army of the unemployed' implied - beyond its moral-normative bias and its empirical validity - that the power relations of labour and capital depend on conditions within and outside the factories. And these conditions are themselves vastly determined by the accumulation of capital.

REFERENCES

Altvater, E. , K. Huebner, M. Stanger 1983: Alternative Wirtschaftspolitik jenseits des Keynesianismus, Westdeutscher Verlag: Opladen

Amoroso, B. 1980: Rapporto dalla Scandinavia, Bari

Bordogna, L. and G. Provasi 1981: I rapporti tra politica e mercato nei paesi capitalistici avanzati: varianti nello sviluppo, differenze nella crisi, in: Stato e Mercato, no. 1, vol. 1, April 1981

Crouch, C. 1979: Industrial Relations in Western Europe: Patterns of Change, in: J. Matthes, (ed.), Sozialer Wandel in Westeuropa. Verhandlungen des 19. Deutschen Soziologentages in Berlin 1979, Frankfurt am Main

Gintis, H. and S. Bowles 1981: Socialist Political Theory and the Critique of Liberal Democracy, Amherst (Mass.) 1980, mimeo; published in: Stato e Mercato, no. 1. vol. 1, April 1981

Kalecki, M. 1943: Political Aspects of Full Employment, in: Kalecki, M. 1971: Selected Essays on the Dynamics of the Capitalist Economy, Cambridge, pp. 138 - 145

Keynes, J.M. 1936: The General Theory of Employment Interest and Money, Macmillan: London (quoted from the reprint of 1949)

Laclau, E. 1981: Politik und Ideologie im Marxismus. Kapitalismus - Faschismus - Populismus, Berlin (Translation of: Politics and Ideology in Marxist Theory, London 1977; with an appended article of 1979)

Maier, C. S. 1975: Recasting Bourgeois Europe, Princeton

Okishio, N. 1974: Technische Veraenderungen und Profitrate, in: H. G. Nutzinger/E. Wolfstetter, (eds.), Die Marxsche Theorie und ihre Kritik, vol. II, Frankfurt am Main

Przeworski, A. 1980: Social Democracy as a Historical Phenomenon, in: New Left Review 122

Robinson, J. 1973: Die zweite Krise der oekonomischen Theorie, in: W. Vogt, (ed.), Seminar Politische Oekonomie, Frankfurt am Main

Skidelsky, R., (ed.), 1979: The End of the Keynesian Era, London

Stamatis, G. 1977: Die "spezifisch kapitalistischen" Produktionsmethoden und der tendenzielle Fall der allgemeinen Profitrate bei Karl Marx, Berlin

Chapter 2

TRADE UNIONS, INDUSTRIAL RELATIONS AND STRUCTURAL ECONOMIC 'RUPTURES'

Otto Jacobi

INTRODUCTION

The change in the trend of economic development in the Western industrial states which has become evident since the middle of the 1970s and changes in the world economic division of labour have produced a phase of economic development which clearly differs from that of the entire preceding post-war period. A new problem-constellation has emerged - one which does not correspond to a Keynesian situation and therefore cannot be solved with the instruments of demand-management. The structural changes in the conditions for growth and employment have led to a change in economic policy strategy. The substitution of laissez-faire strategies for the Keynesian model of socio-economic 'steering' is not determined by the changed constellation of economic problems, but it is, as it were, 'pre-structured' by the fact that neo-liberal economic policies correspond far more closely with the direct interests of capital than does a 'Keynes-plus' programme. Thus, it is not at all accidental that, even if at different intervals and in varying degrees of intensity, laissez-faire strategies have been adopted in all the major Western industrial countries. As the neo-liberal neo-conservative diagnoses maintain that the roots of the economic crisis lie in the excessive demands of wage and salary-earners and the state on the national output and that the market-power of the trade unions and state intervention have robbed innovative market forces of their dynamism, various questions arise regarding the role and function of the trade unions and industrial relations:

- Do the structurally new problem-constellation and the neo-liberal economic strategy contain forces which lead to such lasting changes in the 'external' relations of the trade unions, their internal structure and their self-conception that one can talk of a crisis of trade-union interest organisations?

- Are laissez-faire strategies being complemented by ideas whose objective is to eliminate the potential of the trade unions to intervene in economic activity and the dysfunctional effects of collective bargaining by making structural changes in the respective national industrial relations systems?
- Are neo-liberal and neo-conservative policies capable of overcoming the development crisis by adopting market and state-authoritarian strategies which are thus detrimental to the interaction between state, business and trade unions?

In the remainder of this paper, these questions will be discussed by reference to observable developmental trends since the middle of the 1970s in Great Britain, Italy and the Federal Republic of Germany. By way of a pre-view of the following analysis, its two general findings can be stated here:

- Almost at the same time as the general economic environment has deteriorated, the trade unions have grown weaker. One direct consequence is that because of the changed balance of social forces, individual elements of industrial relations can no longer be exploited by trade unions to their benefit. On the other hand, structural changes in the industrial relations systems through the creation of new legal frameworks and institutions have been partial rather than general and their implementation has taken place slowly rather than quickly.
- Both the degree to which the position of the trade unions has been weakened and the magnitude and direction of the structural changes which have taken place have been affected very substantially by peculiar national conditions.
- In the presence of the highly differentiated and interdependent structure of Western European industrial societies, the neo-liberal and neo-conservative doctrines look like formulae of the palaeolithic period. Their ineffectiveness has still to be found out before the close interaction of politics, economy and interest organisations in the post-war period can be resumed.

STRUCTURAL ECONOMIC 'RUPTURES'

The Provisional End of the Keynesian Era

The identifying characteristic of the new phase of economic development in the capitalist democracies is to be seen in the fact that, at least in the medium-term, but not permanently, the conditions for the effective functioning of the Keynesian model for securing growth and employment through the 'global' steering of the economy by the state no longer exist. There is a lot of evidence for the view that, at the moment, we are experiencing not the end, but at least a standstill of Keynesianism.

The aim of Keynesianism was and is an expanding economy, which, by reducing mass unemployment and expanding the welfare system, creates the pre-condition for compromise settlements of social interest-conflicts and thus guarantees the continuation of the capitalist mode of production. It provided capitalism with an "alternative programme" which is intended to safeguard the private form of capital-realisation through state intervention and, by offering a minimum of welfare and a high level of employment, to ensure mass loyalty to this system (Habermas 1969). Thus, Keynesianism was and is not simply a model for economic diagnosis and therapy, but also a model for neutralising the immanent contradiction of interest between labour and capital and thus for increasing the political stability of capitalist democracies. In this sense, the "Keynesian message" (Robinson 1953) heralds a "conservative revolution"(Hofmann 1962).

The economic essence of Keynesianism is that it proposes a policy of raising demand, via the state, to bring about the re-utilisation of idle production capacity and absorb unemployment. A critical pre-condition for the success of such a policy for stimulating growth is the existence of markets which can expand - markets which are stagnant from a lack of private demand, although there are unfulfilled needs. However, the more successfully production, employment and income can be raised, the more limited becomes the Keynesian model's scope for securing growth and anaesthetising the contradiction of interest between capital and labour. In this sense, Skidelsky is correct in saying: "Keynes found a way of keeping capitalist democracy working, but only by weakening further the long-run conditions for its survival" (Skidelsky 1977, p. 33). The oft-cited metaphor that Keynesianism is the victim of its own success is accurate in two senses for developments in the post-war period.

(1) The more successfully employment could be expanded, the more difficult it became to resolve the distributional conflict. The high-employment situation had released market-related wage-increase tendencies and also strengthened the bargaining power of the trade unions. The explosion of wages and the unions' success in the distributional struggle, often achieved by means of strikes, came increasingly into conflict with the conditions of accumulation in capitalist economies. The Achilles heel of Keynesianism (namely, the incompatibility of lasting full employment with stable monetary values and profit margins that allow investment to a sufficient extent to ensure growth) was revealed, since wage movements could be only partially controlled by means of anti-cyclical fiscal policy, administratively-directed wage- and price-freezes or through incomes policy and trilateral agreements. This was because the latter instruments presented no comparable substitute for the wage-limiting function of an "industrial reserve army". The situation which had arisen was portrayed as early as 1943 by Kalecki with the concept of the "political business-cycle":

> Indeed, under a regime of permanent full employment, the 'sack' would cease to play its role as a disciplinary measure. The social position of the boss would be undermined and the self-assurance and class consciousness of the working class would grow. Strikes for wage increases and improvements in conditions of work would create political tension (Kalecki 1971, pp. 140-41).

The starting-point of this consideration is that a stable equilibrium with full employment through state intervention leads, in the long run, to changes in the economic, and, ultimately, in the social, structure of capitalism and therefore incites the resistance of capital. In periods of high levels of employment, capital has an economic lever at its disposal by exercising investment restraint and passing on costs into prices and can thus force the state into pursuing a restrictive economic policy designed to weaken the bargaining power of the trade unions through unemployment. This is what developed strongly in the 1970s.

(2) Keynesianism was very successful in exhausting the potential of markets to expand. A central role was played here by the internationalisation of the goods, capital and credit markets. However, the more the chances for expand-

ing markets were exploited, the more the potential for growth was exhausted by market-saturation tendencies and increased competition. The new stage of development which has now emerged rests upon tendencies which have grown up over the long-term and can be described with the concept of the innovation and product cycle. According to this concept, industrial products and production processes go through a life-cycle, which begins with innovation and, after a gradual maturing, ends with standardisation - with standardised product characteristics and production stages (Borner 1981). The corollary of this is that a new, maturing, standardised product is connected with far-reaching economic consequences. The development of new products and production technologies is limited almost exclusively to the technologically most advanced economies, so that these countries can gain comparative advantages in competition - advantages based on their technological superiority. As a result of this, they can build up or maintain a high level of wages and social benefits and cope with unfavourable conditions as regards industrial location. At the same rate as industrial technologies, especially mass-production processes, mature, the transferral phase (Verlagerungsphase) of the production cycle, which is based on two mutually complementary motive forces, begins. In the industrial countries, with the standardisation of industrial products and their mass production, market-saturation draws nearer. The Swedish economist, Anell, has described very graphically not only the growth effects of private and public consumption, but also the high level of fulfilment of needs which has meanwhile been achieved (Anell 1981). Demand, especially that for industrial consumer goods, switches in the course of the product cycle from new needs to replacement (or substitution) needs. In the case of numerous common products, sales can no longer, or hardly any longer, be increased. The nearer the market verges on saturation, the more intensively the enterprises seek to introduce labour-saving technologies and more favourable production locations in less developed countries. In order to try and prolong the life of their older product and production-process generation, the big enterprises in particular transfer their manufacturing plant to third countries. The latter, in turn, want to push ahead with the building-up of an industrial structure to link up manufacturing capacities with their raw material resources and reduce their dependency on imports. In addition, however, they are appearing as new suppliers on a range of international goods markets. The further the product cycle progresses, the more the technological gaps (first between the individual industrial countries and then between the classical and the newly-developing industrial countries) close up. While a technological advantage secures market dominance in the early phase of the product cycle, in the late phase cost factors become increasingly important. As a consequence, because their low levels of wages and social benefits (often guaranteed politically by the suppression of trade unions) enable them to offer favourable production costs and conditions, the developing countries are attractive as new locations for industrial production-plant. This is how former "innovators" and industrial pioneers run the risk of losing the competitive advantages they enjoy through their technological superiority and thus of being pushed out of the market.

If one compares the two phases which have led to significant world economic transformations since the end of World War II, it becomes clear that a qualitatively new stage has been reached in the international division of labour. During the first phase, spanning the 50s and 60s, it was characteristic that the Western industrial nations caught up with the economic and technological superiority of the USA. Typical for the second phase that unfolded in the 70s is, in contrast, the displacement of industrial production from the industrial countries to the developing nations. "There was no longer a superior North American technology to copy. Instead the OECD countries were threatened 'from behind' by a number of newly industrialising countries" (Anell 1981, p. 52).

In summary, it can be observed that the production cycle which began in the middle of the 1930s has reached the stage of standardisation (Mensch 1979). Also the OECD study on "Technological Change and Economic Policy" (1980) concludes that the growth potential of the new technologies which had been developed, but had not been applied on a broad scale, during the Great Depression and the war is now exhausted. With the concept of the product cycle, which is not an exogenous determinant of economic growth, it can be made clear that the available resources for economic progress and maintaining social peace and political stability could be fully utilised through the application of Keynesian policy instruments during the long post-war phase - but that they were also, in the end, depleted.

On the Adequacy of Laissez-Faire Strategies

The alternative, in a constellation of economic problems

which cannot be tackled with the instruments of classical Keynesianism, between adopting a 'Keynes-plus' policy (European Trade Union Institute 1979) or returning to neo-liberal strategies remained an academic debate. As the former strategy seeks to undermine even further fundamental capitalist interests, structures and mechanisms of operation, while the latter seeks, in contrast, to renew them, the advance of neo-liberal strategies which has begun on a broad front becomes understandable. And, indeed, these strategies do broach the two central problem-areas of the present phase of capitalist development.

(1) So that laissez-faire strategies can break the bargaining power of wage and salary-earners and the trade unions, unemployment has been revitalised as an instrument of economic policy (the ability of these strategies to achieve this task is backed up by fundamental theoretical, social and ideological convictions). In the context of these strategies, the establishment and maintenance of an industrial reserve army is a necessary pre-condition for the control of the movement of wages and the distribution of income as well as for the disciplining of the trade unions' organisational strength in industrial conflicts. The reduction of labour costs by means of dismissals and redundancies, real falls in income and cuts in welfare-state benefits is also functional in a wider sense.

(2) It is necessary to make the way free for a new cycle of innovation and products. Given that there is no potential for growth left in the older generation of products and processes and given the continuing shifts in the international division of labour, the classical industrial countries are faced with the necessity of making innovations (OECD 1980). It is necessary through technological innovations to set in motion product and process innovations which will enable them, through a high-quality, high-value supply of goods, to remain competitive. The efforts at modernisation which can be observed in all the Western industrial countries are aimed at creating fresh, technologically-based comparative advantages in competition. The German "Council of Economic Experts" (1981, paragraph 459) has summarised the objective of this modernisation strategy as follows:

> The improvement of competitiveness must be achieved through the adoption of new products into the product-range - those products whose production requires special technical knowledge possessed only by a few

> suppliers ... Such products are competitive not because they are particularly cheap, but because of their high utility for their users; in short, because they are particularly expensive. Otherwise expressed: competitiveness in a dynamic economy is the ability to develop new special products and new technical solutions to problems to an extent which permits the achievement of rising incomes together with a high level of employment, although competitors coming up from behind are gradually attaining the technical knowledge and organisational abilities needed to produce these products as well. A high-wage country cannot retreat back into the role of this latter kind of competition.

The neo-liberal economic strategies correspond, in principle, to this constellation of problems. According to them, the cause of the crisis lies not in a shortfall of demand, but in the fact that the market system is over-burdened - which has undermined the innovative capacity and investment-dynamic of the economy. The primacy of investments in neo-liberal thought is a rational approach to the problem in so far as the order of the day is not the closure of a gap in demand, but investment in new labour-saving, market-creating technologies. At the moment, an anti-cyclical policy of steering against the crisis produces only weak employment impulses, while conserving production structures which, in the long run, are not competitive and thereby hold up adaptation to the new international division of labour. The German Council of Economic Experts summarises this position succinctly, but clearly: "The stronger the resistance, the longer the crisis."

Cutting costs by reducing the level of wages and social benefits or by devaluations is, however, merely a defensive strategy of adaptation to a changed competitive situation in the world economy. Cost-saving rationalisation and the creation of new markets are of primary importance. Microelectronics, combined with computer technologies, represents a mature, applicable line of technological development and must be seen as a branch-transcending basic technology which possibly heralds the beginning of a new product cycle. The economic significance of this new basic technology lies in the fact that a stage in the development of the production structure will be reached at which the traditional barriers to automation will be overcome.

It is extremely significant here that, in the medium-term, the new technology will lead primarily to labour-saving process innovations and less to employment-increasing product innovations. In so far as products have been renewed up until now through micro-electronics, this has preponderantly affected normal products, which have been refined by additional functions into qualitatively more valuable products, but thus enter merely into existential competition with other goods which are already on the market. Positive employment effects are to be expected only from completely new products - that is to say, from new emerging goods markets, which meet an unsatisfied demand and therefore expand. At the conference of the "Club of Rome" in early 1982, Guenter Friedrichs, director of the 'automation' department of IG Metall, delivered the following resumé:

> Seen in the long-term, micro-electronics offers both things: improvements in quality which are so great that additional demand is created and completely new kinds of products which actually create new jobs. However, a considerable time-span lies between the phase in which the application of micro-electronics through process innovations predominates and the phase in which product innovations become dominant (Friedrichs 1982, 218).

At the present time, the Western economies are in this phase of transition, so that the prospects of re-absorbing dismissed workers into the labour process must be described as very unfavourable. Otherwise expressed, this means that the critical growth rate - that is to say, a growth dynamic through which unemployment can again be reduced - has risen considerably. To restore full employment, it would be necessary to achieve a rate of production growth which clearly exceeded the growth rates experienced during the phase of prosperity in the 1950s and 1960s. In the medium term, a continuation of the tendency towards "jobless growth" can therefore be expected (Rothwell and Zegveld 1979).

The Possibility of a New Keynesian Situation

The view represented here - that the laissez-faire strategies correspond to a high degree to the present constellation of economic problems - does not embrace the expectation that they will achieve the objectives they have set themselves. The function and also the fate of neo-liberal strategies seem rather to be to allow the purgative effect of the crisis to operate long enough for a situation to be restored in which Keynesian instruments are again appropriate. Neo-liberal strategies can accelerate the depreciation of capital which has become obsolete, reduce the level of wages and social benefits, use mass unemployment for disciplining the trade unions and favour rationalising investments by means of new technologies. However, they themselves constitute an obstacle to the creation of a new period of growth with a high level of employment. As demand components are systematically neglected, deficits in demand emerge, develop their own momentum and grow into independent components of the crisis, so that a prolongation - not a lasting overcoming - of the crisis can be expected. The possible return of a Keynesian situation does not mean that everything will again be as it once was, but that the conditions for the pursuit of an effective Keynesian policy will again be improved.

The expectation that a new Keynesian situation will develop is based on the following assumptions:

- The possibility is not excluded that, as already in earlier phases of capitalist development, a new technology will lead to the emergence also of new markets, which can expand. Micro-electronics is a basic innovation, comparable, for example, with steel, electricity or the automobile (BMFT 1981, Friedrichs and Schaff 1982). Moreover, the possibility cannot be excluded that other technologies, for example biotechnology, will also lead to fundamental innovations in many areas (OECD 1980).
- Environmental protection is a new market, capable of expanding. Politically and economically, it has entered its initial phase.
- It is assumed that it is in the interests of the classical industrial countries not to block the economic development of countries in the Third World - so that they thereby retain or create foreign markets capable of absorbing their exports. As the one or other country beyond the classical industrial countries might succeed in gaining "structural power" (the ability to co-determine the rules of international economic transaction) and many developing countries possess growing "procedural power" (the ability to exploit the rules and mechanisms), the external vulnerability of the export-dependent industrial countries is increasing (OECD 1979). And conflicts between debtor and creditor countries do not make loans safer, but involve the danger of causing a really gigantic Depression. "Nothing would have been more fatal at the moment than a contraction of inter-

> national lending. Credit creates trade, trade secures credit" (Schmidt 1983, p. 29). As the participants only have the choice either of finding new rules for the international economy or of gambling away the world economy as a whole, a more or less utilitarian approach of all participants can be expected (Hankel 1984).

Here, then, a "cyclical" thesis is being advanced. Its essence is that, through the effect of the "purification crisis" (Reinigungskrise), the conditions for the start of a new growth period and thus for a 'new edition' of Keynesian politics will be created. It is therefore assumed that the laissez-faire strategies will be deprived of the use of the growth potential connected with the new technologies and the wealth-promoting expansion of new markets and that the social and political forces opposing them will grow. The historical experience that, in Keynesianism, an economic, social and political alternative is available will become all the more significant, the longer and the more one-sidedly the sacrifices in the purification process are imposed on the broad mass of the population. The expectation is therefore that it will not be possible to reverse or undo the historical stage of development of the capitalist democracies which has produced, with Keynesianism, a "mixed economy" and, with the competition between the parties and the organisations of capital and labour, a "mixed polity" (Offe 1983).

Thus, the present situation can be seen as a crisis of interaction. The economic and technological ruptures have been followed by rival interpretations and definitions of interests (Scharpf 1979). The changed balance of power has favoured those in the conservative camp who are critical of democracy and who have set against the participation of the unions a state-authoritarian, market-oriented counter-model. The exclusion of the unions from policy-making, in their prescribed role as 'social partners' without any power for intervention or veto, however, makes it more difficult to secure social and political stability. The conservative expectation of being able to re-introduce pre-Keynesian political structures is unhistorical and in the long run much more unrealistic than the contrary expectation of being able to reconstruct a framework of interaction between the actors of political, economic and social interests.

THE CRISIS OF THE TRADE UNIONS AND INDUSTRIAL RELATIONS

When, below, a 'crisis of the trade unions' is mentioned, it is meant that the new economic situation has forced the trade unions to make changes in the contents of their policies and in their forms of interest-representation, because the balance of social forces has shifted to their disadvantage. The retreat of the trade unions on to the defensive, which can be observed everywhere, occurred almost simultaneously with the economic crisis. There is obviously no imminent crisis in the sense that there is no immediate threat that the trade unions' historically-won extension of their economic and social functions will be reversed and that they will be reduced to a state of such impotence that - politically - they can safely be ignored. The traditional protective function of the unions has not become superfluous. As the post-industrial society is still a far cry and further economic development will bring a long period of total industrialisation in all fields, a wide range of activities will open up for the trade unions. This view is also supported by the fact that, although the trade unions are not able to make such effective use of the instruments available to them in the national industrial relations systems, structural changes, whereby lasting restrictions are imposed on them by new laws or institutions, have not so far become dominant.

The assumption that the current weakness of the trade unions will not extend to a permanent crisis not only suggests the failure of neo-liberal and neo-conservative strategies but also indicates that the unions, as traditional agencies of reform, are capable of socially innovative processes of learning and renewal.

The Crisis of the Trade Unions

The different forms of the present weakness of the trade unions can be summarised as follows:

(1) The continuing high mass unemployment has brought about a lasting curtailment of the trade unions' market power. The reduction of collective bargaining demands to the objective of protecting the existing social status (sozialer Besitzstand) of workers constitutes an adaptation by the trade unions to an economic situation in which a positive-sum game is no longer being played. The difficulties in attaining this objective indicate that the trade unions have already been forced well into a defensive position. Their ability to imple-

ment their will vis-à-vis their opponent in collective bargaining - that is, their position in the economic market - has been damaged by the fact that industrial action often proves ineffectual. In contrast to the conditions of a prospering economy, the risk involved for the trade unions in strikes has now increased considerably, as the costs resulting for the employers are often smaller than the negative effects which rebound on the employees. The economic costs of strikes in the form of retarded modernisation and increases in productivity weaken the competitiveness of enterprises, branches or even whole economies and thereby worsen the employment situation. The obvious cracks in trade union solidarity are the reverse side of this coin. The establishment of blocs and splits as well as the conflicts between groups about their willingness or unwillingness to strike have led to a considerable increase of rivalry within the unions. This illustrates the extent to which conflicts that were originally external to the unions have been successfully transferred to the level of internal structures. The clearly perceptible decline in the volume of strikes in the last few years is simultaneously an indicator of the increased risk involved in strikes and an indicator of the disciplining effect of the industrial reserve army.

(2) The weakness of the trade unions is especially evident at the micro-economic level. In addition to the general employment situation, technological innovations and changes in work organisation have also weakened the employees' interest-organs in the factory bargaining-process. The enterprises use these changes to restore their authority and managerial prerogatives. The enterprises' purpose is to re-establish unfettered control over the production and labour process; they also pursue a selective personnel policy. In recruiting or rehiring - and particularly in the case of dismissals - not only technical but political criteria too are brought to bear to weaken employees' interest-organs in terms of personnel. There are clearly perceptible tendencies towards professionalising the work of factory interest-organs. There is also evidence that considerations about increasing productivity and safeguarding the competitiveness of factories are playing an increasing role in determining the attitudes of employees' representatives. On the other hand, the entrepreneurs are going on to the offensive and can implement their objectives regarding greater flexibility, mobility and control of the labour force partly by excluding or instrumentalising the factory interest-organs

of the employees and partly by establishing new consultative bodies below the bargaining level.

(3) To safeguard the existence of their organisation and to remain, in their external relations, a recognised party to collective bargaining, the trade unions must attain a membership strength which permits them to represent the entire section of the population dependent on wage-labour. In meeting this requirement, they are being confronted with growing obstacles. Firstly, the earlier tendency towards a growth in membership has been reversed. The membership losses in recent years possibly reflect a growing alienation between employees and trade unions. Nevertheless, they are probably largely attributable to the decline in employment and unemployment. Alongside mass unemployment shifts in favour of the tertiary sector might also have undermined their organisational density and representational monopoly. The organisational strength of the trade unions is endangered, moreover, by an internal process of attrition triggered off by redundancies among the group of traditionally highly-unionised "core" work forces. Overall, it can be assumed that those groups of employees which have so far been less amenable to trade-union organisation are becoming, in relative terms, more significant. The already perceptible aspects of an organisational crisis will become all the more profound, the less the trade unions are able to counter the social-structural trends detrimental to their organisational efforts by extending their areas of action. The danger of a structurally 'self-reinforcing' organisational weakness developing is high.

(4) Trade union strategies oriented towards both class- and reform-politics have become less convincing, and the indicators of a programmatic crisis of the trade unions are growing (Regini 1983). Participation in economic growth is no longer the issue; so the old recipes are less and less useful as orientations for action in practical interest-politics. As modernisation strategies cannot be rejected and are seen by the trade unions, too, as a promising developmental perspective, the unions are increasingly prepared to agree to productivity 'cartels' and to accept advances in productivity even when they are denied concessions in terms of employment, social, and co-determination policy. Parallel to these developmental tendencies on the factory level, there are also signs on the sectoral and macro-economic levels that they are prepared to recognise the safeguarding of competitiveness as the dominant criterion. They thereby run the risk of

becoming an appendage to an uncontrolled capitalist modernisation strategy and turning an admittedly programmatic international solidarity into a relationship of competition. Not only national capitalisms, but also, in their tow, the national trade union movements would then be competing for shares on the world market.

(5) In their relationship to the state, on the political market, the decisive weakness of the trade unions lies in the fact that they are far less able than earlier to control the macro-economic aggregate "wages and distribution". With the loss of this 'action-parameter', a decisive weapon - one which opened the trade unions' way on to the political market - has been blunted. This development is a consequence of laissez-faire strategies. Their objective is to roll back as far as possible the influence of the economic market power of the trade unions on the development of the economy and the influence of their political market power on the economic policy of the state. Only in exceptional cases are the trade unions still a significant force on the political market. Whether the unions will be able to open again the way on the political market depends on their ability to counteract the conservative doctrine together with other traditional and new reform movements by developing a convincing alternative model of social development and by representing hitherto neglected interests of groups in society which would otherwise run the risk of being marginalised.

National Patterns of Trade Union Weakness

While the developmental tendencies described above can be perceived in all the countries being discussed here, their nuances are so different that the crisis of the three trade union movements assumes forms specific to each individual country.

(1) In international comparison, the trade unions in Great Britain have obviously been most enduringly weakened. The collapse of the factory, economic and political power of the British trade unions corresponds to the magnitude of unemployment and de-industrialisation, the severity of the neo-liberal economic policy, and the advance of conservative ideologies and populistic strategies, which have been welded together as in no other Western European country and have changed both the social and political climates. On the political market they have been declared more or less persona non grata. The post-war consensus politics has been terminated by the government, which can afford to reject the trade

unions as a partner in consultations, talks and negotiations. Apart from the weakness of the trade unions, a decisive role is played here - above all - by the polarisation of the balance of political power, which is greatly strengthened by the electoral system. The traditional ally of the trade unions, the Labour Party, is a merely 'spiritual' partner without any political influence. In contrast to the federal system in the Federal Republic of Germany and to the Italian party system, the opposition is largely excluded from the political decision-making process in Great Britain.

The general remark that the bargaining power of the trade unions at the factory or enterprise level has diminished conceals the very different strategies which are being pursued by employers in Great Britain in their relations with the shop stewards as representatives of the work forces (Brown and Sisson 1983). The range of strategies extends from crushing them to ignoring them and attempting to harness the factory interest-organs and, with them, the work force for the achievement of the enterprise's objectives. Often the enterprises can extend their control over the production and labour process and increase productivity by exploiting the competition between trade unions or different parts of the work forces. It seems as if, in an economic crisis particularly, when trade union solidarity is especially necessary, intra- and inter-trade-union cleavages are an 'open goal' for offensive entrepreneurial strategies. While the sharp fall in the frequency and volume of strikes indicates the magnitude of the decline in the trade unions' market power, their heavy membership losses, which are far greater than in the Federal Republic or Italy, prove how much their organisational strength and representational monopoly have been curtailed.

(2) In Italy, the picture of trade union crisis is less unequivocal. Clear tendencies towards their weakening on the factory and economic market are accompanied by the unions' remarkable ability to maintain their capacity for action and remain a party on the political market.

In the factory bargaining-process in particular, the power and influence of the trade unions have clearly declined. The enterprises are increasingly in a position to implement plans for modernisation, rationalisation and increasing productivity and, in the process, to win back prerogatives of control over the production process and work organisation lost to the trade unions in earlier conflicts. More than elsewhere, the entrepreneurs use dismissals and re-hirings as chances to pursue selective, above all politically motivated, personnel policies. The factory organs of the trade unions, themselves interested in their firms' capacity to survive by increasing economic efficiency, are often forced into the function of crisis management. At the supra-factory level, the loss of trade union market power is exemplified particularly by the fact that, in a number of sectors, above all in the engineering industry, the private-sector employers refused for almost two years to conclude new collective agreements. The increased capacity for resistance shown by the employers is, of course, only the reverse side of the decline in the trade unions' capacity to implement their will. An indicator for this fact is the decline in the number of strikes and the number of working-days lost through strikes, although in international comparison the level of strikes in Italy is still above-average (Bordogna 1982). More than in any other country, the loss of the trade unions' economic market power is shown in Italy by the changed forms of strikes. The type of strike which has become dominant in recent years is the demonstration-strike (*sciopero dimostrativo*), which is characterised by its short duration, but high level of participation. While this shows, on the one hand, that the trade unions possess a strong capacity for mobilising their members, it is, on the other hand, an expression of their weakened bargaining position vis-à-vis the employers. Demonstration-strikes are in fact aimed not so much at making the opponent in collective bargaining more prepared to compromise; they are located less on the "mercato contrattuale" than on the "mercato politico" (Cella 1983).

Neither in Great Britain nor in the Federal Republic are the trade unions trying as intensively and successfully as in Italy to open the political market and involve the state in the regulation of labour relations. The foundations of such a strategy on the part of the Italian trade unions are manifold. There is a long, above all theoretically-grounded, tradition in the Italian trade union movement that, while it should primarily represent the interests of the industrial working class, it should *not* do so exclusively, but should also feel responsible for the political, economic and social development of society as a whole. Consequently, the pressure unleashed by the economic crisis to change the contents and forms of implementation of policies did not have a fundamental impact on the trade unions' self-conception. While, in connection with the "hot autumn", the primary interests of the working class were placed in the forefront, there was a progressive transformation on the part of the trade unions in the course of the 1970s from advancing particular to advancing general demands.

> Objectives such as, firstly, social reform and employment, investment and development of the south to follow, and lastly, productivity of enterprises and the economy have been the stages in an attempt to take on that role of 'representative of the general interests of the collectivity' which, according to the classic approach, ought to be the business of political parties (Regini 1983, pp. 246-47).

This points up the special features of the political system in Italy - which is characterised by unstable governments, a low level of efficiency of the state apparatus and a multiplicity of parties. In the Communist Party, the trade unions are flanked by a strong ally which cannot be excluded from the political decision-making process. Moreover, the influence of the trade unions reaches into the two most important parties in the centre-left coalition as well. Added to this is the fact that the political market in Italy is relatively large because, on the one hand, the state sector is far more significant than it is in the West German economy and, on the other hand, in contrast to Great Britain, it does not serve or hardly serves as an instrument of a laissez-faire strategy, which, in any case, in international comparison, is more weakly-developed in Italy.

These remarks may help to explain why, in contrast with Great Britain and the Federal Republic, a tripartite social pact could be negotiated in Italy at the beginning of 1983. Perhaps this was only a truce because in early 1984 the pressure exerted by the employers and the government - since 1983 headed by a Socialist Prime Minister - led to negotiations over modification of the social contract. The crucial point was to further limit the effectiveness of the former agreement on the adjustment of wages to the inflation rate. After the socialist minority supporting this line within the communist-socialist trade union confederation, had been outvoted, this confederation rejected the plans and with only two of the three Italian political trade unions' accepting there was no revival of a tripartite arrangement. Whether the conflict between and within the unions can be overcome remains as uncertain as the prospective success of the union strategies designed to counter-balance the employers' increased market power by shifting their resources to the political market. A concomitant phenomenon of these efforts to reconstruct Italian capitalism has not only been that the splits within the trade union movement have become very evident but that a possibly irreconcilable confrontation between the Socialist and Communist Party has started over which of them will be the predominant popular party on the left.

(3) For the Federal Republic of Germany too, all aspects of a crisis of the trade unions can be identified. However, the German crisis lacks the drama of the British, as neither employers nor the government have been forced to start a general attack on the unions. However, it also lacks the Italian variant of seeking a substitute for a decline in market power. To explain the apparently invisible progression of the crisis of the German trade unions, a dual thesis will be advanced here:

- The co-operative behaviour of the trade unions, which developed in the phase of prosperity, has not only carried on to the present-day, but has also left behind fewer "distortions" which ought now to be set right by a state or entrepreneurs' offensive.
- The modernisation perspective put forward by the earlier Social-Liberal government has provided the German trade unions with a programmatic alternative.

The tradition of co-operative relations between capital and labour has been sustained under conditions of increasing unemployment. The macro-economic orientation of trade union collective bargaining policy made it possible that wages and working conditions could be adjusted flexibly to a situation of economic crisis. The three big strikes in the last 10 years (in 1978 in the engineering industry as a protection against negative social consequences of technological reconstruction and in the steel industry for a reduction of working time and in 1984 in the engineering industry for the introduction of a 35-hour week) have confirmed the German trade unions' role as co-operative intermediary interest organisations. The outcome of the strikes - on the one hand a better protection against de-skilling and the loss of incomes and on the other a reduction of yearly and weekly working time - was a success for the unions but it also showed their readiness to find a compromise formula, which would not affect the employers' policy of reducing the labour cost, of rationalisation and of securing international competitiveness.

The fact, that strikes have been launched at all in a situation of mass-unemployment is no doubt remarkable but does not imply a break with the tradition of West German social history. Because of their external positions the trade unions simply have to demonstrate periodically their ability to strike, in order to pass the hardness test of the employers and to be accepted as partners for co-operation.

In contrast to Italy and, in particular, Great Britain, the position of the employers is extraordinarily strong because they possess unitary and centrally-led associations. An indicator for this is the fact that, in cases of conflict, the duration of strikes is relatively long and the employers generally make use of their right to implement lock-outs.

Even fewer steps towards 'purification' had to be carried out at the level of the factory and enterprise - a subordinate terrain for bargaining processes in any event in the Federal Republic of Germany. In contrast with Italy and Great Britain, the factory interest-organs are not trade union organs, but rather institutions which are committed to the well-being of the factory and to maintaining peace in the factory. Hence there is no reason for the enterprises to restructure negotiating structures within the factory. This is not least expressed in the fact that production- and achievement-oriented selection criteria predominate in personnel policy.

For two reasons, the trade unions will be less present in the future on the political market, which is, in any event, rather a place of consultation than negotiation in the Federal Republic of Germany. For one thing, their influence on the macro-economic aggregate 'wages and distribution' has declined; for another, the preparedness to engage in political exchange has declined on both sides with the installation of the new political leadership.

The crisis of the West German trade unions has a creeping character, but various manifestations of it are becoming visible. It is closely related to the modernisation model put forward already early in the crisis by the Social-Liberal government (Hauff and Scharpf 1975). Given the high level of international dependence of the industrial sector of the West German economy especially, the German trade unions have in any event a fundamental interest in safeguarding the international competitiveness of the German economy. In this modernisation strategy, they were offered far-reaching possibilities for exercising influence in exchange for their being prepared to reduce barriers to social innovation. In effect, the trade unions were thus given a substitute programme as a guide to action - one which has concealed the crisis in their self-conception. However, it is unmistakable that the renewal of the German economy is also going to be carried out without extending concessions to the trade unions and that the unions are thus more 'spiritual' than indispensable partners in the modernisation cartel. Nevertheless, the trade unions are sticking to their position, banking on the hope that, in spite of the high social costs involved, the modernisation strategy ultimately benefits the wage and salary-earners too. This attitude is based on the not unfounded expectation that the German economy will be one of the winners in the struggle for shares on the world market.

Tendencies Towards Change and Continuity in Industrial Relations

How much the economic and employment crisis together with laissez-faire strategies have weakened the position of the trade unions can be explained relatively well. There is also sufficient evidence to show that there have been changes in the weight of individual elements of the industrial relations systems, rooted in the fact that, as a consequence of the changed balance of social forces, a range of instruments have, in effect, been neutralised and can no longer be used to their advantage by the trade unions. However, less evidence can be found at the moment for the related assumption that the state and employers are able to bring about an enduring 'tightening' of the respective industrial relations systems through new juridical or institutional frameworks. The following section will therefore be devoted not only to tracing tendencies towards change in the three countries being discussed here, but also to underlining which of the crucial structural characteristics of the respective systems for regulating industrial relations are distinguishable by their high degree of stability.

(1) For the Federal Republic of Germany, it can be argued that the extent to which the contradiction of interest between capital and labour is legalised and institutionalised has prevented any necessity for structural changes from emerging. The high level of legitimacy and effectiveness which was achieved in the agreements between the parties to collective bargaining and reflected in the extremely low level of strikes could also be conserved in the years of the economic crisis. The German system of industrial relations has demonstrated that it possesses a high degree of flexibility, which

permits it to deal functionally with changed constellations of socio-economic problems and to whittle down new potential for conflicts effectively (Brandt, Jacobi and Mueller-Jentsch 1982). Reference to the following, most important structural characteristics of the German system of regulating industrial relations may help to make it clear why no need has emerged in the Federal Republic to eliminate any of the individual features which accommodate trade union interests, let alone to create new legal forms or institutions:

- centralised trade union structures;
- centralised negotiating structures;
- subordinate ranking of the micro-economic level as a location of bargaining processes;
- autonomous organs for the representation of the interests of enterprise work forces, independent of the trade unions and committed to the well-being of the factory and maintaining peaceful labour relations in it;
- an effective arbitration system;
- a curtailed right to strike, while employers have an instrument for waging industrial action in the form of the lock-out; and
- strong employers' organisations.

The industrial dispute in 1984 over the reduction of the weekly working time has brought out two interesting, if contrary, aspects:

(a) The absence of competing 'political unions' and of rival craft- or sectoral unions as well as the highly centralised organizational structures act (still) as a protective barrier against divisive tendencies in the trade union movement. The strong support for the strike by union members and its disciplined realisation are indicators showing that the employees can still be mobilised and that they are still ready to follow their unions.

(b) The policies the conservative and neo-liberal side is urging - under the heading 'flexibility' - on the parties to collective bargaining to negotiate on a general framework which should be completed in more detailed negotiations on plant level could be the trade unions' undoing. As there are no trade union negotiating committees on plant level but only the work councils who are bound by law to the weal of the company and who are not allowed to engage

> in industrial action, the collective bargaining monopoly of the trade unions would be jeopardised. With the agreements which ended the strikes the employers have succeeded in putting through new forms of flexibility with regard to working time for whole sectors of the industry. The working periods of machines are no longer bound to the working times of the machine operators and there can be different regulations as to weekly working time for individual groups of employees. There will be an increasing tendency of working hours at plant level to differ widely from collective bargaining agreements so that trade union control will be by-passed.

(2) In Italy, whose industrial relations system, compared with that of the Federal Republic, is under-institutionalised, strong tendencies towards eliminating the sectoral and, above all, the factory arenas as locations of trade union activity can be observed. At the same time, there is a high degree of immobility as regards the creation of new legal or institutional frameworks for the regulation of social interest-differences.

The collective-bargaining system, which normally provides for the conclusion, at three-year intervals, of industry-wide agreements and complementary factory arrangements, has run into a crisis in so far as the private-sector employers, particularly in the engineering industry (the key industrial sector in the Italian economy), are refusing to renew the collective agreements with the trade unions. In line with the changed constellation of power, the trade unions have largely lost their former bargaining power on the sectoral and factory levels - and, with this, two central spheres of action. The reverse side of this are the strong tendencies towards centralization on the side of the trade unions. Here a shift of authority has occurred not only in favour of the leaderships of the individual (industrially-organised) trade unions, but also, and above all, in favour of the trade union federations. The conduct of negotiations lies in the hands of the leading organs of the trade unions, which also make the decisions about how union strength for waging industrial action is to be handled, as is clear in the case of the demonstration-strikes. Negotiations with the employers and the state have been shifted to the macro-level of the political market. This strategy illustrates not only that the trade unions are trying to compensate at least partially for the decline in their market power by extending their chances of exercising political influence. It also reflects their conviction that, subject as they are to the dictate of the world market, the difficult processes of adaptation, together with their social consequences, require macro-economic and macro-political steering.

While this centralisation process has 'shut-down' individual structural elements in the Italian industrial relations system, these elements could, however, be revitalised under changed conditions. (This was proved by the mass-mobilisation against the government decree of February 1984 for a reduction of the scala mobile.) This thesis is based on the fact that there have so far been hardly any attempts to introduce a higher level of legalisation and institutionalisation. Thus, while the trade union organs in Italy are weakened in their bargaining power at the factory or enterprise level, they are not endangered by policies seeking to replace them with new institutions of factory interest-representation. Although the strike weapon has been bluntened, there are no tendencies either to curb the freedom to strike (which is hardly legalised at all, compared with the situation in the Federal Republic) or to extend the very restricted right of the employers to impose lock-outs. While there are arbitration processes, no attempts have been made to build up an institutionalised arbitration system. And within the trade union system the higher level of centralisation has not been institutionalised in the form of new provisions in union statutes and constitutions. In this sense, Italy can be regarded as a model case of how the changed constellation of social forces brings about a suspension or another kind of usage of individual elements in the system for regulating industrial relations - but without developing new institutions or forms of legalisation.

(3) Great Britain is a model for strategies which seek to attach an institutional 'anchor' to the present weakness of the trade unions by means of new legal arrangements. At the same time, the policy of the Conservative government also proves, however, that the supreme goal of laissez-faire strategies lies in limiting the freedom of action of trade unions, not in achieving a higher level of legitimacy or effectiveness in the industrial relations system.

> Perhaps the greatest weakness in the Conservative legislation ... lies in the very nature of the policy behind it. It is fuelled by a 'unitarist' (a conveniently neutral word) understanding of industrial relations in

> which trade unions are basically regarded as an unpleasant blemish in the market economy (Mackie 1983, p. 89).

The two Employment Acts, of 1980 and 1982 respectively (as well as the additional legislative proposals announced in the Green Paper "Democracy in the Trade Unions"), have the sole purpose of altering the balance between individual freedom and collective organisation and between employers and trade unions at the expense, in both cases, of the latter (Lewis 1983; Mackie 1983). Both laws aim at limiting the organisational strength of the trade unions and the effectiveness of strikes.

> Although the Employment Acts preserve the traditional form of the law of industrial conflict, the legal freedom to strike has been drastically curtailed by the reduction of immunities for those engaged in picketing, secondary action, and acts in support of union- and recognition-only practices, the narrowing of the definition of trade dispute, and the reintroduction of the liabilities of unions as such (Lewis 1983, p. 389).

It all looks as though the central construction error in the Conservative legislation at the beginning of the 1970s is being repeated. Illustrative for the Conservative stance is the argument that the trade union leadership seduces the rank-and-file into taking militant action, while, on the other hand, it is suggested that one of the chief problems of industrial relations in Great Britain is the lack of control of the trade unions over their members. While the first point of view implies strengthening the legal position of non-members (especially important in Great Britain because of the institution of the 'closed shop'), reducing the level of unionisation and curtailing the responsibilities of factory interest-organs; the second leads to the conclusion that the trade unions must be changed (according to the official document, "Trade Union Immunities") "into more authoritarian organisations, reversing the trend towards the increasing authority of the shop steward and power of the working group at the expense of the authority of branch and national officials" (Department of Employment 1981, paragraph 125). The legislation of the Thatcher Government is characterised by its desire to realise both objectives with essentially repressive instruments. As regards their negotiating position vis-à-vis the employers and the state, the leaderships of the trade unions are dependent essentially on the level of organisation and the unions' strength for waging industrial action, while their ability to make compromises with other parties is dependent on their members' preparedness to follow them. For these reasons, merely restrictive measures are not sufficient.

What is required is rather the functional extension of the trade unions' scope for action. Instead of this, not only are the trade unions excluded from the political market in Great Britain, but there are also no efforts being made to carry out structural reforms in other central elements of industrial relations. No attempt is being made, for example, to replace the decentralised and fragmented and therefore, as it were, under-institutionalised collective-bargaining system by transferring bargaining to the meso- or macro-level - which would bring with it a shift of authority in favour of the trade union leaderships. Equally, nothing is being done to give the leading organs of the trade unions (as in the German example) a monopoly of the right to make decisions on strikes. Neither have any structural changes been made in the factory bargaining system, which is represented in Great Britain by the shop stewards and is at the moment largely 'shut down'. There have likewise been no attempts to establish new institutions of factory interest-representation. This is all connected with the Conservatives' fear that the trade union leaderships might make unfair use of increased powers and functions. Consequently, no changes are being undertaken in those structural elements of the system which have to do with the employers. This holds for the right of employers to impose lock-outs as well as for the employers' extremely fragmented forms of interest-representation vis-à-vis the trade unions. It is typical for the Conservative strategy that it seeks structurally to 'ossify' the present weakness of the trade unions - but not to modernise the system of regulating industrial relations, which is not very efficient when it comes to macro-economic steering and assuaging social tensions. The break with the British tradition performed by the Conservatives' legislation may be great, although it takes on less dramatic proportions when looked at in continental perspective. Although these changes are profound it is not unthinkable that, under a changed balance of political and social forces, the old mode of operation of the British industrial relations system will be revived anew.

The following conclusions can be briefly stated:

(a) Despite basically similar economic problems and increasingly similar economic policy strategies, convergent paths of development have not so far become dominant as regards the role and function of the trade unions and systems of industrial relations. While, generally, a weakening of the position of the trade unions can be observed, the distinguishing features of this process vary from country to country. So far as the systems of industrial relations are concerned, individual elements have been suspended or partially restructured, but these developments have been shaped to a great extent by peculiar national conditions. There are many indications that nationally divergent, rather than internationally converging, patterns of development are to be expected in the future as well.

(b) A striking discrepancy exists between the parallel development of the economic crisis and the crisis of the trade unions, on the one hand, and the difficulties, on the other, in turning the 'conjunctural' weakness of the trade unions into a more permanent phenomenon through the re-organisation of industrial relations. Whether what we have here is simply a time lag, which will be closed with the continuation of the crisis, or whether the systems of industrial relations contain their own conservative forces, permitting them to withstand phases of this nature, cannot be answered unequivocally one way or the other.

(c) Given the expectation that the laissez-faire strategies will fail, the possibility cannot be excluded that the trade unions will develop into a counter-force and become important actors in a situation again more similar to the Keynesian policy model.

(d) The 'cyclical' thesis advanced here rests on the assumption that the trade unions cannot be reduced in the long run to a social force which can safely be ignored. Whether the industrial system as a whole is in danger of being enveloped by the crisis is an entirely different question. That can be debated more aptly with adventurous, speculative theses and prognoses than in this work.

REFERENCES

Anell, L., 1981: Recession, The Western Economies and the Changing World Order, London

Baglioni, G. and E. Santi (eds.), 1982: L'Europa sindacale agli inizi degli anni '80, Bologna

Baglioni, G. and E. Santi (eds.), 1982: L'Europa sindacale nel 1981, Bologna

Baglioni, G and E. Santi (eds.), 1983: L'Europa sindacale nel 1982, Bologna

BMFT - Der Bundesminister fuer Forschung und Technologie (ed.), 1981: Modernisierung der Volkswirtschaft in den achtziger Jahren, Duesseldorf

Bordogna, L., 1982: Conflittualità, in: Cesos - Le Relazioni Sindacali in Italia, Rapporto 1981, a cura di Baglioni, G., Santi E., Squarzon, C., Roma 1982, p. 32 - 39

Borner, S., 1981: Die Internationalisierung der Industrie, in: Kyklos, 34, S. 14 - 35

Brandt, G., Jacobi, O., Mueller-Jentsch, W., 1982: Anpassung an die Krise: Gewerkschaften in den siebziger Jahren, Frankfurt-New York

Brown, W. and Sisson, K., 1983: Industrial relations in the next decade, in: industrial relations journal, vol. 14, 1/1983, pp. 9 - 21

Cella, G. P., 1983: Determinanti della conflittualità, Relazione presentata al Congresso Nazionale dell'AISRI, Riva del Garda

Clegg, S., Dow, G. and Boreham, P. (ed.), 1983: The State, Class and the Recession, London-New York

Department of Employment, 1981: Trade Unions Immunities, London

European Trade Union Institute, 1979: Keynes Plus - A Participatory Economy, Bruxelles

Friedrichs, G., 1982: Mikroelektronik und Makrooekonomik, in: Friedrichs, G. und Schaff, A. (ed.), Auf Gedeih und Verderb, Wien, S. 201 - 223

Friedrichs, G. und Schaff, A. (ed.), 1982: Auf Gedeih und Verderb, Wien

Habermas, J., 1969: Technik und Wissenschaft als "Ideologie", Frankfurt

Hankel, W. 1984: Gegenkurs, Von der Schuldenkrise zur Vollbeschaeftigung, Berlin

Hauff, V., Scharpf, F. W., 1975: Modernisierung der Volkswirtschaft, Koeln

Hofmann, W., 1962: Die saekulare Inflation, Berlin

Kalecki, M., 1943: Political Aspects of Full Employment, in: Kalecki, M., 1971: Selected Essays on the Dynamics of the Capitalist Economy, Cambridge, pp. 138 - 145

Lewis, R., 1983: Collective Labour Law, in: Bain, G. S. (ed.), Industrial Relations in Britain, Oxford, p. 361 - 392

Mackie, K., 1983: Industrial relations law commentary, in: industrial relations journal, vol. 14, 1/1983, pp. 87 -

94 and 2/1983, pp. 87 - 90
Mensch, G., 1979: Stalemate in Technology, New York
OECD, 1979: Interfutures: Facing the Future. Mastering the Probable and Managing the Unpredictable, Paris
OECD, 1980: Technical change and Economic Policy, Paris
Offe, C., 1983: Competitive Party Democracy and the Keynesian Welfare State: Some Reflections Upon their Historical Limits, in: Clegg, S., Dow, G. and Boreham, P. (ed.), The State, Class and the Recession, London-New York, pp. 51 - 71
Regini, M., 1983: The Crisis of Representation in Class-Oriented Unions: Some Reflections based on the Italian Case, in: Clegg, S., Dow, G. and Boreham, P. (ed.), The State, Class and the Recession, London-New York, pp. 239 - 256
Robinson, J., 1953: Essay in the Theory of Employment, Oxford
Rothwell, R./Zegveld, W. (ed.), 1979: Technical Change and Employment, Paris
Sachverstaendigenrat zur Begutachtung der gesamtwirtschaftlichen Entwicklung, 1981: Jahresgutachten 1981/82, Bonn
Sachverstaendigenrat zur Begutachtung der gesamtwirtschaftlichen Entwicklung, 1982: Jahresgutachten 1982/83, Bonn
Scharpf, F. W. 1979: Die Rolle des Staates im westlichen Wirtschaftssystem: Zwischen Krise und Neuorientierung, in: Carl C. von Weizsaecker (ed.), Staat und Wirtschaft, Berlin
Schmidt, H., 1983: The World Economy at Stake, in: The Economist, February 26, 1983
Skidelsky, R., 1977: The Political Meaning of the Keynesian Revolution, in: Skidelsky, R., 1977: The End of the Keynesian Era, London, pp. 33 - 40

Chapter 3

POLITICAL BARGAINING IN WESTERN EUROPE DURING THE ECONOMIC CRISIS OF THE 1980s

Marino Regini

TYPES OF POLITICAL BARGAINING IN POST-WAR WESTERN EUROPE

Throughout Western Europe, the processes of political bargaining, and more generally, the relations between governments and large interest organisations, have recently undergone substantial change. So as to understand the nature of this change, let us proceed from the patterns of political bargaining which had been established during the three decades of economic growth prior to the economic crises of the 1970s.[1]

Essentially, three basic models of government-union relations and economic policy formulation can be identified as characteristic of the 1950s and 1960s. The first was the *concertation* model, in which labour unions were closely involved in the formulation and implementation of economic policies. It implied a high degree of centralisation in bargaining over wages as well as over government policies, and in industrial relations in general. It was this type of arrangement that later came to be re-interpreted as the "neo-corporatist" model (see Lehmbruch 1977).

The second model focussed on the *political isolation* of the union movement, in which the unions' exclusion from the policy-making process meant that no effective political bargaining took place. Wage bargaining, on the other hand, was relatively centralised. (Lange *et al.* 1982).

The third model can best be termed *pluralistic fragmentation.* In this case, wage bargaining was decentralised to the shop-floor level; industrial relations, as a whole, were quite separate from the political system; and the influence which the union movement was able to exert on economic policy, in the form of external pressures, like any other interest group, depended exclusively on its market power.

The above models are, of course, ideal types, and can therefore not be expected to correspond precisely with the detailed historical experience of any single country. Nonetheless, if our objective is to classify countries at a slightly more general level, we can reasonably conclude that the first model is applicable to Scandinavia, Austria, the Netherlands, and partially, to Germany and Switzerland; the second to France, and Italy during the 1950s; and the third to Britain, and, outside Europe, the United States. Most analyses confirm the applicability of this typology to the 1950s and 1960s, though we must also bear in mind that this period also saw major changes in the political bargaining process in some countries. Italy, for instance, was fairly typical of the political isolation model during the 1950s. But during the 1960s, the picture became much more confused as a result of the first tentative steps by the new centre-left government to involve the unions in economic planning, and the gradual process of decentralisation of the industrial relations system. These new trends could not easily be accommodated in any of our three ideal types.

Overall, during the 1970s, the three models seemed even less applicable. The differences which had distinguished the political bargaining processes of various Western European countries became less significant. What was taking place, according to many observers, was a convergence of the various systems along the lines of the neo-corporatist model.

Three factors could possibly account for the apparent dominance of corporatist trends. First, the countries which had adopted the concertation model at an early stage showed that they were much better able to cope with the economic crisis and to deal with the problems of "governability" than were other countries (Schmitter 1981). Their relative success generated widespread interest in their institutional arrangements, which, it was felt, other countries would wish to imitate. Second, two major Western European countries, Great Britain during the period of the Social Contract (1974-79), and Italy at the time of _solidarieta nazionale_ (1977-1979)[2], made conspicuous moves in the direction of a concertative arrangement. Finally, the defeat of dominant coalitions which had been responsible for the political isolation or outright repression of labour in France, Spain, and Greece, added to the impression that concertation was going to become the prevailing pattern of relations between interest organisations and the state.

As we shall see later, the patterns have changed yet again in the 1980s. In the 1970s, however, the very success and expansion of concertation provided the context for the enormous growth of neo-corporatist literature (e.g. Schmitter and Lehmbruch 1979). Indeed, this literature provided an attractive and fairly convincing interpretation of the growing role of large interest organisations in economic policy-making, and of the changes in the character of these organisations which accompanied such involvement. The entire process, so the argument ran, would be encouraged by the state so as to allow the transformation of interest organisations from agents of class mobilisation and interest representation into partners of government in co-operative policy-making.

This strategy of "government by agreement" (Salvati 1982) with the major interest organisations, is usually explained in terms of the need for Western European states to solve a series of problems associated with advanced industrialisation (Lehmbruch 1977; Panitch 1977; Offe 1981; Schmitter 1981). These problems concern, first, the impossibility of averting class conflict through the outright repression of union activity, which, in turn, creates the need to regulate such conflict by shifting it into the political arena. The state, in fact, is in a position to grant power and material benefits to the representative organisations of both capital and labour in exchange for their taking a moderate stance in industrial relations, thus transforming a zero-sum conflict into a positive sum one. The second problem is the increasing propensity of organised interests to make demands upon the state, which results, according to the "overload" theorists, in a crisis of governability. Some governments, however, can successfully deal with this problem by co-opting the most powerful groups into the policy-making process, thereby inducing them to abstain from exercising their veto power *ex post*. The third problem focuses on economic growth, a major issue of the 1970s. Some scholars have outlined a scenario in which, faced with a crisis of a welfare state which has hitherto confined its actions to indirect support of economic development, governments are now eager to take a more "directive" role in order to ensure sufficient levels of capital accumulation (Winkler 1976). Democratic governments, though, are normally too weak to perform such a role unaided. Hence, they try to involve major interest organisations in this process so as to increase their authority and legitimacy.

POLITICAL BARGAINING AND THE ECONOMY

According to neo-corporatist theorists, the centralised political bargaining that is a feature of concertation, and that often finds institutional expression in tripartite organisations, performs important functions for the stability of the capitalist state. But under what conditions does it play such a role? Much of the neo-corporatist literature has been devoted to this very question. Time and again, scholars have emphasised the importance of organisational conditions (a high degree of centralisation and concentration of interest organisations, combined with their representational monopoly); politico-institutional conditions (the presence of a pro-labour party in government, and the existence of credible state apparatuses, capable of implementing tripartite decisions); and finally, ideological conditions (the prevalence of a consensual culture - typical of either social democracy or consociational democracy - as opposed to a conflictual culture). Unfortunately, the necessarily limited number of cases which form the basis of these observations, along with the detectable determinism in much of the literature, has led many people to conclude, wrongly, that these conditions are pre-requisites for stability (see Regini 1984 a).

Much less attention has been paid to how economic conditions themselves influence the development of concertation. One can argue that the success and diffusion of political bargaining in many Western European countries owed a great deal to the exceptional period of continuous economic growth from the end of the Second World War up until the oil crisis of 1974. Crouch (1978), for instance, argues that the ample availability of resources during a period of constant economic growth predicated upon Keynesian policies, was a crucial factor for the development of a stable system of concertation. It enabled participants in the system to obtain compensation for the self-imposed limitation of their market power. In addition, the expectation of continuous growth for the forseeable future made it much easier to bridge the gap in trust which is always apparent between two opposing parties, and which risks paralysing political exchange. Under conditions of constant growth, then, unions could agree not to exert their full market power, giving up immediate benefits in return for future benefits, which by their very nature are uncertain (Pizzorno 1978). So long as growth is constant, the uncertainty of these future benefits is insignificant. If the future state of the economy can be accurately predicted, then so too can the costs and benefits of exchange.

Though these general analyses seem reasonable, they are only partial. There is little doubt that continuous economic growth facilitates the actions of those actors who have decided to engage in a relationship of political exchange. Conversely, however, the same growth can also encourage the parties not to respect the constraints of the exchange. In a period of growth, the temptation not to honour centralised agreements is, in fact, higher (as is evidenced by the diffusion of wage drift), and preoccupations about the macroeconomic consequences of such transgressions is distinctly lower, than in a period of economic depression. In an economic crisis, it is vital for all actors to calculate precisely the compatibility of their own actions or goals with the needs of the economy. The latter are more easily accepted as shared "general interests." Thus, the effect of economic conditions on the institutions of concertation are neither as clear nor unequivocable as we have been led to believe. A slow down in growth may make political bargaining more difficult, but, at the same time, it also makes it even more crucial for the health of the economy.

In order to set out the probable scenarios, however, we must also consider the more specific aspect of the effects which a prolonged crisis is likely to have on the power of the unions and on their capacity to aggregate interests and guarantee consent. It is these latter characteristics, in fact, which have made the unions' role so crucial in the concertative process. In what specific ways, then, do various aspects of the crisis affect the premises of centralised political bargaining in the West European context? Two of the following aspects have already been raised in the previous discussion.

(a) High inflation and consequent uncertainty as to the future state of the economy threaten the very "heart" of concertation, which is the trade-off between self-limitation of market power and future benefits. Accordingly, it becomes less rational to await long-term benefits, which, in any case, cannot be accurately predicted. The unions, therefore, are presented with a dilemma from which there is no satisfactory exit. Whatever they choose to do threatens to undermine the bases of their power. If they agree to moderate their demands in consideration of the economic crisis, agreeing to consensual management irrespective of the declining likelihood of future benefits, they risk alienating their own rank and file, who are the principal source of their power. If, on the other hand, they refuse to participate in any such agreement, they risk having themselves labelled as the principal "guilty" party in the inflation process. Such a development would reduce their legitimacy and endanger their recognition as a privileged partner in political bargaining with the government.

(b) The growing public deficit which is usually associated with economic crisis also makes political bargaining more difficult. The public resources to be traded in the bargaining process (welfare, fiscal benefits, public employment) can no longer be easily provided. Thus benefits cannot be offered to the bargaining partners in exchange for the willingness to restrain their own market power, nor can compensation of various kinds be made available to excluded groups. The dimensions reached by the "fiscal crisis of the state" may even make it necessary for the unions to accept or, possibly, to request reductions in public expenditure. These cuts inevitably conflict with some general interests of workers (their "social wage"), and also with the particular interests of certain groups within the union movement (public employees, pensioners, etc.). Here too, then, the unions are likely to be faced with a crisis of representation which lessens their power and authority, while it diminishes their capability to aggregate interests and guarantee consensus.

(c) Apart from the above two aspects, other manifestations of the current economic crisis have perhaps an even more profound and longer lasting impact on concertation. The period of prolonged recession, relaxing the tensions on the labour market, has inevitably reduced workers' bargaining power. It has obviously encouraged employers to pursue a strategy of de-regulation, that is attempting to break down the rules and institutions which have so limited their autonomy of decision. However, the reduction of workers' contractual power has not been homogeneous or even. Inevitably, certain groups of workers are more protected by laws than others. Some have skills which are in short supply on the market. Others have a crucially important position in the productive process. All these are relatively advantaged compared to other groups. The net result is that while the recession cuts into the power base of the unions in general, it also reduces their capacity to represent the _aggregated_ interests of workers. It becomes much more difficult to mediate between a plurality of demands, yet it was this very ability to mediate and aggregate that gave the unions their 'oligopolistic position" in political bargaining with the government (Regini 1984 a).

(d) Finally, the crisis has had an impact on unions through the related restructuring of the economy. Industrial restructuring and the technological innovation that has gone with it, the growth of services and especially of the advanced tertiary sector, the diffusion of small firms and of the "hidden" economy are all developments which can be interpreted as responses to the problems of productivity and competiveness which have been highlighted by the crisis. The overall effect of these changes has been to fragment the social base represented by the unions. Their capacity to mobilise all workers around shared objectives (or even around a grand design which was suited to the hegemonic groups inside the working class: Accornero 1985) was essential to channelling into an organisational form, not just the protest of the masses but also their potential co-operation. It was, therefore, a crucial resource that the union could trade in the political market. As the unions' capacity has become diminished in this regard, they cease to have the political weight they once had in the past, and they become less useful to the government as mediators of consensus.

THE FUTURE OF POLITICAL BARGAINING IN THE ECONOMIC CRISIS OF THE 1980s

Having discussed the specific ways in which the present crisis has affected the premises on which political bargaining was based in the post-war era, we can now concern ourselves with outlining the probable scenarios for the 1980s.

Though the trends cannot yet be clearly discerned, many indicators reveal a decreasing stability and efficacy in neo-corporatist arrangements, a decline in concertation between unions and the state, and a reduced capacity on the part of the unions to exert political pressure. A number of observers now believe that the trend towards a model based on concertation and centralisation, which was the dominant trend in the second half of the 1970s, has now been stemmed. They see a general crisis in corporatist arrangements, and the types of political bargaining associated with them.

The most recent analyses of national case studies confirm this crisis of relations between unions and the state. The British case is clearly the most extreme example in

Western Europe. But even in West Germany, prior to the change in government of 1982, there were clear signs of instability in the system of political exchange that had dominated the 1970s. The existence of politically favourable conditions seems to make little difference. Though socialist governments have recently come to power in France, Spain, and Greece, there appears to have been no significant development of concertative relations between government and unions.

In general, the major tendency at the present time is the expansion of those areas of industrial relations in which market relations, rather than institutional mediation, predominate, and also the increasing de-regulation of labour relations. Thatcherist neo-liberalism is the ideological mouth-piece of this tendency, but it is also present in different forms and different measure in other countries. Most observers of industrial relations are agreed about the general direction in which the system is moving. They are less agreed about the precise and particular scenarios that are emerging in the 1980s. Mainly, their differences focus on questions of emphasis of the impact and consequences of the changes that are occurring, rather than fundamental differences in the basic analysis. We can, however, usefully group the emerging interpretations into a few major strands, as a means of organising our discussion.

A Drastic Loss of Relevance (and Tendency to Break-up) of Concertation and a Substantial Reduction of the Unions' Political Role

The first scenario is based on arguments substantially shared by many observers. The general weakening of the unions, resulting from the developments discussed above, has the overall effect of making their consent less necessary, It also diminishes their capacity to aggregate the different interests of the workers. Such a situation exposes the institutions of concertation (i. e. those of centralised political bargaining), but also all other forms of market regulation, which have hitherto been crucial to effective management of industry and the economy as a whole, to the danger of attacks by the government and employers. More generally, it results in their effective loss of relevance.

(a) Some scholars (Carrieri and Donolo 1983) emphasise the role that governments are playing in the above development. In fact, it can be argued that political bargaining is in crisis throughout Western Europe, on the grounds that governments are now less reliant on unions' consent, and also because they now find themselves in the position of being obliged to pursue policies which conflict with the interests and priorities of the union movement. As regards the first aspect, one is likely to see various state bodies becoming autonomous of union control. Put another way, public authorities are likely to become relatively independent in their decision-making, compared to their previous position of dependence on union consent. Such a development could be attributed not just to the general weakening of unions' organisational ability, the decline of their bargaining power in the market-place, and the declining power of left-wing political parties that had been favourable to union interests. More important would be the intensification of industrial restructuring, which, with its effect of numerically reducing the working class and removing decision centres from the productive units, has made the traditional instruments of bargaining obsolete and reduced the need to rely on the consent of the unions. There are already several indicators of the "isolation" of the unions, mainly concerning the more widespread practice of governments to issue unilateral regulations and decisions (for example, the dismantling of tripartite institutions in Britain, and decisions on wages and prices in France and Belgium).

As for the second aspect concerning governments' being forced to pursue policies out of line with union interests, one is likely to find all governments, irrespective of their ideological orientation, being obliged to give priority to the dictates of efficiency and international competiveness in order to find a way out of the crisis. This "functional imperative" necessarily conflicts with the logic of the workers' movement, orientated towards safeguarding, even amidst numerous concessions, the previous conditions of welfare.

(b) Other scholars note primarily the resurgence of neo-liberalist ideas among employers. The latter are eager to get rid of the costly arrangements of "joint regulation," which, given the changed power relations, are no longer necessary. They seek to reappropriate their traditional managerial prerogatives in the work-place, and their political hegemony in society as a whole.

As Streeck (1984) demonstrates in the West German case, employers became keen, during the 1980s, to abandon the old neo-corporatist arrangements. The institutions of concertation and co-determination had originally been established in a period of relative power equilibrium between capital and labour. They reflected, therefore, a situation in which the working class was powerful in the labour market and also in organisational terms. Under such conditions, union participation in the management of the economy and of individual firms was accepted by employers *obtorto collo*, because not to have done so would have implied even greater costs. However, the present recession with its attendant high unemployment, altering power relations to the disadvantage of the working class, has caused employers to rethink their strategy. They are now led to believe that the regulation of class conflict can once again be left to market forces, and that there is no longer any need to rely on the kind of consensus that has involved high costs in the past. This scenario is extreme, and probably employers throughout Western Europe would be hesitant to pursue this course of action to its limits. This hesitancy has been noted in research carried out in Britain recently. Also, it was apparent in Italy during the events which preceded the accord of 22 January 1983 on wage indexation: first, employers pursued a "hard" line in an attempt to abolish the *scala mobile* - the wage indexation system; later, though, they took a "soft" line, reaching agreement with the unions on a basis which, to most employers, reflected not the actual power relationship in the market-place, but instead the will of the government. A more realistic scenario which employers probably have in mind is one focussing on the segmentation of union power and of industrial relations in general. It seems clear that one cannot completely ignore the need for unions' consent, since they still represent certain "powerful" sectors of the work-force. An alternative, however, is to move towards a redimensioning of the role of working class representatives. Employers can be more selective and discriminate in their strategies towards various sectors of the working class. While in those firms in which workers are powerful, it will still be necessary to seek the co-operation of unions, elsewhere employers will try to extend those areas in which managerial discretion is not subject to limits. Such a development would imply not only a decline in the overall power of unions, but would also encourage the development of micro-corporative forms of unionism in the traditional sense of privileging the security and interests of "inside" and already protected workers, to the exclusion of more general class interests. The above scenario, then, is the probable strategy of management in those countries in which the union movement has acquired notable positions of institutional power, both in the work-place and in the political system. The institutions which reflect this power cannot be abolished completely. Instead, the aim of management is to erode the capacities of aggregation and of control that the union movement has gained replacing them with a more segmented industrial relations system, which corresponds, in turn, to the segmentation of the market power of workers in various firms and sectors of the economy.

A Sharpening of Differences Between West European Countries as Regards the Possible Institutional Solutions to the Crisis of Concertation, and the Political Future of the Union Movement

This second scenario does not contest the analyses (and predictions) of the first, but they are not considered applicable to all Western European nations. Instead, it predicts two opposite solutions to the present crisis of political bargaining. The previous scenario is seen as most probable in those countries where the institutions of concertation are less solid and have not fully taken root. But in those countries where unions have acquired substantial power resources, and where they have successfully shaped the institutions of concertation, they are likely to be able to resist the crisis, and, in fact, turn it to their advantage, by expanding their role through a further process of regulation of the market. The best expressed argument of this type is that of Goldthorpe (1984), which can be synthesised as follows.

Contrary to the thesis of a convergence of advanced industrialised countries towards a common pluralist model, two quite different responses have emerged in the post-war era to the threat that competition among powerful organised interests has posed to governability and satisfactory economic performance. The first response took the form of attempts to create a neo-corporatist order, founded upon the inclusion of major interest organisations in the formulation of economic policy. The second, in contrast, was a solution based on dualism, that is the expansion of those sectors of the economy in which market forces were relatively free to operate. The expansion in these sectors compensated for the constraints and lack of flexibility prevalent in other sectors of the economy.

As for future developments, it is argued that this division is becoming more acute, and that Western European countries are therefore moving in two quite radically different directions. In certain countries (among which Sweden is the prime example), where concertation has become firmly established as a result of a strong class-based union movement which succeeded in shifting distributive conflict into the political arena (Korpi 1983), we are likely to see repeated renegotiations on the substance of the social contract, leading in the direction of a progressive attack on capitalist institutions. Within this context, unions will continue to promote the long-term general interests of the working class, as opposed to the immediate interests of particular groups. In other countries, where dualistic tendencies predominate, there will be no possibility of any such radical transformation of the economy. In addition, unions will be forced to withdraw to the defence of their members' sectoral interests.

A General Redefinition (but not a Break-up) of Concertative Institutions and of the Unions' Political Role

The preceding scenarios contain useful insights. The first, however, seems to err on the side of excessive pessimism, and also shows excessive haste in drawing general conclusions from a too limited number of complex events. It is still too early to perceive any clear-cut trends from these events. The second scenario seems to suffer from the same limitations as the first, combined also with a little too much optimism as far as regards the countries in which the institutions of concertation and the power resources of the workers' movement are firmly established. These institutions and resources, we must remember, are still subject to the same negative effects of the crisis as are those in other countries.

The variety of circumstances and the complexity of the processes we are considering suggest that we should perhaps formulate a more cautious and balanced scenario. The factors serving to weaken the unions, though undoubtedly significant, do not seem sufficient at the present time to eliminate *tout court* the utility of their consent. Nor are they sufficient to eliminate the unions' capacity to trade their resources in institutions of concertation, though this capacity may be somewhat diminished. The extreme example of Britain may be the only exception to this general line of argument.

What, then, are the prospects for political bargaining, and more generally for the role of unions as political actors? At the national level, it is fairly clear that social contracts in all countries will be renegotiated to take account of diminished union strength. But a renegotiation of this kind does not necessarily imply a loss of relevance and still less a breakdown of concertative arrangements. The consent of the unions, though less crucial and increasingly limited to a more restricted and fragmented representative base, will continue to be important for the formulation of several policies, especially incomes policies.

At the local level, opportunities for political bargaining may even increase, and new instruments of co-operation may then come into existence. Management's need for flexibility and the elimination of practices that prevent the free operation of the market do not necessarily imply that there is no need to collaborate with local labour forces. Even at the national level, the Italian experience, for example, provides evidence of a diffusion rather than a reduction of the role of centralised political bargaining, with the period of solidarietà nazionale (1977-1979) and then with the agreement on labour costs in January 1983. This experience, despite the difficulties encountered in agreeing an incomes' policy in 1984, might well constitute not an anomaly with regard to the general Western European situation, but instead the anticipation of a new common trend (Regini 1984 b). A characteristic of the Italian case is the peculiar type of coexistence of the two trends considered contradictory in the second scenario. Dualism became widespread in Italy, earlier and with greater success than elsewhere (Berger - Piore 1980). But this development did not prevent the simultaneous establishment of centralised political bargaining, admittedly without any stable and clear-cut results. Despite the deepening of the recession and the subsequent weakening of the unions, dualism has not triumphed. It has not led to the break-up of the industrial relations system, nor to its "Japanization", as Streeck (1984) seems to predict for West Germany. There has also been no general attack of a neo-liberal kind on union power, as in Great Britain. Centralised political agreement remains an important unifying aspect of the overall industrial relations' system. The other major aspect, that of the progressive differentiation of union relations at the sectoral, local and work-place level, is quite different, but manages to coexist quite happily with the first.

Two final considerations can be made about this apparently unnatural coexistence. First, we maintained that the weakening of the unions, owing to the factors discussed in the second section, does not necessarily put an end to centralised political bargaining, or even diminish its relevance. It certainly obliges unions, however, to accept a worsening of the "terms of trade." In the case of the January 1983 agreement in Italy, this worsening took the form of a restriction of the range of interests represented (from those of the entire working class to those of regularly employed workers), and the giving-up of certain long-term goals (employment, investments, development of the Mezzogiorno). In other circumstances, or in the near future, one could have different solutions. What should be noted, though, is that the unions' capacity to aggregate interests and influence economic policy is maintained through a renegotiation of the terms of trade. So long as the factors remain that cause the weakness of the unions, there is no country in which such terms of trade can be turned to the advantage of the union movement.

Our second consideration concerns the growing differentiation of union relations at the sectoral, local and workplace levels. Though somewhat speculative, this development is the probable outcome of maintaining a level of centralised political bargaining. It can take a "hidden" form, as in Italy, or it can be guided and controlled. The respective spheres of competence of centralised political agreement and of decentralised, or even fragmented bargaining can be regulated. The extent to which the central sphere is responsible for workers' living conditions and their degree of control over the economy, and how much is left instead to the variability of market conditions and eventually to new concertative institutions at the decentralised level, can be subjected to precise rules. It does not seem unlikely that on this question of the separation of general interests from particular interests, and the establishment of a more flexible approach in dealing with the latter, we may soon see the powerful and highly centralised unions of other Western European countries moving in the direction recently taken by Italian industrial relations.

NOTES

1. This research was made possible by a grant from the Ministero della Pubblica Istruzione, entitled "Scambio politico e conflitto sindacale in Europa".
2. The Period known as 'national solidarity' or 'national unity' was one in which the Italian Communist Party (PCI), i.e. the major party of opposition since 1947, entered a parliamentary coalition of six parties, supporting the government. Faced with a deep economic crisis and with the threat of terrorism, the six parties, including the PCI, reached a 'programmatic agreement' on a series of policies, which obtained the parliamentary abstention of the PCI in 1977 and then its vote in 1978. 'National solidarity' officially ended in 1979, with the elections of that year. For a

comparison between this period and the British "Social Contract", see Regini (1984 a).

REFERENCES

Accornero, A. (1985), Social Change and Trade Union Movement: Italy in the 1970s, in O. Jacobi et al. (eds.), Technological Change, Rationalization and Industrial Relations, London, Croom Helm

Berger, S. - Piore, M. (1980), Dualism and Discontinuity in Industrial Societies, Cambridge University Press

Carrieri, M. - Donolo, C. (1983), "Oltre l'orizzonte neo-corporatista. Alcuni scenari sul futuro politico del sindacato", Stato e mercato, 9

Crouch, C. (1978), The Changing Role of the State in Industrial Relations in W. Europe, in C. Crouch - A. Pizzorno (eds.), The Resurgence of Class Conflict in W. Europe Since 1968, vol. 2, London, Macmillan

Goldthorpe, J. (1984), The end of convergence: corporatist and dualist tendencies in modern western societies, in J. Goldthorpe (ed.), Order and Conflict in Contemporary Capitalism, Oxford University Press

Korpi, W. (1983), The Democratic Class Struggle, London, Routledge & Kegan Paul

Lange, P. et al. (1982), Unions, Change and Crisis, London, Allen & Unwin

Lehmbruch, G. (1977), "Liberal corporatism and party government", Comparative Political Studies

Offe, C. (1981), The Attribution of Public Status to Interest Groups: Observations on the W. German Case, in S. Berger (ed.), Organizing Interests in Western Europe, Cambridge University Press

Panitch, L. (1977), "The development of corporatism in liberal democies", Comparative Political Studies

Pizzorno, A. (1978), Political Exchange and Collective Identity in Industrial Conflict, in C. Crouch - A. Pizzorno (eds.), op. cit.

Regini, M. (1984 a), The Conditions for Political Exchange: How Concertation Emerged and Declined in Italy and Great Britain, in J. Goldthorpe (ed.), op. cit.

Regini, M. (1984 b), "I tentativi italiani di 'patto sociale' a cavallo degli anni ottanta", Il Mulino, 2

Salvati, M. (1982), "Strutture politiche ed esiti economici", Stato e mercato, 4

Schmitter, P. (1981), Interest intermediation and regime

governability in contemporary Western Europe and North America, in S. Berger (ed.), op. cit.
Schmitter, P. -Lehmbruch, G. (eds., 1979), Trends Toward Corporatist Intermediation, London, Sage
Streeck, W. (1984), Neo-corporatist Industrial Relations and the Economic Crisis in West Germany, in J. Goldthorpe (ed.), op. cit.
Winkler, J. (1976), "Corporatism", Archives Europeennes de Sociologie

PART TWO

"Great Britain: The Impasse Broken?"

Chapter 4

BRITISH INDUSTRIAL RELATIONS: THE LIMITS OF CORPORATISM

Richard Hyman

THE CORPORATIST PROBLEMATIC

For students of West European politics, the notion of corporatism has for many years now been central to discussion of the relationships between state, economy, and economic interest organisations. Writers on industrial relations, though traditionally suspicious of novel intellectual fashions, have more recently embraced the term within their own vocabulary as aspects of these same relationships have entered their field of vision. For industrial relations empiricists, indeed, one attraction is doubtless that 'corporatism' is typically employed as a descriptive category or empirical generalisation, not rooted in any explicit theoretical framework.

This theoretic innocence is however a frequent source of ambiguity and confusion. For different authors, 'corporatism' denotes an economic system, a form of state, or a structure of interest representation; or an imprecise amalgam of all of these. Some treat corporatism merely as a tendency, dominant within specific societies at particular historical moments; others as a universal and irrevocable trend within western polities. This is in part a reflection of the divergent intellectual and pragmatic concerns which have encouraged the adoption of corporatist analyses. Political scientists have aimed to interpret the erosion of traditional demarcations between polity and economy: the extension of state functions within the sphere of production and circulation, the growing involvement of economic institutions and actors in the machinery of state. Industrial relations students have sought to comprehend the diminishing autonomy of their own area of analysis: increased governmental and legislative intervention in employment affairs, the expanding political role of trade unions and employers' organisations. Those who define their interest as the analysis of class struggle have focused on new forms of legitimation and external containment of workers' organisations. All these phenomena bespeak new modes of integration between state and civil society (some would add: as a response to the crisis of capital accumulation); but the meanings and emphases of 'corporatism' and 'incorporation' vary substantially according to the features of this integration under examination.

Accordingly, one may be sceptical whether discussions of corporatism have genuinely advanced understanding and enlightenment. Yet if too much intellectual capital is now invested in this 'growth industry'[1] to permit a moratorium on the usage of the term, it is at least essential to define its meaning with precision. In the context of this paper, the notion of corporatism is used to denote an institutional framework within which organised economic interests are directly represented in the formulation and application of state policy, displacing or by-passing the traditional parliamentary process. Three corollaries are of particular significance for industrial relations. Firstly, the representational status of trade unions (or of certain favoured organisations) is enhanced. This follows partly from their formal involvement in the machinery of government, but may also reflect legislative support for union recognition and collective bargaining. Secondly, union participation in policy-making is at least implicitly conditional on an acceptance of the overriding priority of profitability and capital accumulation, and on a readiness to resolve differences which occur within this basic consensus through conciliatory means. And thirdly, hierarchical authority within union organisation is reinforced, providing disciplinary sanctions to inhibit or contain rank-and-file aspirations and actions which threaten leadership collaboration in corporate arrangements.

Corporatism and the British Industrial Tradition

Industrial relations in Britain have traditionally diverged sharply from the corporatist model. As pioneers of industrial capitalism, British entrepreneurs fought against traditional restrictions on 'market forces', demanding the state's withdrawal from civil society. Confident of their own ability to dominate both in domestic relations with labour and in overseas competition in product markets, capitalists opposed state economic intervention - beyond the vital background role of securing imperial markets and suppressing working-class challenges to their own economic power.

The nineteenth-century *laisser-faire* tradition shaped the formation of British industrial relations institutions. The first trade unions faced severe legal repression. But by the second half of the nineteenth century many employers had come to recognise that British unions were moderate and conciliatory organisations which posed little threat to their own interests; and that legalisation might indeed reinforce their conservative tendencies. From the 1870s a system of labour law was thus established which was to distinguish British industrial relations for the following century. The key legislation permitting unions to organise and conduct strikes was negative rather than positive in character: rather than establishing *rights* the law prescribed *immunities* from common-law prosecutions. The conduct of industrial relations was thus to be largely outside the jurisdiction of the courts, symbolising a majority view among unions and employers alike that the less legislative or governmental interference in their common affairs the better.

The consequent detachment between 'politics' and industrial relations is in sharp contrast to corporatism. Equally marked is the absence of those corollaries of corporatism which were identified earlier. The law has traditionally imposed no obligation on employers to recognise or negotiate with trade unions; indeed they have been free to dismiss employees for the very fact of union membership. Collective agreements themselves have not possessed any legal status: they are private treaties, not collective contracts, and do not override the individual contract of employment. Given the lack of statutory support for union representation, there has been no reciprocal requirement of 'responsible' behaviour. Thus union 'responsibility' cannot plausibly be interpreted as part of a corporatist trade-off. Finally, the disciplinary role of British trade unions has always been less significant than in most other countries. Union leaders with control of only limited financial resources and a relatively small body of full-time officials have been highly dependent on the energies and commitment of innumerable 'lay' officers and representatives, and this has entailed major restraints on bureaucratic or authoritarian tendencies.

Yet if the *laisser-faire* tradition was the obverse of corporatism, most commentaries on the politics of British industry in the 1970s identified an increasing corporatist drift. This trend was typically attributed to material pressures: the specific requirements of late twentieth-century capitalist production, the changing structure of British capital, the deteriorating performance of the UK economy. The product of two decades of seemingly bipartisan political initiative, corporatist structures were widely regarded as immune to both the trend from Keynesian to monetarist economic policies and the vagaries of party ideology.

The experience of the 1979 Thatcher government, with its frontal attacks on trade unions, on state welfare, and on the very notion of active economic management by government, has rudely shaken such complacency. But there is as yet little evidence of serious re-evaluation of the corporatist interpretations of the 1960s and 1970s, or of persuasive analyses of the continuities and discontinuities in government policy since 1979. The aim of the discussion which follows is to assess the key developments in Britain in the past two decades; to stress the historically contingent character, the incompleteness, and the internal contradictions of those corporatist arrangements which were established, and hence their underlying fragility; and thus to provide a basis for an understanding of Thatcherism.

Tripartism in the 1960s

The *laisser-faire* tradition outlined above has been subject to adaptation and erosion throughout the present century; in particular, the extensive integration of state and economy during both world wars had repercussions which survived the process of post-war 'decontrol'. Nevertheless, the changes which have occurred since 1960 have been particularly marked. Four aspects in particular may be identified: alterations in the structure and priorities of capital; the expansion of state employment; the creation of tripartite machinery of economic planning; and the extension of state legislative and administrative intervention in industrial relations.

Corporatist developments must be located in their material context: a point far too often neglected in academic discussions. In recent decades there has occurred a dramatic concentration and centralisation of capital in Britain.[2] Increasingly monopolistic in character, the dominant sectors of modern British capital bear little resemblance to the Victorian model of competitive capitalism. Concerned above all else to obtain a stable and predictable macro-economic environment within which to make long-term investment decisions, and anxious to externalise the costs of training and research, major industrialists have increasingly viewed the state as the necessary provider of their infrastructural requirements as well as the source of direct grants and subventions.

The economic role of the state itself has been substantially affected by its development as a major - indeed *the* major - employer of British labour. This reflects in part the nationalisation of private industry, initially in accordance with the programme of the 1945-51 Labour Government, more recently to rescue the casualties of capitalist crisis; in part the growth of the 'welfare state', of social services provided by national or local government; in part the general expansion of the administrative apparatus of the state. Today these areas of activity account for roughly a third of total British employment, and about half the total number of trade unionists.[3]

The third major area of change has been the increasing commitment of British governments to the idea of economic planning. This trend was signalled by the establishment in 1962 of the National Economic Development Council (NEDC) composed of senior ministers, employer representatives, and TUC nominees; tripartite machinery ('little Neddies') was also created for individual branches of industry. It is significant that this initiative was taken by a Conservative government: the symbolic abandonment of *laisser-faire* by the party of British capital may be seen as the outcome both of concern with the relatively poor growth rate of the British economy, and of the decision to seek membership of the Common Market (where planning was regarded as the norm).

Initially, planning was presented as a recipe for growth, and it was this which gave specific delineations to what would remain a continuing issue: the link between economic planning in general and incomes policy in particular. Government efforts in the 1950s to control wage and salary movements had relied on aggregate fiscal and monetary measures which were widely viewed as a cause of poor economic growth; direct intervention in pay determination was increasingly urged (by academics, employers and politicians) as a preferable alternative. Accordingly, the birth of the NEDC coincided with government guidelines for a national incomes policy and the formation of a National Incomes Commission.

However the TUC rejected pay restraint, and there was opposition to participation in the NEDC itself. But the Labour government elected in 1964 achieved greater success. Union support for a Labour pay policy was won in advance of the 1964 election on the basis that it would represent, not wage restraint but a 'planned growth of incomes'. Most unions remained remarkably loyal even though, during most of the period Labour was in office, real post-tax incomes barely increased; indeed in 1966 the TUC 'reluctantly acquiesced' in a formal wage freeze. At national level, unions appeared less concerned with the content of incomes policy than with their own status in its operation: the paramount consideration was that the policy should remain 'voluntary', an exercise in union self-restraint, rather than externally imposed by government wielding statutory powers.

Associated with incomes policy were new forms of state involvement in the sphere of production. The ideology of 'planning for growth' rested on a commitment to raise labour productivity; and a variety of new government agencies encouraged a vogue for 'productivity bargaining'. The 1960s also saw the development of an 'active manpower policy' on the part of government. The 1964 Industrial Training Act set up Training Boards in specific industries, funded by levies on employers, together with a central council; all included TUC and employer nominees. The 1965 Redundancy Payments Act (originally drafted under the Conservatives) sought to weaken workers' resistance to job loss and hence encourage labour mobility by providing a state-backed system of redundancy compensation; a structure of Industrial Tribunals, with union and employer representation, was created to adjudicate disputes on the application of the Act.

The role of the state as promoter of industrial relations 'reform' also requires emphasis. The Royal Commission on Trade Unions and Employers' Associations, appointed by the Labour government in 1965, spoke of a conflict between the 'formal and informal systems' of industrial relations in Britain, and called for a series of structural reforms designed to achieve 'the orderly and effective regulation of industrial relations within companies and factories' (Donovan 1968). There followed the establishment of a further tripartite agency, the Commission on Industrial Relations (CIR), empowered to conduct investigations and make recommendations on both general issues and conditions in specific firms or industries.

How far did the development of union-employer-state relations in the 1960s, symbolised by the proliferation of tripartite institutions, justify analyses in terms of corporatism?[4] Institutional symbolism can obscure the fact that the growth of tripartism was both uneven and asymmetrical. Traditionally the economic strategies of post-war governments - and hence normally their broader social objectives - have depended on the production and investment decisions of private companies. In the absence of direct and detailed control over such decisions, economic policy has rested on various forms of positive assistance and encouragement to capital. The position of labour is quite distinct. The routine activities of trade unions challenge profitability and hence the economic priorities of governments, which thus seek negative curbs on union activity.[5] Within tripartite administration of economic policy, employers co-operate insofar as they see this as consistent with their own interests; while unions collaborate as a result of material or ideological pressure, or as part of an explicit or implicit trade-off.

What is also clear in the context of Britain in the 1960s is the partial and limited nature of corporatist tendencies. The vogue for planning gave birth to the NEDC in 1962, a Department of Economic Affairs under the 1964 Labour Government, and a National Plan published with much ceremony in 1965; but its practical effects were negligible. British planning was unambiguously indicative rather than dirigiste in character; and corporate decision-makers put little faith in the indicators - thus contributing to their invalidation. The main area of more forceful state intervention was pay determination, where the objective of containing labour costs reflected employers' own interests.

The tentative nature of 1960s corporatism is evident in the three specific areas outlined earlier. In formal terms, the position of the unions as an 'estate of the realm' was undoubtedly enhanced; the special postage stamp issued for the TUC centenary in 1968 constituted the ultimate accolade. The representational monopoly enjoyed by the TUC on tripartite bodies induced almost every union of any significance not already affiliated (mainly professional and white-collar associations in the public sector) to join its ranks. But there were no moves towards statutory backing for collective bargaining or union recognition.

Certainly there is evidence of a move towards a trade-off involving union moderation in wage bargaining in return for participation in economic planning. An eloquent advocate of the strategy of collective bargaining at the level of government was George Woodcock, general secretary of the TUC, who regularly insisted that voluntary limitation of pay claims was an acceptable price to pay for securing full employment and expanded welfare services. There were also moves towards greater central discipline within this exceptionally decentralised trade union movement.[6]

Yet in retrospect, what is notable is how little success

was achieved in the 1960s by what Panitch (1976: 246) terms the 'quasi-corporatist project' to transform trade unions into 'agencies of social control over their members'. Labour's incomes policy was vociferously opposed by a minority of unions from the outset; by 1967 a majority were against the legislative sanctions underlying the policy; and this growing disaffection helped ensure the violent reaction to the 'penal clauses' in the government's 1969 industrial relations proposals. In 1968 the TUC launched the first of an annual series of Economic Reviews, which detailed a macroeconomic strategy very different from that of the government itself: emphasising expansion, egalitarianism, and greater state control over private capital. Finally, 1969 and 1970 saw 'explosions' in which the number of strikes, and the level of pay increases, rose rapidly. At least for many leftist commentators, a strategy of incorporation at leadership level had been fractured by the autonomous militancy of the union rank and file.

Crisis and Contract in the 1970s

In the 1970s the ailing British economy lurched from crisis to crisis, its inherent structural weaknesses accentuated by the world recession. Registered unemployment in the UK rose to a peak of a million in early 1972, and after a brief recovery climbed to new record levels in the second half of the decade. Apart from a short-lived 'mini-boom' in 1973, production stagnated and in some years declined. The annual rate of price inflation was over 10 per cent for most of the 1970s, with a peak of 27 per cent in 1975.

The Conservative Government elected in 1970 was explicitly committed to reverse the trend of industrial policy of the previous decade. To restore the impact of market forces, many of the institutions of Labour's intervention in economic planning were abolished.[7] Formal incomes policy was abandoned, though rigid pay restraint was imposed in the public sector. The most dramatic change, though, was the transformation of labour law through the Industrial Relations Act of 1971, introduced after a minimal gesture of consultation with those affected.

This abrasive re-assertion of nineteenth-century principles of *laisser-faire* and aggressive anti-unionism was short-lived: in 1972 came the government's 'U-turn'. In the face of deepening recession and acute financial problems for major companies, it passed an Industry Act providing powers for selective intervention, financial assistance and acquisition of shares in private companies. State initiatives within the labour market were extended by the Employment and Training Act of 1973, which established the Manpower Services Commission as a new exercise in tripartism. And after major disputes in 1972 seriously damaged the government's credibility, a new accommodation was sought with the trade unions.

After the defeat of Heath in 1974, a new phase of intensive relations between state and unions ensued. Opposition to the Conservative Government had healed the divisions between TUC and Labour Party leaderships; and unity was consolidated with the formation of a joint Liaison Committee. The outcome was a series of agreements on the economic and social programme of a future Labour government. Planning would be far more directive than in 1964-70, with powers to control prices and to intervene in company investment decisions. State welfare provision would be considerably extended. There would be a 'fundamental and irreversible shift in the balance of power and wealth in favour of working people and their families'. And as an immediate priority, the Industrial Relations Act was to be replaced by legislation in line with union aspirations. In popular discussion, this broad agenda soon acquired the title of 'social contract'.

In the field of labour law the unions' objectives were largely satisfied. The Trade Union and Labour Relations Act of 1974 (with amendments in 1976) and the Employment Protection Act of 1975 repealed the 1971 legislation, restoring the traditional immunities for trade union action and creating a number of new rights for workers. More significant was the range of collective rights contained in the legislation: machinery for union recognition and for awards against firms not observing the 'general level' of conditions in their industry; protection of union members against victimisation; provisions for disclosure of information and for time off for union workplace representatives. (In approving these initiatives the TUC, almost without debate, abandoned its traditional opposition to 'positive' labour law.) The Health and Safety at Work Act of 1974 extended previous legislation, and provided for union representation in a new structure of safety committees. The Sex Discrimination Act of 1975 (which complemented the 1970 Equal Pay Act) and the Race Relations Act of 1976 allowed complaints to an Industrial Tribunal against discrimination in employment.

Without exception the new statutory rights proved far more impressive on paper than in practice; their symbolic effect was nevertheless substantial. Moreover, the legislative initiatives were associated with a rash of new tripartite machinery (dismissively labelled 'quangos' by critics of this trend).

At workplace level there were parallel developments. The process of 'reform' articulated by the Donovan Report, and already actively embraced by some leading employers, involved extensive formalisation, rationalisation and centralisation of domestic bargaining. The tightening of internal management controls; the introduction of new payment systems, job evaluation schemes and 'productivity' agreements; and the implementation of more legalistic bargaining and disciplinary procedures, all restricted the negotiating opportunities of first-line shop stewards. At the same time the stratum of senior stewards and convenors at plant or company level expanded rapidly and acquired new powers and responsibilities. As part of the process of formalising relationships, employers were increasingly willing to aid union organisation through the closed shop and deduction of union subscriptions from wages - often as a means to more 'orderly' workplace relations. The need for workplace negotiators to follow 'due procedure', to rely more on legalistic principles and 'rational' argument in handling cases and less on the mobilisation of collective action, was moreover strongly urged in the shop steward training courses which grew rapidly, with state funding, in the latter 1970s.

In all other respects the achievements of the 'social contract' - at least for the unions - were of little note. The 'industrial strategy' which was initially portrayed as such a potent instrument turned out to be a paper tiger, particularly after the right regained unquestioned ascendancy within the government in mid-1975 and Benn was removed from his post as Industry Secretary. The 1975 Industry Act was a pale reflection of the original grand design: the planning agreements - through which government and unions were to help shape company production and investment decisions - were a dead letter, since firms were under no pressure to make such agreements; the tripartite National Enterprise Board (1975), designed to give a public stake in the most dynamic sectors of the economy, was starved of resources; the Sector Working Parties grafted onto the NEDC machinery in 1976 proved to be mere talking shops.

In broader socio-economic policy, radical hopes were likewise disappointed. Following a well-worn British tradition, the commitment to egalitarianism was side-stepped by appointing a Royal Commission. Public expenditure on social welfare fell victim to the sterling crises of 1975 and succeeding years, and the direct constraints of the International Monetary Fund over budgetary policy, initiating a regime which can at best be termed 'soft monetarism'. Cutbacks in social expenditure programmes in 1975 led the following year to 'the most deflationary budget for many years' (Clark et al. 1980: 38). Most areas of spending by central and local government and the nationalised industries became subject to 'cash limits': a strict monetary budget allocation in place of the previous flexible funding.

While union pressure was ineffectual in halting this adverse trend in economic policy, the government was far more successful in its pressure on the unions: their 'privileged' involvement in the 'social contract' became 'less an index of their power than of their subordination' (Coates 1980: 59). In the financial crisis of summer 1975 the government insisted on the introduction of a rigid set of wage controls, and after hasty discussions the TUC agreed to a £6 limit for pay increases. In the following year a second phase of controls was agreed, providing a ceiling of 5 per cent for wage rises. But by 1977, with earnings falling behind the cost of living, pressure built up in many unions for an immediate return to 'free collective bargaining'.[8] The TUC refused to approve the government's limit of 10 per cent for 1977-8, but neither did it lead any concerted opposition. A year later, however, the government's declaration of a further 5 per cent ceiling and its attempt to impose this in public sector negotiations provoked a series of major strikes, notably in local government and the health service. In an attempt to repair the breach, a 'concordat' was agreed between government and TUC in February 1979. But the reiteration of the need for a 'close and constructive partnership' failed to restore the government's economic credibility, and three months later the general election resulted in a heavy defeat.

In appraising the experience of the 1970s, it is clear that any corporatist interpretations which stress state control over (or fusion with) private capital are one-sided and exaggerated. It has been seen that radical proposals for directive planning were quickly aborted: 'measures which might have fostered an extension of corporatism were rejected and state intervention was limited to subvention' (Cox 1981: 89). The elaborate developments in labour law did not in practice entail serious external regulation of managerial control of the labour process.[9] A far more significant corporatist project, a statutory right for union representation on company boards of directors, formed part of the original 'social contract' understandings but came to nothing. A Committee of Inquiry on Industrial Democracy was appointed in 1975 and submitted detailed and complex proposals (the Bullock Report) two years later, urging the necessity of 'putting the relationship between capital and labour on to a new basis which will involve not just management but the whole workforce in sharing responsibility for the success and profitability of the enterprise'. But the whole idea of statutory worker directors was rejected by the minority of employer representatives on the Bullock Committee, bitterly resisted by the CBI, and quietly abandoned by the government.

The changing posture of the CBI is itself an important aspect of the 1970s. Traditional sectors of large-scale national capital were probably most favourable towards corporatist developments, and had exerted major influence in employers' organisations. The professional functionaries of the CBI tended to acquire close understandings with their counterparts in government and the TUC, while their own status was boosted by tripartism. But the rapidly expanding sector of transnational capital resisted enmeshment with a single national state; while small-scale capital often clung to traditional _laisser-faire_ principles (Strinati 1979). Moreover small-scale employers were typically emotionally and ideologically committed to the Conservative Party and to its sharp rightwards shift under Thatcher's leadership; and perceiving the form rather than the substance of the 'social contract', they tended to experience 1974-9 as a period of exceptional privilege for the unions when the balance of power swung intolerably in their favour. The first national conference held by the CBI, in the autumn of 1977, was the occasion for a 'rank-and-file revolt': only months after CBI leaders had published proposals for a 'national economic forum' linked to Parliament within which employers and unions would collaborate in policy formulation, the demand from below was for a far more abrasive anti-union and anti-corporatist bias. Thereafter the official CBI stance moved substantially away from consensus and collaboration.

If the notion of corporatism is to be applied to the latter 1970s it must thus relate primarily to the relationship between state and unions; and it is indeed significant that the 'social contract' was a _bilateral_ arrangement between Labour and the TUC, rather than a simple extension of tripartism. Some commentators have interpreted this relationship as essentially one of union subordination or 'incorporation': as symbolised by the introduction of the £6 pay limit after brief negotiations with a few TUC leaders (the 'NEDC six'), and the enforcement of this and the 1976-7 policy on potentially dissident unions. Even after the end of formal agreement on pay policy, the TUC indirectly aided restraint: as, for example, in its refusal to mobilise support for the firemen's strike at the end of 1977, and its attempt to contain the eruption of conflict in the winter of 1978-9. More generally, the subdued character of TUC criticism of the drift to monetarism, public sector cuts and a wage-control-based economic policy helped reinforce the view that there was no credible policy option to the left of the austerity programme of the Labour government.

Yet how adequately can this be characterised as corporatism? The £6 pay policy was only narrowly approved by the TUC General Council, and although opposition was less the following year there remained a core of unions resistant to the whole principle of restraint and soon able to win majority support against its continuation. Some union leaders did present a sustained left-wing critique of government economic policy. And the whole 'corporatist' image of the 'social contract' evoked suspicion: as one union leader put it in 1976,

> if we are going to bargain continuously and effectively on all major issues of the day with which our members are concerned, then it is possible that we will become mesmerised by the process itself, rather than considering the results it achieves.... It is dangerous for the Movement to accept incorporation in the apparatus of the State, articulated through what may be a loyalty to a Labour Government.[10]

Trade unions in Britain (as elsewhere) have traditionally been susceptible to appeals to 'national interest', have always qualified the oppositional and disruptive aspects of their representation of working-class interests within a pragmatic appreciation of the external power of capital and the state; and have been particularly sensitive to appeals for moderation and loyalty from Labour governments. In this sense, the period of the 'social contract' may be regarded as merely an elaboration of the <u>normal</u> inhibitions on trade union militancy: an episode in which the particular contradictory interrelationship of representation and restraint probably owed as much to the distinctive material environment as to the specific institutional entanglements of the unions. To focus on one facet of this ensemble of relations, applying the label 'corporatism', obstructs rather than advances understanding.

The Thatcher Government: Corporatism Discarded

'Despite their instability,' Panitch has argued (1981: 40), 'corporatist structures exhibit a tenacious durability, spanning the rise and fall of particular governments'. According to Jessop, writing before the 1979 election (1978: 46), corporatism is fully compatible with

> monetarist policies within the political executive. For, in addition to their role in the restructuring of capital, control over the money supply and state expenditure is also being used to create the conditions required for reorganising the labour movement itself and integrating it more effectively into the state apparatus. Thus the monetarist policies of the Labour government should be seen as complementary to its corporatist strategy.

Thus many commentators discerned a 'logic' to corporatist tendencies which would prove resistant to the ideological antipathy of a Conservative government under Thatcher. Writing on the eve of the 1979 election, Thomson (1979: 48) noted that 'the Conservatives have made considerable contributions to the unions' role in the corporate state' and argued that 'the Tories are unlikely to dismantle much of the structure' established in the previous years. 'After all, they cannot afford to be seen to be anti-union.'

Few predictions can have been so rapidly discredited. In its break with the socio-economic consensus underlying the policies of all former post-war governments - committed regardless of party to a managed welfare capitalism - the Thatcher government in office has executed its declared intentions. Dismantling the Keynesian mechanisms of demand management raised UK registered unemployment from 1.3 million at the date of the election to over 3.3 million in September 1982, a level of 14 per cent. Unregistered unemployment (particularly among women) together with school leavers involved in cosmetic 'work experience' schemes would add at least another million to this total.[11]

The government's antipathy to the 'welfare state' has brought the National Health Service to the brink of collapse and pushed educational standards back to pre-war levels.

Rigorous powers have been assumed to curb local authority expenditure, resulting in drastic cutbacks in social services and in subsidies for housing and public transport. The dismantling of welfare services - which have represented a major growth area for female employment in post-war Britain - has a particularly serious impact on women, both as employees and as clients: since it is women who are forced to assume the now privatised burden of care for pre-school children, the old, the sick and the disabled. And indeed, some government ministers in preaching a return to 'traditional family values' aim explicitly to force women out of the labour market.

Government policy defines a close connection between Keynesianism, state welfare, and trade unionism: and in particular what is termed 'public sector monopoly unionism'. The tendency to present unions as a scapegoat for economic stagnation and crisis, attractive to governments since the 1960s, has been radically reinforced; the corporatist project has thus been firmly rejected. The novel insight of Thatcherism is that national consensus on social policy may be more readily pursued in opposition to trade unions than in collaboration with them.

In line with this perspective the government has challenged, not merely the legislation of 1974-76, but the whole framework of labour law established between 1871 and 1913. The Employment Acts of 1980 and 1982 constitute a more far-reaching though more piecemeal attack on trade unionism than the ill-fated Industrial Relations Act, outlawing most forms of strike, picketing and closed shop, and exposing unions to heavy financial penalties. The 1984 legislation requires individual ballots in key union decisions (thus assailing the principle of collective participation as the basis of union solidarity) and closely circumscribes union political activities. Special restrictions on strike action in 'essential services' are also contemplated.

Secondly, many of the positive protections contained in Labour's legislation have been diluted or eliminated, as have such long-standing provisions as the 'fair wages clause' in government contracts. The Wages Councils, which have sought to provide some statutory minimum to earnings in the lowest-paid industries since the beginning of the century, face abolition. Most Industrial Training Boards have been closed down, and public funding for trade union education drastically reduced.

Thirdly, Thatcher's ministers have been even more

anxious than those of the early Heath years to discard the cosy etiquette of consultative relations with union representatives. Openly contemptuous of the whole philosophy of tripartism, one of the government's first acts was to initiate a review of the 'quango' system; this resulted in the abolition of a number of such bodies (though it proved impracticable to eliminate as many as had been expected). But in those that survived, TUC nominees could no longer pretend to exert any discernible influence; indeed their views were treated with such obvious disdain that there was significant pressure at the 1982 TUC to withdraw from the NEDC, the major symbolic relic of tripartism. Thatcher's second election victory in June 1983 at first strengthened the majority view that consultative links, however ineffectual, must be maintained; but the government itself eventually forced a change of policy in 1984 by its gratuitous attack on union membership rights at GCHQ.

The fourth main challenge has occurred within public sector industrial relations. Like its predecessor in 1970, the Conservative government has disavowed an incomes policy but has imposed rigid pay curbs for its own employees through cash limits. The system of budgetary controls initiated by Labour has been intensified, and percentage allowances for wage increases have been specified at levels considerably below the rate of inflation: the choice for unions has thus been falling real incomes or even faster job losses. In the nationalised industries, government willingness to fund investment programmes (or to offset operating losses) has been directly proportionate to management rigour in attacking established collective arrangements. The proposed legislation on strikes in 'essential services' will represent a further stage in the attack on public sector unionism.

It is evident that the government's anti-union strategy has achieved considerable success. Trade union membership, which rose consistently throughout the 1970s, has fallen by some 17 per cent since 1979. The annual number of strikes is roughly half the 1970s average: an indication of demoralisation in the face of falling real incomes and deteriorating conditions of work. Declining combativity may be attributed in part to sheer fear of unemployment; but in part to positive acceptance of the need for 'sacrifice' in time of economic crisis. Fragmented resistance by sections of public sector workers, often seemingly deliberately provoked, is skilfully utilised by Thatcherism's ideological exponents to demonstrate the unreliability of 'public sector monopolies' and the 'anti-social' character of trade unionism. The government has consistently argued that the official union movement's claim to represent the views of the mass of workers has always rested on bluff; at decisive moments it has appeared to prove its point.

Conclusion: the Contradictions of Corporatism in Practice and Theory

The notion of corporatism, with its connotations of the assimilation of 'organised producer interests' into the policy formulation and administration of the state, is typically employed with two main directions of empirical reference. The first involves the integration of the state and private capital in the control of an increasingly planned economy. The second involves the absorption of trade unions within the processes of economic management: as a means either of socialising and humanising capitalist priorities (the rationale for social-democratic approval and conservative denunciation); or for subordinating working-class interests to these priorities (as left critics allege); or both (as some interpreters suggest).

Interpretations of both sets of relations as corporatist typically lack historical specificity. Often the analysis of capital-state interaction implies a somewhat naive developmental model, in which capitalism's contradictions are progressively eliminated through Keynesian demand management, monopolisation of ownership and state-sponsored planning. Yet the eclipse of Keynesianism in the 1970s reflects not merely the triumph of conservative ideology but the material contradictions of orthodox demand management as a strategy for capital. The Keynesian recipe is addressed to the problem of the realisation of surplus value but not its production; indeed 'full' employment, by fostering the confidence of labour, may well undermine surplus value production by eroding capitalist discipline over the labour process. At the other pole of the circuit of capital, demand-sustaining activities of the state impose a fiscal burden which threatens the profitability of capital, especially when constrained by international competition. Integration with the state in its post-war pursuit of macro-economic stabilisation was undeniably attractive to national monopoly capital, particularly if producing for relatively sheltered domestic markets yet experiencing problems of profitability. Transnational capital, as suggested earlier, is however far less disposed to integrative relations with individual nation-states; while capital in competitive sectors is perhaps most inclined towards monetarist solutions (which have always been favoured by finance capital). More generally, the conjunction of a rising tax burden and declining profitability is almost inevitably fatal for corporatist/Keynesian structures.[12]

Debates on the role of trade unions within corporatist institutions typically focus on the dialectic of representation and restraint. For Panitch (1981: 34-5), it is precisely the contradiction between these two functions in the operation of wage controls which ensures 'the fragility of corporatist political structures'. Crouch (1979: 188-9) discerns a similar tension:

> the problem is that unions will become unable to deliver their members' consent to restraint if they never offer them anything to make acceptance of co-ordination by the union leadership worthwhile .... The consequence of this is a continual slippage away from corporatist arrangements to free collective bargaining on the part of union leaderships. This means that union consent to participation in corporatist relations has to be continually regained by governments through concessions - either concessions to compensate unions for the difficult time they will have at the hands of their members, or concessions that will be experienced as such by the members.

This formulation - despite its reified treatment of 'unions' - makes clear that a process of corporatist trade-off may involve, not real concessions to working-class interests but such symbolic gestures as the consolidation of the status of union leaders. Indeed, a corporatist strategy may well involve a reinforcement of the disciplinary powers and representational monopoly of union leaders, so that rank-and-file protest may be more readily de-fused or suppressed.[13]

What is particularly notable in Crouch's analysis, however, is his insensitivity to the material context of 'bargained corporatism'. It is evident that the fiscal crisis of the state, and the declining profitability of private capital, must reduce or eliminate the margin for substantive concessions to trade unions. But the ideological currency of political exchange is also historically variable. It has been seen that the manipulation of anti-union rhetoric may be a source of electoral support for governments seeking to excuse the failure of their economic policies; while the pursuit of national consensus may seem more likely to succeed if workers are addressed as individual citizens rather than as members of collective organisations. Even symbolic concessions to trade unions through corporatist institutions may involve too high a cost for employers or governments in some circumstances; for by consolidating the legitimacy of definitions of worker interests opposed to those of capital and the state, such institutions contradict the rhetoric of universal sacrifice in the 'national interest'. The 1983 election demonstrates how effectively an anti-corporatist ideological offensive has eased the detachment of trade union members themselves from a 'labourist' identity.

A further contradiction of corporatism is of particular relevance to recent British experience. Such writers as Panitch, Crouch and Strinati have viewed corporatist institutions as self-limiting primarily because the material sacrifices or restraints imposed on rank-and-file union members provoke eventual resistance and revolt. This interpretation[14] owes much to the experience of industrial struggle in Britain in the late 1960s and early 1970s; but is it universally valid? With some inspiring but isolated exceptions, recent years have been notable for their lack of generalised rank-and-file combativity; hence the government argument that 'militant' union activists and leaders are unrepresentative of their own members.

It can be plausibly suggested that this lack of grassroots assertiveness, though in part of course attributable to mass unemployment, is itself in part the product of previous corporatist relationships; and that in consequence, corporatist strategies on the part of capital or the state are no longer necessary. Capitalist production divides and fragments workers; bourgeois ideology asserts the unity of nation rather than of class. The cultivation of a distinctive working-class identity and consciousness involves firstly a lived experience of collective activity and interests, and often secondly a sustained effort of mobilisation. Trade union participation in corporatist relations is profoundly corrosive of this process. In the 1970s, structures of workplace representation which had often evolved spontaneously over many years became increasingly integrated in formal bargaining relationships with management. Positions of shop-floor leadership which stemmed originally from day-to-day accountability and responsibility to the membership and from the regular mobilisation of collective activity, became increasingly dependent instead on employer support and sponsorship. As the traditional organic relationship with the base began to atrophy, so workplace organisation became more bureaucratic in character and more vulnerable to withdrawal of management support. British Leyland, where the shop steward leadership had lost its former relationship with the membership as a collectivity while becoming enmeshed in routinised mechanisms of grievance administration and joint consultation, provides a stark example of the consequences of such dependence. But far more generally, employers forced by economic circumstances to restructure production along lines which challenge deeply-held union principles, have been able to exploit the representational gap between workplace membership and leadership (Hyman 1979).

At an aggregate level, such processes explain how British trade unionism in the 1970s became quantitatively ever stronger yet qualitatively weaker. Membership expanded despite mounting unemployment largely as a result of employer sponsorship (the closed shop from above and check-off arrangements); but such membership represented a paper attachment rather than felt participation in an active collectivity. This trend may be seen alongside the contrast posed by Woodcock after the establishment of the NEDC: 'we left Trafalgar Square a long time ago... to deal... with affairs of the moment in committee rooms, with people who have power'. This transition implied the demobilisation of trade union membership; as a corollary, the status of union leadership became less an expression of the active will of the collective membership, more the product of recognition by partners in corporatist arrangements. This implies that the representational credibility of national unions is sustained less by their internal relations with their own members than by their external relations with 'people who have power'. Yet as has now been brutally demonstrated, state and capital no longer need to make either real or formal concessions to representatives who have ceased to represent.

Participation in corporatist arrangements, to the extent that it undermines the active collectivism which made 'state-induced collaboration' necessary, is thus potentially self-destructive. This may be seen as the most fundamental source of instability of corporatism as practice; but it serves also to underline the inadequacy of 'corporatism' as an analytical category. British experience in the past two decades demonstrates that institutional accommodation between capital, the state and labour is partial, tentative and contradictory; and that the very dynamics of their interrelationship (particularly in the context of international capitalist instability) tend constantly to disrupt the balance of forces on which arrangements at any given moment rest. Moreover the shifting material and ideological circumstances of workers themselves, their mutual relations and their organisational attachments, constitute the elemental base to institutional superstructures.

British experience, then, indicates that 'corporatism' can at most designate a process, a tendency or a strategy, always subject to contrary forces; used to congeal conceptually an essentially fluid and many-layered social relation it becomes an ahistorical obfuscation. Yet this conclusion is consistent with the proposition of Kastendiek et al. (1983: 8) that while it is impossible to identify the emergence of a corporatist system, it is nevertheless possible to pursue analysis in terms of corporatist strategies and structures. However, any systematic investigation of strategies must confront the familiar problem: who does what, and with which, and to whom? For a technocratic state functionary, a corporatist strategy may involve harnessing the disciplinary and representational resources of unions and employers' organisations to ensure the success of government economic programmes. For a representative of capital, a corporatist strategy may be a method of directing state policy towards projects which enhance the profitability of particular companies or sectors. For a trade union official, a corporatist strategy may be the pursuit of state endorsement of the status of a specific organisation and its leaders (against rival unions, hostile employers, or rank-and-file dissent), or an alternative means of securing certain material goals. Among the three main 'parties' to corporatist arrangements there exist, of course, a variety of divergent strategies (reflecting both material and ideological differentiations); while any given strategy is typically ambiguous and contradictory. But it is clear that the corporatist strategies of any one party can achieve success, in general, only by frustrating those of others; despite the harmonistic rhetoric which at times accompanies tripartite institutions, corporatist bargaining approximates to a zero-sum game.

The essentially conflictual character of corporatist strategies is partially camouflaged by the diversity of social processes involved: representation, consultation, direction, influence, responsibility. The elision of many of these distinctions in much popular discussion of corporatist arrangements helps fog the realities of control and domination. Confusion often stems also from a failure to distinguish procedural from substantive demands and concessions. Particularly in the case of trade union representatives, the personal and organisational status and legitimacy attained through participation in corporatist institutions may constitute a dominant motive and justification, overriding considerations of material advantages (or disadvantages) accruing to the membership.

Advantage and disadvantage: it is of crucial importance that the interplay of corporatist strategies necessarily involves a constant process of negotiation and trade-off. Any (neo-)corporatist structure, as Martin insists (1983: 101-2), is inevitably the locus of 'a bargaining relationship, varying only in degree from pluralist forms of group-government dealing'.[15] But - as with 'pluralism' - the agenda of bargaining, the resources of the parties and the character of the outcomes can vary substantially according to context. Such contextual differences give rise to a contrast between what may be termed 'hard' and 'soft' corporatist strategies. Thus Heath after the climacteric of 1972, or Labour at the outset of the social contract, was obliged to come to terms with the strength and grassroots assertiveness of trade unionism; this encouraged a 'soft' strategy, offering real concessions in return for union restraint. Similar considerations motivated employers, in the early phase of productivity bargaining and procedural reform, to make significant concessions in terms both of pay and organisational facilities in exchange for guarantees of 'orderly' industrial relations. But economic crisis and trade union weakness have been associated with a hardening of those corporatist strategies that remain. To the extent that the state still seeks to utilise the disciplinary powers of trade unionism (which in many respects it has attempted to weaken) it is by legislative coercion rather than reciprocal concessions of even a symbolic kind. Among employers (leaving aside those that have launched a frontal attack on workplace unionism) a 'hard' corporatist strategy is evident in the widespread imposition of joint consultation arrangements where negotiation was formerly the rule (Terry 1983: 90).

Union strategies have of course followed a reverse trajectory. British unions, as Fox has noted (1978: 43), have been particularly committed to a 'utilitarian calculus'. Tripartism in the 1960s was thus pursued or justified for essentially instrumental reasons, as a new level of collective bargaining. But the 'hard' corporatist strategy was never pressed vigorously in the face of state and employer resistance, and in a period of union weakness consultation with government is pursued virtually as an end in itself, irrespective of outcome.

This is to suggest, then, that the notion of 'corporatist strategy' does not greatly advance understanding of recent British industrial relations. The meaning of corporatist strategy varies according to institution or actor, and alters also with the changing historical context. In Britain in 1983, it is difficult to identify more than elements or residues of 'corporatist strategy' among the programmes and practices of state, employers and trade unions. Indeed one reflection of crisis is the dissolution of strategy itself into shifting sequences of ad hoc policies and tactics. It is above all the contradictory and emergent character of strategy which must be comprehended within any adequate theorisation of contemporary class struggle and its containment.

NOTES

1. See Panitch 1980. Many of the points in these introductory paragraphs are influenced by Panitch's discussion, though the definition of corporatism which is offered also owes something to Jessop 1978.
2. See for example Prais 1976; Channon 1973.
3. Employment in health, education and local government increased between 1948 and 1974 from two to almost four million; union membership roughly trebled. Associated with these trends was a significant occupational shift (from manual to white-collar employment and unionism), with the rise to prominence of several unions organising in these sectors; female employment and unionisation also rose rapidly. For an assessment of these developments see Hyman 1980, 1983.
4. Such an interpretation was proposed by such commentators as Shonfield 1965, Harris 1972.
5. See for example Offe and Wiesenthal 1980.
6. See Winchester 1979: 109.
7. Most notably, the Industrial Reorganisation Corporation and the main provisions of the 1968 Industrial Expansion Act.
8. Most notably, the conference of the largest British union, the Transport and General Workers, insisted on such a policy against the opposition of its general secretary Jack Jones, a leading architect of the 'social contract'.
9. See for example Collins 1982.

10. Alan Fisher, general secretary of the National Union of Public Employees, quoted in Clark et al. 1980: 40.
11. Since the autumn of 1982 the government has altered the basis of calculation of unemployment statistics, removing some 200,000 workers from the register.
12. There are parallels with the argument of Booth (1982: 200) that 'corporatism in twentieth-century Britain appears to be little more than a technique of economic management operating within capitalism and developed during periods of national economic difficulty. When international slumps have overtaken the British economy, corporatist structures have been easily and painlessly dropped.'
13. See for example the discussions in Offe and Wiesenthal 1980 and Sabel 1981.
14. The interpretation, it should be added, is one with which the present writer has been explicitly associated.
15. Hence it is only by contrast to the fascist corporate state that Crouch's 'bargained corporatism' can be said to constitute a distinctive type.

REFERENCES

A. Booth (1982) 'Corporatism, Capitalism and Depression in Twentieth-Century Britain', British Journal of Sociology, 33, 2, pp. 200-23

W. Brown (ed.) (1981) The Changing Contours of British Industrial Relations, Oxford: Blackwell

D. Channon (1973) The Srategy and Structure of British Enterprise, London: Macmillan

CIS (Counter Information Services) (1981) Anti-Report 1981, London: CIS

J. Clark, H. Hartmann, C. Lau, D. Winchester (1980) Trade Unions, National Politics and Economic Management, London: Anglo-German Foundation

D. Coates (1980) Labour in Power?, London: Longman

H. Collins (1982) 'Capitalist Discipline and Corporatist Law', Industrial Law Journal, 11, 2-3, pp. 78-93 and 170-7

A. Cox (1981) 'Corporatism as Reductionism: the Analytic Limits of the Corporatist Thesis', Government and Opposition, 16, 1, pp. 78-93

C. Crouch (1977) Class Conflict and the Industrial Relations Crisis, London: Heinemann

C. Crouch (1979)The Politics of Industrial Relations, London:

Fontana
A. Fox (1978) 'Corporatism and Industrial Democracy' in Industrial Democracy: International Views, Coventry: SSRC Industrial Relations Research Unit, pp. 3-54
W. Grant and D. March (1977) The Confederation of British Industry, London: Hodder and Stoughton
N. Harris (1972) Competition and the Corporate Society, London: Methuen
R. Hyman (1975) Industrial Relations: a Marxist Introduction, London: Macmillan
R. Hyman (1979) 'The Politics of Workplace Trade Unionism', Capital and Class, 8, pp. 54-67
R. Hyman (1980) 'British Trade Unionism: Post-War Trends and Future Prospects', International Socialism, 2, 8, pp. 64-79
R. Hyman (1981) 'Green Means Danger? Trade Union Immunities and the Tory Attack', Politics and Power, 4, pp. 129-46
R. Hyman (1983) 'Trade Unions: Structure, Policies and Politics' in G. S. Bain, ed., Industrial Relations in Britain, Oxford: Blackwell, pp. 35-65
R. Hyman and T. Elger (1981) 'Job Controls, the Employers' Offensive and Alternative Strategies', Capital and Class, 15, pp. 115-49
B. Jessop (1978) 'Capitalism and Democracy: the Best Possible Political Shell?' in G. Littlejohn et al., eds., Power and the State, London: Croom Helm, pp. 10-51
H. Kastendiek, H. Kastendiek and H. Reister (1983) Incorporation of the Trade Unions?, Frankfurt: Institut fuer Sozialforschung
R. M. Martin (1983) 'Pluralism and the New Corporatism', Political Studies, 31, pp. 86-102
K. Middlemas (1979) Politics in Industrial Society, London: Deutsch
C. Offe and H. Wiesenthal (1980) 'Two Logics of Collective Action', Political Power and Social Theory, 1, pp. 67-115
L. Panitch (1976) Social Democracy and Industrial Militancy, Cambridge: Cambridge University Press
L. Panitch (1980) 'Recent Theorizations of Corporatism: Reflections on a Growth Industry', British Journal of Sociology, 31, 2, pp. 159-87
L. Panitch (1981) 'Trade Unions and the Capitalist State', New Left Review, 125, pp. 21-43
S. J. Prais (1976) The Evolution of Giant Firms in Britain,

Cambridge: Cambridge University Press
C. F. Sabel (1981) 'The Internal Politics of Trade Unions' in S. Berger, ed., Organizing Interests in Western Europe, Cambridge: Cambridge University Press, pp. 209-44
A. Shonfield (1965) Modern Capitalism, London: Oxford University Press
D. Strinati (1979) 'Capitalism, the State and Industrial Relations' in C. Crouch, ed., State and Economy in Contemporary Capitalism, London: Croom Helm, pp. 191-236
D. Strinati (1982) Capitalism, the State and Industrial Relations, London: Croom Helm
M. Terry (1983) 'Shop Steward Development and Managerial Strategies' in G. S. Bain, ed., Industrial Relations in Britain, Oxford: Blackwell, pp. 67-91
A. W. J. Thomson (1979) 'Trade Unions and the Corporate State in Britain', Industrial and Labor Relations Review, 33, 1, 36-54
H. Urwin and G. Murray (1982) 'Return to Trafalgar Square', New Statesman, 3 September, pp. 6-8
H. L. Wilensky (1981) 'Democratic Corporatism, Consensus and Social Policy' in OECD, The Welfare State in Crisis, Paris: OECD, pp. 185-95
D. Winchester (1979) 'Power and Influence in the TUC' in J. Purcell and R. Smith, eds., The Control of Work, London: Macmillan, pp. 100-32
J. Winkler (1977) 'The Corporatist Economy: Theory and Administration' in R. Scase, ed., Industrial Society: Class, Cleavage and Control, London: Allen and Unwin, pp. 43-58

Chapter 5

THE PROSPECTS FOR THE CORPORATISATION OF MONETARISM IN BRITAIN

Bob Jessop

In this paper I discuss the prospects for corporatism and monetarism in Britain and, in particular, for their combination in a corporatist monetarism. Let me make it clear at once that I am not arguing that such a system of political economy, with its apparent contradictio in adjecto, is bound sooner or later to arrive in Britain. My argument does not seek to resuscitate Pahl and Winkler's now ailing prediction of a 'coming corporatism' (1974) simply through adding yet one more adjective to the growing list of terms that qualify current discussions of corporatism. Indeed the careful reader will already have noted that the present paper is concerned, not with the prospects for a monetarist corporatism, but, rather, with those for a corporatist monetarism. More precisely still it is concerned with the prospects for the corporatisation of monetarism in Britain.

Before examining this question directly, I undertake two detours: one theoretical and one empirical. In a theoretical detour I consider whether one can delineate a dynamic of monetarist economies analogous to that developed by Martin for Keynesian economies. This establishes an abstract theoretical possibility for a corporatist monetarism. In an empirical detour I review the recent experience of capitalist democracies in bringing inflation under control. This establishes some concrete historical examples of a monetarist corporatism. I then consider what light these detours throw on the prospects for monetarist counter-inflationary policies in Britain under the present Thatcher government.

A Theoretical Detour: Monetarist Political Economy

Let us begin by clarifying the meaning of 'monetarism'. This can be understood in at least three different senses: a narrow, technical sense; a broader, technico-economic sense; and a more general political sense. In its narrow meaning monetarism refers to a set of policy prescriptions involving control over the money supply to influence the rate of inflation in a (national) economy. In its broader, technico-economic sense, monetarism refers to a general counter-inflation strategy concerned not only with the monetary expression of inflation but also with its real causes. Finally, the more general sense of monetarism refers to the resurgence of neo-liberal economic philosophy, advocacy of a social market economy and a strong nightwatchman state, and state-sponsored promotion of market forces as the dynamic principle of the economy. Which of these interpretations is appropriate is generally clear from the context but it is worth emphasising at the outset that my discussion of the political dynamic interprets monetarism in its broader, technico-economic sense of counter-inflationary strategy. It does not imply that all monetarist policies are associated with a social market economy, a strong state, and neo-liberalism. Indeed it is an important part of my argument that counter-inflationary policies can be articulated with a wide range of accumulation strategies, state forms, and ideological ensembles.

The Political Dynamic of a Keynesian Economy

In an important article on Keynesian policies in Sweden, Andy Martin suggests that there is a distinctive dynamic to the pursuit of full employment in social democratic societies. He identifies three stages or phases in the development of a Keynesian political economy. He also argues that the move from one stage to another is (a) required by the intensification of particular economic contradictions or dilemmas inherent in Keynesianism and (b) conditional on the presence of specific political and ideological relations. It is worth noting in this context that Martin interprets Keynesianism as a general commitment to full employment rather than as a particular package of policy measures. The three stages are:

- The first stage of Keynesian political economy involved the use of deficit finance in a contra-cyclical manner as a means of macro-level demand management which is intended to create or maintain full employment. At this stage market forces are still important both in allocating capital to particular branches of production and in determining what is produced as opposed to the general level of demand.
- Since this stage typically generates stagflationary

tendencies, there is a move to a second stage. This involves wage restraint through incomes policies (rather than the market discipline of rising unemployment), price restraint through an 'inflation tax' (indirect taxation), and a stimulus to economic growth through active manpower policies. In practice even this does not fully eliminate stagflationary tendencies, however, because inflationary pressures still remain and the level and pattern of investment are still left to market forces.

- In response to continuing economic difficulties arising from wage drift, structural unemployment, and public sector expansion, there are moves in the direction of a third stage. This involves the socialisation of profits and investment through worker-controlled or tripartite funds financed initially from private profits. This is intended to encourage continued wage restraint through compensatory economic control and to promote private sector investment so that international competitiveness and full employment are restored.

The move from one stage to another depends on political conditions which are less common among national economies with each step. Thus, while many are called to stage one, few are chosen to go to stage two, and, as yet, only one has embarked on the move to stage three (Martin, 1978). My concern here is not to criticise this model (either for its Swedocentrism or its conflation of Keynesianism with its social democratic form). Instead I want to develop an analogous model for the dynamic of a monetarist (anti-inflationary) political economy.

The Political Dynamic of a Monetarist Economy

This dynamic derives from the character of banking capital and the nature of the capital-labour relation. Martin's analysis took for granted that the state was excluded from the private core of industrial capital.[1] It also took for granted that unions would be inclined to exploit full employment in their bargaining activities. Similarly my account of monetarism rests on the nature of financial markets and their reactions to monetary restraint. Financial capital is just as concerned to protect its prerogatives and increase its rates of return as industrial capital. The state has no part in the origin of bank money or the creation of private credit but must nonetheless guarantee the smooth operation of the national money system as a whole. This leads to a number of difficulties which generate the dynamic of a monetarist political economy.

In the following model I assume that monetarism follows a stage-like development akin to that sketched by Martin for Keynesian full employment policies. This inevitably involves a gross simplification of actual historical experiences and I consider the problems involved in applying this model later. For the moment, however, I will speculate on possible stages of monetarism.

A first stage would follow from an unacceptable level of inflation and the growing political influence of a monetarist alliance. Following the preliminary pursuit of a tight money policy according to one or another of the various monetarist prescriptions, however, monetarism may encounter structural and/or conjunctural obstacles that require movement beyond the initial narrow, technical stage.

It is an argument much beloved by monetarists that resort to deficit finance to maintain full employment requires increasing deficits on each occasion to produce the same level of employment and thereby results in an accelerating rate of inflation. It is pleasantly ironical to record that an analogous charge applies to monetarism. For resort to tight money or deflation in order to reduce the rate of price increase requires an increasingly restrictive and deflationary policy stance to produce the same result and thus leads to an accelerating rate of unemployment. This problem is rooted in the nature of financial markets and their reactions to monetary restraint. For the efficient use by the state of general instruments of monetary management to restrict monetary expansion requires that the financial system cannot generate money substitutes, cannot activate idle balances, and cannot draw on international funds. Yet, when faced with monetary restraint, each particular financial capital will want to exploit any such opportunities in the interests of profit maximisation. And, to the extent that a significant number of financial capitals resort to such activities, this will undermine monetary restraint and thereby harm the interests of capital as a whole in a non-inflationary economic environment. In turn this will exercise an upward pressure on the rate of inflation and/or require greater monetary restriction to counteract such actions.

Indeed one American commentator has noted that

> the financial system has seen aggressive innovation and aggressive exploitation of existing institutional arrangements with each succeeding burst of tight money (sc. in the USA). Once restraint ends and relaxation returns, the new financial mechanisms tend to remain and the areas of induced growth do not return to their former positions. They tend to be amalgamated into the system permanently, and permit a greater amount of credit to be supplied than before the squeeze at any given rate of interest and any given level of bank reserves, other things being equal. Thus, each succeeding period of tight money tends to require a greater harshness to achieve a degree of restraint similar to that achieved in a previous period of tight money. (Miller, 1978, p. 112).

Thus, to the extent that this pattern is repeated, each successive bout of tight money policy would have greater deflationary impact. It would be coupled with greater increases in unemployment, more bankruptcies, a larger drop in output, and so forth. Alternatively the efficiency of monetary restraint will decline and other counter-inflationary measures will be needed.

This is a structural problem inscribed in the very heart of capitalist financial systems. Further difficulties can arise from the differential impact of monetary restraint. This will vary according to a wide range of factors, such as gearing ratios (or reliance on external finance), capital intensity, durability or turnover time of capital goods, elasticity of demand, inventory-sales ratios, access to foreign credit, etc. But there can be no guarantee that those financial institutions, industrial concerns, branches of industry, etc., which are hardest hit by monetary restraint are those least essential to the overall performance of the national economy. This suggests that supplementary measures may be required to protect strategically important economic agents against the vagaries of generalised monetary restraint.

Moreover, as monetarists recognise (albeit somewhat late in the day in many cases), control over the money supply (even where successful) merely controls the growth of nominal gross domestic product. It cannot determine the trade-off between inflation (i.e., a rise in the general price level) and real output (i.e., the overall volume of goods and services) within nominal GDP. In particular it is still open for variations both in the response of firms to a corporate liquidity squeeze (lower investment, de-stocking, cutting unit wage costs through redundancies and/or lower real wages) and in the balance of forces between capital and labour to influence the price/output mix (cf. Gowland, 1982, pp. 186-7). In turn this suggests that measures may be required to influence corporate behaviour and the balance of forces between capital and labour in order to alter the trade-off between these two variables.

Finally it should be noted that reductions in public expenditure intended to reduce the public sector borrowing requirement can generate increased state spending elsewhere in the public domain. For, in so far as the state acts not only to guarantee the national money but also acts as 'financier of last resort' for the unemployed and/or strategically significant but potentially bankrupt enterprises, it will need to compensate for the effects of tight money and spending cuts by doling out the unemployed and/or subsidising vital but uneconomic enterprises.

In short, for structural and conjunctural reasons alike, a purely macro-level, arms-length, laissez-faire programme of monetary restraint using general instruments could well generate a series of economic and political problems that require movement beyond such simple techniques.

Assuming continued commitment to counter-inflationary policies, it would seem that a second stage of monetarism is required. This would be concerned with the real causes of inflation rather than the monetary expression of real inflationary pressures. It would be concerned, in short, with the supply-side of the economy as well as with monetary aggregates. The crucial question is: movement to what? At least two paths seem plausible.

A second stage could aim to create the conditions in which market forces can operate according to the principles of laissez-faire and free competition in the hope that this would ensure general equilibrium at a stable general price level. Or it could attempt to rationalise the impact of monetary restraint at the meso- and micro-level and/or to tackle the 'real' (as opposed to monetary) mechanisms generating inflationary pressures. The state would necessarily be involved in promoting either alternative - whether in a short-term, transitional role or in a longer-term, directive capacity. Thus, from the viewpoint of state involvement, a second stage could take the form of a state-sponsored process of recommodification and/or the form of direct or indirect state intervention in real economic activities. This option can also be expressed as a choice between (a) a policy mixture which involves deregulation of the private sector, privatising the public sector, and commercialising any residual state activities by introducing market criteria and (b) a policy mixture which involves government regulation of the private sector, national economic planning (to include nationalisation where appropriate), and decommodification of the public sector so that it escapes narrowly-defined profit-and-loss criteria. A second stage could, in short, involve either privatisation or socialisation. But the continued pursuit of the anti-inflation policy would, at least in the short-term, involve increased state intervention.

Almost by definition a second stage monetarism based on deregulation, privatisation, and commercialisation is incompatible with corporatist institutions and/or strategies. For corporatist institutions and/or strategies involve the visible hand of concertation among the 'social partners' of capital, labour, and the state. In contrast deregulation, privatisation, and commercialisation involve the subordination of economic activities to the invisible hand of market forces. In this sense the political preconditions of a privatisation strategy should involve the dismantling of any corporatist institutions and/or the abandonment of any corporatist strategies. Conversely a second stage monetarism based on regulation, planning, and decommodification is not as such incompatible with corporatist institutions and/or strategies. Nor does it require them. But a plausible case could be made that such a counter-inflationary strategy would benefit from its articulation with certain forms of corporatism.

From Stages to Strategies

It seems clear that there are inherent limitations in the efficiency of Keynesian demand management techniques in securing full employment and in the efficiency of tight money policy techniques in controlling inflation. Whether these limitations are realised and then transcended in a stage-like manner as postulated by Martin or are countered more or less ab initio through a combination of macro-level techniques with additional measures is an essentially historical, conjunctural question. That some form of supplementation is required should be apparent from an abstract account of the respective 'logics' of Keynesian or monetarist solutions to the problems of full employment and inflation in capitalist economies. In this sense the key set of questions is not whether there is a unique, unilinear 'logic' of Keynesian or monetarist strategies.

Instead it involves the conditions under which full employment or stable prices can be secured. Martin's analysis is still relevant here but it needs to be re-interpreted and supplemented. So too does the monetarist policy model sketched above. The most appropriate and useful solution would involve redefining Martin's stages and my 'paths' as alternative strategies which could be pursued sequentially but which could also be combined and recombined in various ways.

The scope of Keynesian and monetarist policies also causes complications. Both Keynesianism and monetarism were initially intended as responses to cyclical or conjunctural phenomena. Keynesian techniques were initially developed for contra-cyclical economic purposes (even though their subsequent use has often been politically motivated and/or proved pro-cyclical in impact). Monetarism in its narrowest sense can also be seen as conjunctural. For it attributes inflation to temporary government failures to control the money supply rather than to deep-rooted, long-term structural causes in the 'real' economy. This suggests that both Keynesianism and monetarism in their technical, macro-level variants will be relatively ineffective in dealing with structural problems. Whatever the situation might have been in Martin's Swedish exemplar, the crisis of Keynesianism in Britain is related to the long-term, structural character of the British disease. A contra-cyclical, konjunkturpolitische policy cannot be expected to resolve long-term, structural problems. Nor can a tight money policy.

The advocates of monetarism may sometimes suggest that a neutral, ordnungspolitische policy can resolve both cyclical and structural crises by permitting the free play of market forces. But it is now more common to find them admitting that 'monetarism is not enough' (Institute of Economic Affairs, 1983). Thus Milton Friedman recently conceded that, 'while monetary restraint is a sufficient condition for controlling inflation, it is a necessary but not sufficient condition for restoring Britain to full economic health'. My earlier arguments suggest that it is not even a sufficient condition for controlling inflation (although it is often beneficial in this respect) and is no better equipped than Keynesian contra-cyclical policies to resolve structural crises. In short, whatever the merits of Keynesian or monetarist prescriptions for managing full employment and the general price level in an otherwise expanding economy, major problems will develop and require treatment when they are applied to a declining economy such as that in Britain. A fortiori this will be true when dealing with the closing stages of a long-wave of economic development and the transition to a new phase of growth with its new set of institutional and strategic preconditions. In both cases a more complex policy mix will be required to secure economic growth as well as full employment and/or stable prices.

An Empirical Detour: Full Employment and Stable Prices

If abstract models have limited utility, do concrete cases tell us anything? Mrs. Thatcher has identified a holy trinity of successful monetarist economies in Austria, Switzerland, and Germany. Yet these economies also display significant corporatist and/or consociational features. Several recent studies have also shown that low rates of inflation since the first oil crisis are found disproportionately among economies which rate highly on corporatism, social democracy, union centralisation, and similar measures. There is little prima facie evidence that a purely technical policy of monetary restraint can eliminate inflation and some evidence to suggest that other policy mixes can help not only to control inflation but also to secure full employment. To illustrate this I draw on recent studies by David Cameron (1984) and Enzo Tarantelli (1983).

Unemployment and Inflation

Cameron notes that there was a strong inverse relation between unemployment and consumer price inflation across twelve capitalist democracies during the 1960s. This would seem to confirm arguments about the orthodox expectations about the trade-off between unemployment and inflation. But he also notes that this relationship was reversed in the period 1964-66 through to 1979-81. He concludes that nations are not inevitably fated to suffer either high unemployment or high inflation in some law-like Phillips-curve trade-off but can influence their position on both dimensions to some extent. What is interesting for present purposes is that some countries manage to combine relatively low unemployment with relatively low inflation (Germany and the smaller European nations which have frequently experienced social democratic rule and/or some variant of corporatism) and other countries have managed to combine high unemployment and high inflation (notably Britain and its former colonies in the period 1964-81).

In interpreting these and other findings Cameron suggests that, "compared to governments dominated by other ideological <u>tendances</u>, then, governments dominated by leftist parties not only are more likely to preside over higher rates of employment but, also, are more likely to achieve that essential objective of conservative politics - price stability - by inducing labour to forsake the use of the strike as a weapon in collective bargaining and to restrain its increases in wages" (Cameron, 1984, p 161). He also notes that the success of leftist governments in these respects is strongly correlated with the presence of the structural or organisational preconditions of corporatist bargaining and tripartite crisis management in the sense that there are significant inverse correlations between these conditions and variables such as unemployment, inflation, rate of increase in both nominal and real earnings, and strike activity.

Without detailed policy studies these findings can only be indicative but they do suggest that counter-inflationary policy may sometimes depend on corporatist or social democratic arrangements. They also suggest that regimes committed largely to tight money policies to squeeze out inflation may not prove the most successful in battling with inflation. If we recall here that such policies may also reveal declining efficiency, then the prospects of pure monetarism seem transformed.

Evidence bearing more directly on this question has been supplied by Enzo Tarantelli (1983) in a study of actual policies pursued to counter inflation since the first oil price rise shock. Tarantelli also establishes a strong correlation between neo-corporatism and successful counter-inflationary policies; and between neo-corporatism and the maintenance of full employment. Indeed, if these two variables are combined into the so-called 'misery index' (or Okun index), which is based on the simple arithmetic sum of rates of inflation and rates of unemployment, neo-corporatist economies perform significantly better than non-corporatist economies throughout the period 1962-82. Moreover, as economic conditions deteriorated through this period, neo-corporatist economies performed even better in comparison with their non-corporatist competitors. Tarantelli himself distinguishes five different groups of countries in terms of their economic performance:

1. Countries combining incomes policies and monetary restraint and thereby combatting inflation with only a limited increase in unemployment. These countries comprise Austria, Sweden, Norway, and, to a lesser extent, Denmark.

2. Countries which have combined incomes policies with more severe monetary restraint; this has moderated inflation and produced modest increases in unemployment. Included here are Germany and Japan.
3. Countries where incomes policies have not succeeded and where a deceleration in inflation was achieved only through severe monetary restraint and high costs in unemployment and lost potential output. Included here are Belgium, Holland, Finland, Australia, and New Zealand.
4. Countries where the rate of deceleration of inflation was lower than expected but which have enjoyed, since the end of 1975, a relatively higher growth rate and some decline in unemployment. Included here are the USA and Canada.
5. Finally, countries where (a) the first oil crisis was superimposed on an ongoing inflation initiated by wage-cost push, (b) there was no sustained deceleration of inflation despite higher unemployment between the first and second oil crises (Italy and Britain), or (c) deceleration of inflation was obtained with very high costs in terms of unemployment and lost output (France).

Clearly these data do not directly test my earlier model of the dynamics of a counter-inflationary political economy. They do suggest that combining tight money policy with incomes policies and corporatist political exchanges focusing on an active Strukturpolitik can play a role in reducing inflation and in enhancing the productive capacities and competitive strength of national economies. In this sense they point to the potential for a monetarist corporatism in resolving the problem of inflation without intensifying that of unemployment.

Monetarist Corporatism and Corporatist Monetarism

Both the theoretical and empirical detours suggest that there is nothing intrinsically implausible about combining monetarism and corporatism. But they do point to different forms of combination. The abstract theoretical model points to the corporatisation of monetarism, i.e., the supplementation of pure monetarist techniques by corporatist concertation or other forms of regulation, planning, and decommodification. The concrete historical evidence points to the monetarisation of corporatism, i.e., the supplementation of corporatist strategies for full employment and economic growth with a more explicit concern with monetary control. Although these may be formally symmetrical movements towards a common strategy, they reveal a substantive asymmetry in terms of their political preconditions. It is one thing to reinforce corporatism and social partnership with monetary restraint during a period of inflationary expectations and real inflationary pressures. It is another to move from a pure monetarist strategy (especially if it is articulated with the broader economic and political philosophy of monetarism) to a second stage involving a corporatist form of socialisation rather than a market-driven form of privatisation. The political preconditions are different in each case and this affects the relative prospects of monetarised corporatism and corporatised monetarism.

The Political Preconditions of Monetarism

These studies are politically significant because they imply that there is a broad range of counter-inflationary strategies. The abstract model of monetarism suggests an inherent dynamic to monetarism which operates regardless of the will of specific economic interests and/or the wishes of particular governments. In this respect it is analogous to Martin's model of Keynesian dynamics. But it differs from that model in outlining alternative second stages. In turn this modifies arguments about the political preconditions of moving from the first to the second stage. For, rather than suggesting that the political preconditions are increasingly restrictive as movement occurs from one stage to the next, the possibility of alternative stages means that different societies might be able to pursue different counter-inflationary strategies. Certainly a brief comparison of monetarist strategies in Chile or Brazil with those in Austria or Britain would indicate this. Only by considering the political preconditions for each alternative could one determine whether or not the corporatisation of monetarism in Britain is necessary and/or possible under the present Conservative Government. Likewise the empirical studies illustrate the actual range of counter-inflationary policies pursued in different societies and also point to the need for more concrete analysis of the British case.

Thus both the theoretical and empirical detours call for a careful analysis of the ways in which the Thatcher government has managed the economic and political repercussions of its monetarist counter-inflationary strategy. It is certainly more and more evident that Thatcherism has adopted more than a purely technical, macro-level monetarist strategy and is also concerned with real factors affecting inflation and output on the supply side of the economy. Indeed it is possible to distinguish a shift in strategy between the first and second Thatcher governments. Thus, as Tim Congdon, an ardent advocate of monetarism, has noted, "in Mrs. Thatcher's first term the emphasis was on the restoration of financial control, through reductions in public sector borrowing and money supply growth, as an essential prerequisite for curbing inflation; in their second term it seems that the main priority will be tax cuts to encourage the supply side of the economy" (1984, p. 65). To this one should add that the primary emphasis in this second stage is on a policy mix based on deregulation, privatisation, and commodification. What are the political preconditions of this movement and how likely are they to persist?

Thatcherism and Monetarism

The Thatcher government was certainly not the first to employ monetarist techniques in combatting inflation in Britain. The shift to monetarism as an instrument of economic policy was promoted some three years earlier by the preceding Labour administration. Indeed the latter was also relatively successful in reducing the rate of growth of the money supply, reducing public spending, expanding the economy, and containing unemployment - certainly more successful in these respects than the incoming Thatcher regime (Riddell, 1983, p. 57). In this sense it is tempting to suggest that a period of 'monetarised corporatism' preceded the more pure monetarism of the Conservative government and, as might have been inferred from the empirical studies cited earlier, proved more successful than the latter. But to suggest this would mean ignoring the crisis of corporatism which characterised the Labour administration and neglecting how the latter was then obliged to adopt monetary restraint faute de mieux to compensate for the failures of the superficially corporatist Social Contract period. Thus it is more appropriate to see this period as combining monetary restraint and second-stage Keynesian techniques to produce a 'monetarily restrained Keynesianism' rather than as a period of effective 'monetarised corporatism' (cf. see Fforde, 1983).

The Background to Thatcherism

The experience of the postwar years and especially those of the immediately preceding Conservative and Labour administrations prepared the political ground for the Thatcher experiment. The economic and political crisis of the postwar settlement in Britain and its supposedly Keynesian welfare state framework produced a situation in which monetarism seemed a realistic (if not the only) alternative. The Keynesian welfare state (hereafter 'KWS') became increasingly crisis-prone as the long-wave of global capital accumulation was exhausted and Britain's distinctive structural weaknesses became more severe. The politically-mediated 'stop-go' cycle of the postwar period became more evident in the seventies as did the succession of liberal and corporatist political strategies. The growing crisis of the KWS witnessed a trade-unionist and 'economic-corporate' offensive by the labour movement (from the 1972 miners' strike through the 1974 elections and the early days of the Social Contract to the referendum on continued membership of the EEC in 1975). This produced significant legislative and economic gains but did not involve any fundamental reorganisation of capital, the state system, or the power bloc to the long-term advantage of labour. Beneath the conjunctural fluctuations of economic and political power, the political and ideological hegemony of capital was only temporarily threatened and its economic dominance (especially that of the City and international capital) was not checked.

After the exhaustion of the labour movement's offensive, there came a period of relative stabilisation. The Labour Government presided over this and began to introduce monetarist techniques and deflation. Even more crucial was the mobilisation that occurred in civil society. Class forces were not so much in a state of paralysis as re-grouping for the next round of struggle. Whereas the labour movement outside Parliament was going on the retreat and moving even further into an economistic and defensive war of manoeuvre (symbolised, par excellence, in the 'Winter of Discontent'), the right was preparing for an offensive in which a political and ideological war of position was given priority and the rollback of the earlier 'economic-corporate' gains of the labour movement was also placed on the political agenda.

Thatcherism proved significant because it became the focal point around which the counter-offensive mobilised. This was all the more urgent because the international recession and the death-throes of the already flawed KWS demanded forward movement merely to stabilise the economic and political systems. This was also widely recognised on the left and encouraged a movement away from defense of the

KWS status quo ante towards demands for a siege economy based on corporatist planning; but only the right engaged in the necessary war of political and ideological position to advance its alternative strategy. In particular Thatcherism developed not only a monetarist approach in the broadest sense but also articulated it with an authoritarian populist rhetoric opposed to social democracy and the KWS (cf. Hall and Jacques, 1983).

Thus the incoming Thatcher government immediately embarked on a radical monetarist programme in the hope that it would promote economic recovery by eliminating inflation. Whatever its errors of timing and its initial inconsistencies with the government's fiscal policy and public sector pay concessions, this programme can hardly be described as half-hearted or ad hoc in the manner of the preceding Labour administration. More recently the Government has proclaimed a strategy involving deregulation, privatisation, and commercialisation. In part this involves a post hoc rationalisation of the increasingly self-evident limits of a narrowly monetarist approach and the accompanying search for alternative sources of government revenue. This can be seen in the privatisation of public sector assets but is also evident in deregulation and commercialisation. But the new strategy also reflects a deliberate transition to a second stage in which supply-side questions have become more important than monetary control and the medium term financial strategy. Overall it would appear that the Conservative Government is pursuing the first path of monetarist political economy that I outlined above and has set its face firmly against a counter-inflationary strategy based on a combination of monetary restraint with regulation, national economic planning, and decommodification.

Stages of Monetarism?

What evidence is there that the Thatcher government has undergone a stage-like movement towards a privatisation strategy? Any answer to this question must examine whether the Conservative Government pursued a first, technical stage whose contradictions then provoked a second, privatisation stage. And, in the spirit of Martin's analysis of Keynesian dynamics, we must also consider the political preconditions of this movement.

The first stage of Thatcher's economic strategy was both less and more than pure monetarism. It was less than pure monetarism because it was inconsistent and it was more than pure monetarism because it was coupled with some fiscal measures on the supply-side. The incoming Thatcher administration was as much concerned with political consolidation as it was with economic stabilisation. Thus measures were taken whose economic impact was inconsistent and contradictory but whose political purpose was to consolidate political support. This can be seen in (a) direct tax reductions for everyone and especially those on higher incomes, (b) public sector 'comparability' pay awards above the rate of inflation, (c) increased public expenditure on defence and law and order. Some of these measures were financed by increases in indirect taxation and public sector prices with negative effects on inflation. Thus the rate of inflation and the public sector borrowing requirement were both threatened by the particular policy mix pursued. Matters were made worse because the government failed to hit its own monetary targets (in part because of the financial intermediation predicted by Miller) and was not prepared to countenance the high interest rates required to bring them back under control (even so the minimum lending rate reached 17 per cent in 1979-80 and would have gone higher but for political pressures against); because it abolished exchange controls thereby losing control over private sector access to foreign credit (although the rising exchange rate linked to high interest rates did have a beneficial effect on domestic inflation); because its squeeze actually led to an increase in £M3 because of distress borrowing from banks by the private sector; and because its resort to high interest rates coupled with the petrocurrency status of sterling led to a high exchange rate, declining competitiveness, further de-industrialisation, and rising unemployment.

Once simple reliance on monetary restraint (targetting £M3) was abandoned in the autumn of 1980, the Thatcher government embarked on a new round of policy measures based on reductions in public spending and wage restraint. Subsequently a fresh stage emerged in which fiscal incentives became more important. This change in strategy was consolidated in two phases: the Cabinet 'wets' were defeated over economic policy in late 1981 and wider, popular support came with the 'halo effect' of the Falklands War in 1982. The government was now confirmed in its programme of privatisation, labour market restructuring, and youth training (Riddell, 1983, p. 50).

There have been stages in the Thatcher government's counter-inflationary programme; but there have so far been three rather than two phases. First came monetary targetting to reduce inflation - this must be regarded as a failure even though inflation fell for other reasons. Then came reductions in public spending - these failed because spending is difficult to control when unemployment, defence, law and order, debt interest, etc., are rising and when a significant part of public spending is determined by local authorities. Most recently we have seen supply-side policies which assume (a) that the money supply adjusts passively to trade rather than itself actively determining price inflation and (b) that labour market inputs and incentives are the crucial, real factors in determining inflation and output (cf. Thompson, 1984, p. 282). In this sense a second-stage monetarism has emerged with an increasing concern for the real economy, i.e., labour markets, competition, training, output, etc., rather than for the ineffective manipulation of monetary aggregates. In addition this second-stage monetarism (albeit representing a third phase of government policy) is unambiguously privatising in character as defined above. This leads to the question of the political preconditions favouring this strategy rather than one of a socialisation path and, possibly, a corporatised monetarism.

Political Preconditions of Thatcherism

Postwar Britain has witnessed several cycles of corporatist and liberal economic and political strategies. What is significant about Thatcherism is its apparent ability to avoid a corporatist U-turn after a period of liberal strategy. In part this can be explained by the continued dominance of worldwide recession accompanying the collapse of the postwar boom. For periods of global recession are typically associated in Britain with liberal strategies in contrast to the corporatist strategies associated with international expansion (see Booth, 1983). But something more has maintained the conviction politics of Thatcherism. At least three further factors are involved. There is the ideological restructuring of popular politics associated with disenchantment with the KWS and with the rise of authoritarian populism (cf. Jessop et al., 1984). There is the channelling of material concessions to significant sections of the labour force (notably in the technologically advanced private sector) and the small business community. And there is the complex crisis of the British state system which has enhanced the ability of the Thatcher government to pursue its policies. It is this last factor which merits particular attention in the context of our concern with economic crisis, trade unions, and the state.

The Dual Crisis of the British State

The coalition of interests mobilised behind the Conservative monetarist initiative provided the Thatcher Government with the initial economic authority to implement radically new policies. Likewise its electoral mandate provided political authority and the linking of monetarism with an authoritarian populist rhetoric provided ideological legitimacy. But these relatively conjunctural factors were reinforced by the 'dual crisis' of parliamentarism and corporatism in the postwar British state. For there are simultaneous, albeit unevenly developed, crises in the spheres of parliamentary representation and corporatist (or functional) representation. The development of the KWS and other forms of intervention in postwar Britain has undermined the role of parliamentarism but no effective alternative (such as corporatism) has been developed. Yet, without suitable forms of 'democratic' consultation and/or regulation corresponding to different spheres and forms of state intervention, the effectiveness of state policies is undermined and their legitimacy is questioned. This was increasingly true of Britain in the sixties and seventies.

The combination of parliamentary and corporatist modes of interest intermediation and their specialisation in different political and economic tasks is supposed to enhance the adaptive capacities of the political system (cf. Lehmbruch, 1980). But in Britain neither mode of political representation can function in the appropriate manner. Each is subject to a complex crisis affecting its institutional form, representational ties, and its economic and political rationality. In turn this is overdetermined by the dynamic of class (and non-class) relations and the economic and political strategies pursued by different social forces. The combination of these crises intensifies the effects of each. This aggravates the problems confronting the British state in securing its operational unity, economic and political efficacy, and overall legitimacy.

This is reflected in the increased decisional autonomy of the state elite but is also associated with the declining economic and political efficacy of state intervention through rational-legal administration of measures in accord with the substantive rule of law and/or through corporatist means. These crises created the opening for the enhanced decisional autonomy of the Thatcher government to pursue its programme in the face of a crisis-prone party system and an unstable and ineffective corporatism (cf. Jessop, 1980).

In particular the trade union movement and business associations remain so decentralised and fragmented that they cannot play any efficient (as opposed to 'dignified') long-term role in the formulation, coordination, and implementation of an effective incomes policy or an active structural policy. This is reinforced in the British case by the separation of the industrial and political wings of the Labour movement and the dominance of the City and multinational corporate interests within the Conservative Party. In both cases this has complicated the problem of coordinating functional representation and parliamentary representation.

Given the continuing structural crisis of the British economy and the failure of Keynesianism and post-Keynesian techniques, it is hardly surprising that monetarism found increasing favour in some quarters. For it allegedly cut through the knotty problem of how to regenerate the British economy when tripartism and state intervention had failed. In future it would be unnecessary to consult trade unions and make them concessions in return for non-binding and undeliverable sacrifices. Nor would it be necessary to establish elaborate bureaucracies for discriminatory state intervention whose attempts to use taxpayers' money and ad hoc rules to promote economic growth were supposedly throwing good money after bad and destroying business confidence in the stability of its decision-making environment. At the same time monetarism could be sold to the electorate in terms of its purported tax cuts, reduced inflation, increased incentives, etc., and its homely connotations of sound housekeeping and restored responsibilities for the family at the expense of the 'granny state'.

To the crisis of corporatism must be added the crisis of the parliamentary and party systems. Three aspects of this crisis are particularly important. The growing difficulties facing the successful pursuit of the KWS economic strategy are reflected in the breakdown of the inter-party consensus on accumulation (leading to divergent economic strategies) and the exacerbation of intra-party conflicts (notably within the Labour Party but also in growing conflicts between an emergent 'new right' and the disorganised 'right progressive' or 'One Nation' tendency in the Conservative Party). The third aspect is the conjoint impact of the crisis of the KWS and inter- and intra-party conflicts on the social bases of the political party system and its capacities to integrate diverse social and economic groups into the capitalist order. This is reflected in the growing volatility of electoral support for the established parties (and, judging by recent evidence, the Liberal-SDP Alliance) and the development of significant marginal groups whose interests and/or demands find no channels of representation within the established parliamentary and party systems. Together these three aspects call into question the capacities of the prevailing system to perform their integrative, legitimatory, and accumulation functions.

Given the crisis of the Conservative Party there was a space for the resurgence of petty bourgeois ressentiment and its increasing influence in the counsels of the Conservative Party (cf. Edgar, 1983). At the same time the crisis of representation within the Labour Party and the more general process of partisan dealignment meant that there was an increasing mass of potentially floating voters. This encouraged a growing resort to populism, i.e., direct appeals to the 'people' over the heads of their representatives in competing parties and Parliament. This 'populism' is of a quite specific kind. It is not concerned with an active populist mobilisation - which would be threatening to the decisional autonomy of Thatcherism. Instead it is concerned to outflank organised opposition from government backbenchers (especially the so-called 'wets') as well as from the labour movement. For, if Thatcher represents the people directly, opposition can be presented as undemocratic. The same populist thrust is seen in union politics with attempts to mobilise grass-roots support against trade union leaders and, most recently, in the NCB's use of opinion polling to assess the views of miners and their wives during the course of the miners' strike in 1984-5. In this sense Thatcherite populism is predominantly plebiscitary and ventriloquist in character: Thatcher speaks in the name of the people against all sectional interests, including those in her own party (cf. Hall, 1983).

Whilst Thatcherism has systematically demoted the role of functional representation in political and economic crisis-management, it has not presided over a reassertion of parliamentary control mediated through the political party system. The Conservatives certainly won a land-slide victory in 1983, which enhances their capacities to control the Commons; but this control is very much one that is orchestrated from above by a small Prime Ministerial clique within (but not necessarily of) the Cabinet together with Mrs. Thatcher's official and irregular advisers. In the last five years the concentration and centralisation of power in the state administration has accelerated at the expense of parliament and parties. Britain is moving towards a presidential system of government with government legitimacy dependent on the popular prestige of the Prime Minister and her ability to appeal directly to the people. Moreover, alongside the resort of populism, there is also increasing resort to raison d'etat to justify decisions. Populism and prerogative powers further enhance the decisional autonomy of government. But, as the series of so-called 'banana skins' since the general election indicates, decisional autonomy does not guarantee good government. In this respect the crisis of parliamentarism and the party system continues and the formulation and implementation of policy (including economic strategy) lacks the necessary democratic regulation from the party system as well as from functional representation.

This affects monetarism as well as other areas of government policy. For, although monetarism appears to offer a way out of the impasse of economic policy created by the dual crisis of the state, it does so only by divorcing economic policy making from any effective anchorage in formal political and economic representation. This has certainly enhanced Thatcherism's room for manoeuvre in pursuing its monetarist strategy in the face of rising unemployment, continued de-industrialisation, rising levels of taxation, increasing proportions of state spending in GDP, deterioration in the non-oil balance of trade, and so forth. It has thereby permitted the Thatcher government to pursue a strategy of deregulation, privatisation, and commercialisation against the odds indicated by the postwar mould of British politics.

Thatcherism, Monetarism, and the Unions

So far I have concentrated on the general development and political preconditions of Thatcherism. Its approach to the trade union movement and the response of the latter have been neglected. A detailed account of Conservative industrial relations policy is provided by Crouch (this volume) and it would be otiose to repeat such an analysis here. Likewise Hyman (this volume) provides an account of the union response. Accordingly I want to concentrate here on how these features fit into the second stage monetarism outlined above and their implications for the prospects for a corporatised monetarism.

The Thatcher government's strategy has always been inimical to the trade union movement. It has also benefited from the inter-related crises of functional representation, social democracy, and the party system in its pursuit of anti-union legislation, strike-breaking, and labour market restructuring.

Government strategy towards the unions is at least three-pronged: (a) weakening their industrial and political influence through the reassertion of market disciplines and the virtual dismantling of functional representation in corporatist and quasi-corporatist settings: (b) reforming their internal organisational framework through proposals for the Verrechtlichung of the trade union's leadership and decision-making processes in conjunction with increased media and governmental intervention in rank-and-file opinion formation; and (c) breaking the links between trade unions and the Labour Party in financial, organisational, and policy-making terms. The first two prongs have met with some success and it remains to be seen whether the financial ties to the Labour Party will be broken under the system of ballots on the political levy. There have been worries in the short-term that the reduced power of trade unions will prove purely conjunctural and that an economic upturn would re-invigorate industrial militancy. But in the medium-term a combination of supply-side measures and populist appeals to a re-educated work-force could operate alongside the economic re-structuring which is decimating traditionally militant and well-organised industries to weaken the overall industrial and political influence of the labour movement. All of this suggests that the present deregulation, privatisation, and commercialisation strategy will not fail on the resistance of the trade union movement. It also suggests that union pressures for a U-turn towards a socialisation strategy (as defined above) and thus, at least potentially, towards a corporatised monetarism will continue to be weak until such time as a Labour government is returned to office.

This said, some qualifications are in order. Firstly, the present government is opposed to macro-level corporatism and aims to confine unions to legally-delimited collective bargaining within the confines of market rationality. But it is not opposed to industrial or plant-level participation or concertation at the initiative of employers and the latter is still an important element in management strategies in some firms. In this context we could see the emergence of a sectoral and selective corporatism confined principally to technologically advanced parts of the private sector. Secondly, it must be noted that the Verrechtlichung or 'juridification' of the unions is a double-edged weapon. For, in so far as unions are reformed (with or without the active compliance of union leaders), they can claim a legitimate right to be consulted on certain matters on the ground that they have become democratic and abandoned party politics. As long as they are unreconstructed, Thatcher can 'justifiably' ignore them; as 'new model unions' imbued with a new realism and fashioned in the Thatcherite mould, they could lay claim to re-integration into corporatist decision-making structures and, paradoxically, could even prove more effective in these circumstances than they did as unreconstructed unions. Lastly, even if the financial link between unions and the Labour Party is broken, this is likely to hurt the latter more than the former.

None of these qualifications undermines the more general conclusion that the dual crisis of the British state and the pattern of economic recovery will enable the Thatcher regime to sustain its commitment to a privatisation strategy as defined above. Whether or not this is successful in combining reduced rates of inflation with economic recovery and reductions in employment remains to be seen. My own view is that the decisional autonomy which enables the Thatcher Cabinet to impose its strategy on Parliament, local authorities, the business community, and the Labour movement alike will also prove counter-productive in securing the legitimacy and efficacy of this strategy in the face of continued deflationary pressures, the increasingly urgent demands to reduce public expenditure (if necessary through further reorganisation and surgery on the welfare state), declining oil revenues, and continued unemployment. The fact that a corporatised monetarism is not currently on the agenda does not mean that the present monetarist strategy will succeed.

CONCLUSIONS

Let me try to summarise the basic ideas underlying this paper. Firstly, Britain is suffering from a long-term structural decline in her domestic economy and from a world recession associated with the end of a long-wave of expansion. In this context neither purely technical, macro-level Keynesianism nor purely technical, arms-length monetarist policies can resolve the economic difficulties confronting Britain on their own. Instead more active, structural policies are required.

Secondly, Britain is also suffering from a 'dual crisis' of parliamentary representation and corporatism coupled with a crisis of social democracy. Thatcherism attempts to resolve the crisis of corporatism by adopting a market-oriented economic strategy and ignoring the would-be industrial partners; to resolve the crisis of social democracy by instituting a new form of common sense and a new hegemonic strategy; and to resolve the crisis of parliamentarism not so much through the reassertion of the party principle as through a combination of prerogative powers and populist appeals. But a purely market-oriented strategy is not enough in Britain to restore full employment as well as to control inflation (as even the Thatcher government admits in lamenting the lack of an entrepreneurial culture comparable to that in the United States); the new common sense has achieved only limited popular impact and is vulnerable in the area of welfare state issues; and the recent Conservative successes at the polls indicate a further deterioration in the party system which questions the popular mandate. It is primarily the continued dual crisis which grants Thatcherism sufficient decisional autonomy to pursue its privatisation strategy without effective resistance from the trade union movement or substantial popular support mediated through the party system. The dull compulsion of economic relations and the awful majesty of the law underpin this decisional autonomy but do not thereby guarantee it any success in achieving its substantive economic objectives.

Thirdly, abstract theoretical arguments suggest that successful counter-inflationary measures need not follow a privatisation path and that, pace Mrs. Thatcher, there is an alternative. Indeed indirect empirical evidence suggests that the successful combination of counter-inflationary measures with measures to achieve economic growth and relatively low unemployment depends on corporatist political exchanges and an active rather than passive state role. Yet Britain is in the paradoxical situation of having had pre-oil shock inflation associated with the failure of corporatism and having to cope with the effects of oil-shock inflation without the corporatist underpinnings which have helped elsewhere to control inflation without serious repercussions on employment and output. Equally Britain lacks the supply-side conditions which would permit the immediate success of a counter-inflationary strategy based on a privatisation strategy. This has produced the current impasse of Thatcherism, namely, a combination of low inflation with relative economic stagnation. This situation appears contrary to pure monetarist expectations but makes sense in terms of supply-side analyses.

Fourthly, failed corporatism was gradually replaced by 'monetarised Keynesianism' in the last Labour administration and a failed monetarism was unsuccessfully corporatised in the preceding Heath government. Two possible solutions to the impasse of Thatcherism are a more deliberate move towards privatisation at the expense of increased repression (the social market economy and the national security state) and/or adoption of an interventionist, corporatist approach (active supply-side intervention plus selective corporatism). The government's clear preference is to reinforce its medium term financial strategy through a programme of deregulation, privatisation, and commercialisation and through changes in the fiscal regime to encourage private investment and productive labour in preference to (collective) consumption and unproductive (un)employment. Neither the organisational preconditions of a socialisation path nor the political will to pursue such a path currently exist in Britain. Indeed the present government is taking steps to ensure that these preconditions will be even further diminished and to transform the political climate so that corporatist solutions are rejected in future.

Finally, although the Conservative government is currently emphasizing a privatisation strategy there are secondary elements of the alternative strategy. Indeed the germs of a more significant interventionist/corporatist strategy are being laid. A two nations corporatist monetarism is not impossible in Britain within the next few years but I doubt whether it would resolve the crises referred to above.

NOTE

1. In the sense that the state cannot control the exercise of managerial prerogative by forcing firms to undertake unprofitable activities and usually finds it difficult to stop them pursuing profitable activities.

REFERENCES

Booth, A., 1982: 'Corporatism, Capitalism, and Depression in twentieth-century Britain', British Journal of Sociology, 1983

Cameron, D., 1984: 'Social Democracy, Corporatism, Labour Quiescence and the Representation of Economic Interest in Advanced Capitalist Society', in J. H. Goldthorpe, (ed.), Order and Conflict in Contemporary Capitalism, Oxford

Congdon, T. 1984: 'The Budget', The Sunday Times, 25th

March
Edgar, D. 1983: 'The Rise of the Popular New Right', New Socialist, September-October
Fforde, J., 1983: 'Setting Monetary Objectives', Bank of England Quarterly Bulletin, June
Gowland, D. 1982: Controlling the Money Supply, London
Hall, S. and Jacques, M., (eds.), 1983: The Politics of Thatcherism, London
Jessop, B., 1980: 'The Transformation of the State in Postwar Britain', in R. Scase, (ed.), The State in Western Europe, London
Jessop, B. et al., 1984: 'Thatcherism, Authoritarian Populism, and Two Nations', New Left Review, 147
Lehmbruch, G., 1980: 'Liberal Corporatism and Party Government', in P. C. Schmitter and G. Lehmbruch, (eds.), Trends Toward Corporatist Intermediation, London
Martin, A. 1978: 'The Dynamics of Change in a Keynesian Political Economy: the Swedish Case and its Implications', in C. Crouch, (ed.), State and Economy in Contemporary Capitalism, London
Miller, 1978: The Micro-Economic Consequences of Macro-Economic Policy, Oxford
Pahl, R. and Winkler, J. T., 1974: 'The Coming Corporatism', New Society, 10 October
Riddell, P. 1983: The Thatcher Government, Oxford
Scharpf, F. W., 1984: 'Economic and Institutional Constraints of Full Employment Strategies: Sweden, Austria, and West Germany', in J. H. Goldthorpe, (ed.), Order and Conflict in Contemporary Capitalism, Oxford.
Tarantelli, E. 1983: 'Patterns of Economic Policy in Response to the Oil Shock' (mimeo), Bank of Rome
Thompson, G. 1984: 'Rolling Back the State', in G. Mclennan, D. Held, and S. Hall, (eds.), State and Society in Contemporary Britain, Oxford

Chapter 6

CONSERVATIVE INDUSTRIAL RELATIONS POLICY: TOWARDS LABOUR EXCLUSION?

Colin Crouch

It has become a commonplace of British discussions of the politics of industrial relations that there has been a major change of direction since the return to office of the Conservatives in May 1979. The commonplace perception is, for once accurate. The first task of this paper is to demonstrate the nature and extent of the change: the second is to analyse it and trace its implications: the third is to explain it. Finally, there will be a brief look at some of the obstacles still faced by the new strategy.

A SUMMARY OF CONSERVATIVE POLICIES

The government's policies may be usefully grouped under five headings:

A. Actions Designed Simply to Weaken the Power of the Unions and/or of Workers in Relations with Employers

Behind specific policies one needs to recall the general weakening of union influence which has occurred everywhere in the western world following the prolonged recession that has succeeded the second oil shock in 1978. The first, 1973, oil shock had opposite consequences: it followed immediately after the general rise in union militancy and confidence of the late 1960s, the unemployment associated with it was relatively minor, and in most countries governments seemed to remain more or less committed to full employment. In that context governments sought to restore economic strength through intensive co-operation with unions. After 1978, not only did the recession bite far deeper into economic activity, but political and industrial elites were far less confident that they were dealing with merely a temporary interruption to the post-war full-employment economy - and policies of co-operation with unions had had a chance to demonstrate their weaknesses. In Britain the consequent weakening of union influence has been intensified by the following actions:

(a) the general macro-economic policy of refusing to take direct action to reduce unemployment, the introduction of public spending cuts and deflationary policies during a period of declining demand, and refusal to take emergency actions to prevent bankruptcies. The power of labour was thereby reduced, not only by the sheer market force of its excess supply, but also by the effect on workers' expectations of the government's obvious unwillingness to rescue public- or private-sector firms that found themselves in difficulties through paying large wage increases or through being hit by prolonged strikes. However, this policy has not been applied quite as strictly as this implies. In a number of cases the government has either continued subsidies, albeit at reduced levels and at the cost of considerable redundancies, to loss-making firms (e.g. British Leyland, the British Steel Corporation) or has made resources available to head off industrial conflict (e.g. when the Welsh miners struck over threatened pit closures in 1981).

(b) the imposition of fairly strict 'cash limits' on public-sector pay, giving management and unions the choice between agreeing pay rises below the level of inflation or financing higher rises by reducing manpower. This weakened public-sector unions by preventing them from squeezing more money from government through political bargaining. Again, the policy has not been ruthlessly pursued: in various years workers in water supply, the National Health Service and the railways have been able to secure increases in pay supported by additional government finance. It is also notable that employment has generally remained more stable in the public services than in manufacturing industry.

(c) the introduction of legal changes to make the use of union strength more difficult. The Employment Acts 1980 and 1982 made most forms of secondary picketing actionable by aggrieved parties. The 1982 Act also reduced the range of actions covered by the immunity of trade disputes from civil action (e.g. secondary action to secure union recognition in a particular company, and political action were both removed from immunity). The same Act removed the right of legal redress from workers given instant dismissal without legally prescribed notice for engaging in strikes or other forms of industrial action. Workers were given a disincentive to strike by the Finance Act 1980, which (a) changed the rules for allocating social security benefits to strikers' families so that unions were assumed to be paying strike pay up to a specified level, irrespective of whether they were doing so and (b) postponed income-tax rebates due to strikers until after the dispute had ceased.

(d) minor reductions in the legal rights of individual workers. The Employment Act 1980 curtailed rights to protection against unfair dismissal and also limited the maternity leave entitlements of women workers. These legislative actions supplemented the de facto weakening of the position of workers against their employers already induced by rising unemployment.

B. Legal Measures to Increase the Power of Union Members and/or Workers in General Against Union Organisations

Behind this strange set of policies has been the mounting evidence of dislike among workers of compulsory unionism and of unions' political involvement with the Labour Party (for early warnings of the fragility of members' tolerance of their unions' political activities, see Moran, 1974). In the 1980s these facts have been reinforced by two developments. First, soon after the government took office workers, fearing unemployment, began to demonstrate reluctance to follow union strike calls from their unions. Second, in the general elections of 1979 and, in particular, 1983, the Labour Party was unable to attract the votes of a majority of union members. (This last may be less relevant to the question of unions' political affiliations than at first appears. Many unions, especially of white-collar workers, are not affiliated to the Labour Party anyway, and it is among these sectors that recent union growth has been concentrated. The available opinion-poll evidence does not tell us anything about the strength of Labour support among the members of affiliated unions alone.) These have been issues on which the government has been happy to take action:

(a) a right of workers not to join a union where 'closed shops' exist has been introduced and reinforced. The Employment Act 1980 made it actionable to expel an employee from employment because of refusal to join a trade union. The Employment Act 1982 made it possible for unions to be joined as co-defendents in actions over such dismissals, provided for government compensation for workers dismissed for refusal to join a union during the years 1974-80, and made it illegal for trade contracts to stipulate that contracting firms must employ only union members.

(b) unions have been encouraged to use secret ballots in elections for officials and votes on strike calls. The Employment Act 1980 offered government subsidies to enable unions to bear the costs of such ballots. This accompanied several incidents in 1979 and 1980 when employers (notably BL and the BSC, two nationalised concerns) used ballots of workers to try to demonstrate opposition to strike calls by unions or by shop stewards. A similar tactic of appealing over the heads of union leaders to workers (with the assumption that the former were unrepresentative) was attempted in 1981 in a series of ministerial speeches encouraging workers to accept low pay rises. At the time of writing the 1983 Trade Union Bill seeks to require secret ballots for elections of national union officials. It will also render actionable any official strike begun without a prior secret ballot of the workers involved - though it would not be required that a majority actually voted in favour of a strike.

(c) action requiring unions to secure membership support for political affiliations. The Trade Union Bill 1983 would require unions to re-submit a decision to affiliate to the Labour Party to a secret ballot of the members every ten years. Earlier plans to permit unions to affiliate to the party only those members who have made a positive declaration of their willingness to be so affiliated have been dropped following undertakings by the Trades Union Congress that unions would publicise arrangements for 'contracting out' of affiliation.

C. Actions to Reduce the Institutionalisation of Conflict and to Reduce the Range of Industrial Relations Issues Subject to Agreed Regulation and Established Understandings

(a) a number of institutions designed to ensure the fixing of pay and conditions without recourse to conflict, especially in the public services, have been abolished. The Standing Commission on Pay Comparability, established by the Labour Government in 1979, was abolished in 1981. The Pay Research Units, set up in 1953 to fix the incomes of civil servants according to pay movements in a number of comparators in the private sector, was also abolished in 1981, this being the occasion of a prolonged strike. At the time of writing the government is seeking to replace it with a system which would have regard to the labour market for civil servants as well as to comparisons. The National Water Council, designed to co-ordinate pay rates in water supply, was abolished in 1982, the intention being that regional water authorities should negotiate individually, though the first major strike ever to take place in the industry, which followed this decision, was eventually settled on a national basis. In 1980 the government announced the ending of an agreement made by the Labour Government in 1977 after a national firemen's strike that in future fire service pay should be linked to that of the police. However, this attempt was withdrawn after a further strike and a revelation that in 1977 the Conservative opposition had committed a future Conservative government to accept the system.

More generally, the government and the Confederation of British Industry tried, with considerable success, to discourage the concept of a 'going rate' for wage settlements in favour of agreements tied more specifically to conditions in individual companies and regions. The government has made one attempt to introduce settled machinery in place of unregulated bargaining. Following a major strike in the NHS in 1982, the government proposed a system of arbitration for fixing health service pay. The government proposed to reserve to itself as the employer the right, with the consent of parliament, to ignore the rulings of the arbitrators: but any group of workers undertaking strike action in opposition to an arbitration award would lose the right to receive any increase in pay flowing from the award. At the time of writing this proposal has not yet been accepted by the health service unions.

(b) stemming from this last, the government has pursued a policy of studied inconsistency in wages policy. It disavows an incomes policy in the private sector, where it believes that, given appropriate general economic policies, market forces are automatically effective; in the public sector, however, it has erected cash limits. In turn, cash limits are not necessarily adhered to. If a group demonstrates considerable industrial strength, concessions are made to it. This has been done on a number of occasions (e. g. water supply in 1980 and 1983; mining in 1981 and the railways in 1984).[1] Since the government is not interested in securing union co-operation in or agreement to restraint, it has no obligation to pursue consistency and has thus gained an important freedom of manoeuvre not available to normal incomes policies which are constrained to follow some kind of distributional rationale.

(c) several devices for protecting the wages of low-paid groups have been revoked or weakened. The Employment Act 1980 revoked the provision in the Employment Protection Act

1975 that enabled a union to apply to the Central Arbitration Committee to have terms and conditions 'generally prevailing' in an area of employment applied to non-conforming firms. This provision, which replaced a much older one, was designed to ensure the extension to firms in which unions were weak of terms and conditions negotiated in the same industry. (It also served to prevent employers in non-union firms from under-cutting employers who negotiated with unions.)

In 1982 the government repudiated the Fair Wages Resolution of 1946, which in turn had replaced a 19th century resolution, committing the government to paying its employees and to enforcing on its contracting firms pay and conditions no less favourable than those generally prevailing in related private-sector employment - that is, a general commitment to be a 'good employer', a provision particularly useful to low-paid grades in the manual civil service. Repudiating this resolution involved the UK government denouncing Convention 94 of the International Labour Office, which commit governments to 'fair treatment' of their own employees. Afterwards the government imposed 10 per cent wage cuts on some of its lowest-paid staff (e.g. office cleaners).

In 1982 the government announced that it would henceforth expect Wages Councils to take account of the alternative employment prospects of workers in their industries and to bear in mind that employment in those industries was often, in compensation for its low wages, relatively secure. Wages Councils fix minimum rates of pay in agriculture and in a number of low-paying industries. In its 1983 election manifesto the Conservative Party said the government would consider abolishing the councils if they kept pay artificially high. In the same year the Secretary of State for Employment, Mr. Norman Tebbit, referred back wage awards from two councils in the retail trade on the grounds that they had not considered the likely employment effects of their decisions. The councils accordingly slightly reduced their awards.

Finally, one can include under this heading the use of training and manpower policy to reduce the pay of young workers. The government believes that union rates have kept the wages of apprentices and other trainees too high, reducing the incentive to firms of employing them. It has therefore used institutions of training and job creation to impose new low wage levels not vulnerable to union negotiation on such workers. This was done first through the Youth Opportunity Projects and since 1983 through the Youth Training Scheme, which has greatly increased the opportunities for training available to young people, but in exchange for a fixed wage considerably below existing trainee pay. Given the vulnerability of many training schemes during the recession, several existing schemes, including some for craft apprentices, have, with reluctant union consent, been moved into the YTS umbrella.

D. Actions Designed to Reduce the Legitimacy of Trade Unions as Participants in National Political Life

Behind these striking developments lie the decline in union membership since 1979 and the evidence of widespread public disquiet at the influential political role played by the unions during the last Labour Government. This is not without its ambiguities. As Nielsen (1984) has shown, British public opinion seems to commend peaceful union co-operation with governments in income restraint, but to condemn union involvement in political decision-making. Government policies relevant to this issue have been:

(a) a drastic reduction in the range and number of contacts between ministers and union leaders. These relations, which had grown steadily since 1940, declined immediately the government took office. While Mr. James Prior was Secretary of State for Employment (1979-81) something of the old pattern was retained. For this, *inter alia*, he was vociferously attacked by other Conservative politicians, most prominently Mr. Tebbit. Mr. Tebbit replaced him in September 1981 and proceeded to put government/union relations on a far more unfriendly basis. In its turn the TUC boycotted all contact with the government over its proposals for union and employment legislation. This lasted until autumn 1983, when, in the wake of Labour's crushing election defeat, they accepted consultation with Mr. Tebbit and then his successor, Mr. Tom King, over the proposed legislation on union affiliations to the Labour Party. Contacts between the TUC and the Prime Minister, Mrs. Margaret Thatcher, have been distinguished by their infrequency and acerbity; they have normally consisted solely of reiterations of opposed points of view. The one partial exception concerned brief talks following the urban riots by young people, mainly black, in the summer of 1981.

(b) a reduction in the unions' participation in official bodies. The government has announced that unions would henceforth no longer be regarded as a major interest meriting representation on public bodies considering matters of general importance: their advice would be sought solely on questions directly affecting their role as representatives of the labour force. As a result there has been an end to the long-standing practice of 'balancing' representatives from capital by those from labour. Within the industrial relations field <u>per se</u>, however, existing institutions have been left in place: the Manpower Services Commission has become an increasingly important agency for the development of labour-market policy in which the unions participate; the Health and Safety Commission remains tripartite; and the Advisory, Conciliation and Arbitration Service continues its work, though with somewhat reduced powers in contrast with the situation under the Labour government. The National Economic Development Council, which has survived more changes of government than any other institution in this field, continued to provide a regular if ineffective meeting place for government, CBI and TUC until the TUC began to boycott it as part of its protest against the government's banning of union membership among employees of General Communications Headquarters in 1984.

(c) a gradual abandonment of the doctrine that union recognition by employers constitutes 'good industrial relations'. This has been a diffuse policy, emerging in ministerial speeches, implied by some of the moves to privatise public (in particular local) services, but never stated as a clear policy. The only legislative actions have been:

(i) the repeal, in the Employment Act 1980, of provisions in the Trade Union and Labour Relations Act 1974 giving ACAS a role in securing union recognition in companies where employers were resisting it; and
(ii) the removal, in the Employment Act 1982, of legal immunity from secondary action designed to enforce recognition.

Beyond that the only case of overt 'deunionisation' by the government itself was its decision to ban union membership among its employees at GCHQ, a military intelligence-gathering unit. In what proved to be a very bitter dispute, staff were offered £1,000 if they resigned their union membership and dismissal if they did not. Ministers, especially the Prime Minister, made it clear that one of the reasons for the ban was an alleged incompatibility between union membership and loyalty to the security of the nation. This was clearly a 'delegitimating' move, and angered union leaders. However, the government has so far not followed the advice of some of its influential supporters to engage in a full deunionisation drive as practised by many US employers (e.g., see The Economist, December 18, 1982).

E. Finally, all Proposals for Co-determination have been Rejected

All discussion of this topic, a major theme of the 1970s, stopped when the government came to office. The government, encouraged by the CBI, has taken the lead within the European Community in opposing the Vredeling and Guertsen initiatives for employee rights to information disclosure and representation within firms. On the other hand, employers have been encouraged to introduce what are known as 'employee involvement' schemes, in which management establishes consultative devices or provides information of its own choosing to the workforce. The studied use by the government of the term 'involvement' and the equally deliberate avoidance of terms like 'participation' or 'democracy' emphasises that the government does not wish to encourage power sharing, but devices that will enable managements to make workers appreciate the 'industrial facts of life'. There is also no implication at all that these schemes should involve union representatives.

The most succinct means of summarising Conservative policy, uniting all these strands, is to speak of an attempt at weakening union organisations: by economic and legal means; by giving their members more control over them and rights to opt out of them; and by undermining the institutions through which unions exercise influence (including dispute settlement institutions, membership of national bodies and as intermediaries in worker participation). It should be noted that increasing the rights of union members within their unions is not necessarily a measure to weaken unions; but given the approach to their members adopted by several British unions it amounts to that in practice.

While this policy is internally highly consistent, it has not been applied with great consistency. Where union power has been too great for political challenge, the government has been prepared to relapse into older styles of industrial relations. Such a stance has been made possible by the general weakening of the unions by the recession, reducing the number of exceptional cases with which the government has to make compromises.

AN ANALYSIS OF CONSERVATIVE POLICY

During the 1970s several observers interpreted developments in industrial relations policy in Britain and elsewhere as movements towards a form of 'liberal', 'pluralist' or 'bargained' corporatism. This referred to policies that depended on an exchange between political influence for trade union leaderships and their co-optation as economic and social *Ordnungsfaktoren*, responsible for ensuring that their organisations and memberships acted in reasonable conformity with the *desiderata* of national economic success.

Such strategies bear some resemblance to the more established concept of 'pluralist' or 'institutionalised' industrial relations, which refers primarily to the mutual acceptance by organised labour and capital of each other as permanent bargaining partners, and associated agreements to accept but also to regulate and insulate the conflicts of their relationship - in particular to insulate them from politics. Pluralism can however be distinguished from corporatism in several respects. The demands it makes on organised interests are clearly fewer; it does not require the same degree of centralised co-ordination - indeed, it rather requires a limited decentralisation in order to achieve a disaggregation and better insulation of conflict; and corporatist industrial relations can hardly be described as insulated from politics, as they require the 'social partners' to take cognisance of 'national interests' and usually offer them a political *quid pro quo* for this.

Both corporatism and pluralism can be sharply distinguished from a third form of industrial relations, which we shall denote by the appropriately French term '*contestation*', since it has been most clearly pursued as a strategy by employers, unions and governments in that country (and, until the 1960s, in Italy). It comprises minimal mutual recognition, resort to conflict as the major means of resolving disputes, maintenance of no understandings at all about mutual tolerance, and no attempt at avoiding the politicisation of disputes. For its part, organised labour looks forward to the transcendance of the present system of employment relations, and therefore sees industrial relations as such as simply a means of mobilising the workers for this eventual transcendance. For their part, employers and governments consider it feasible to exclude organised labour entirely from all important decision-making and try to marginalise it within the society. From employers and governments, therefore, contestation involves a policy of labour 'exclusion'.

This very brief theoretical sketch (a fuller statement of which will be found in Crouch, 1985) provides a framework for the analysis of the Conservative policies outlined above. Do they constitute a break with the neo-corporatism of the 1970s? And if so, in favour of what?

The policies listed under A above are not necessarily incompatible with continued pursuit of a neo-corporatist strategy; within neo-corporatist co-operation governments may try to make labour's voice less powerful and thereby win co-operation on easier terms. The simultaneous pursuit of neo-corporatist and limited monetarist policies by the social-liberal coalition in Germany after 1973 and by the Labour Government in Britain during the social contract are examples of this, as is the 'hard-currency' policy of the Austrian socialist government. Monetarist corporatism is not essentially contradictory until it reaches the point where the attack on unions' power makes the political exchange so unattractive to them that they cease to co-operate.

Policies under B should give us more analytical clues, but this is rendered difficult by their extraordinary function in British industrial relations. If many unions had not taken such a cavalier attitude to their members' views, the policies would not have been pursued. And when militancy returns to the work force after some economic recovery, these policies may become extremely inconvenient for Conservative strategy. It is remarkable how often British politicians make fixed assumptions about the relationship between union leaders and their members, when in fact that relationship is likely to change with economic and social developments. From the early 1960s onwards it was assumed that union leaders were likely to reach 'reasonable' agreements with governments, and that the danger of disruption came from shop-floor militancy. It is significant that it was in 1960 that the Ministry of Labour first started publishing statistics on the proportion of British strike activity that was 'unofficial', that is, not officially recognised by a union. (From year to year the proportion varied within the range 92 per cent to 97 per cent). This was the beginning of the period of intensified attempts at corporatist co-operation with union leaders.

From 1979 the present government has abruptly altered this analysis. Following some incidents in which workers, afraid of redundancy and unemployment, rejected union strike calls, the government view now is that it is union leaders who impose militancy on a reluctant work force. Significantly, in

1981 the government stopped publishing the regular data on unofficial strikes. Unofficial shop-floor movements are no longer seen as a problem, and policy tries to increase the power of members against leaders. The most surprising example of this appears in the provision of the 1983 Trade Union Bill, mentioned above, for official strikes to be actionable at law unless they have been preceded by a ballot; unofficial strikes would not be subject to the same restriction.

Neo-corporatist industrial relations policy requires some 'protection' of union leaders from their members. The fact that the government is removing most of this protection is evidence that it is making a fundamental break from the corporatist experiments of the preceding 20 years. It envisages no need to rely on co-operation from union leaders in restraining shop-floor militancy. This contrasts very strongly with the previous attempts at legislation by a Conservative government, the Industrial Relations Act 1971, which tried to strengthen the power of union leaders over their members.

When we consider policies under C, it becomes even clearer that the government is rejecting neo-corporatism, and is even withdrawing from the institutionalised conflict characteristic of pluralist industrial relations of the classic Anglo-American form. The government's reasons for trying to reduce the importance of conflict regulation are clear. It believes that these institutions have imparted rigidities to pay and conditions, making them unresponsive to market forces, especially in the public sector; and that efficiency would be improved and unemployment reduced only when labour has become a market commodity.

These are of course well known risks of institutionalisation. They have in the past been considered worth-while because:

(i) under pluralist systems it is usually assumed that labour's strength will not be consistently or uniformly high, enabling the strain on the labour market to be absorbed, perhaps through dual labour markets;

(ii) under corporatism it is assumed that unions will co-operate to ensure that labour is neither over-priced nor inefficient;

(iii) under both, labour market rigidities have been considered to be a lesser risk than the uninhibited conflict threatened by an absence of institutionalisation.

Conservative Industrial Relations Policy:

The present British government faces a different equation. With respect to (i) it confronts a union movement which, during the 1970s possessed a stubborn ability to keep unit labour costs high despite both the specific British economic decline and the general world recession. Corporatist co-operation (ii) was shown in the late 1970s to be both difficult and fragile, as we have discussed above. On (iii) the government has taken a calculated risk that fears, based on the experience of the first half of the century, about the likelihood of civil disorder in the absence of institutional arrangements, are outdated. Several factors sustain this belief: the absence of broad-based solidarity as opposed to local action revealed by the recent history of industrial conflict; the electoral decline of left-wing forces, including the Labour Party; the early response of workers to the post-1979 economic climate; the fact that the groups with traditions of militancy and solidarity are isolated in declining industries and regions. The coal miners provide something of an exception to this last point, the long-term problems of energy supply rendering the decline of their industry temporary. But this problem is averted, partly by North Sea oil, and partly by certain government policies, e.g. the rejection of any idea of a national energy policy, by European standards an unusually low level of subsidy to the coal industry, and a programme of pit closures which is politically as well as economically motivated.

All these arguments apply as well to the policies being pursued under D, which demonstrate more clearly than anything else the rejection of corporatist experiments. Before they came to office in 1979 the Conservatives were ambivalent on these matters. They, and the CBI, used to cite <u>konzertierte Aktion</u> as an important source of German success in industrial relations. (Nobody seemed to notice that at the time the DGB was boycotting the meetings of KA!) This potentially conflicted with other party statements that the Labour government had allowed the unions to become too closely involved in policy discussions. After they came to office the Conservatives resolved the conflict by simply ignoring the concerted action option, with, as mentioned above, a partial and temporary survival in the conduct of Mr. James Prior, when he was Secretary of State for Employment. Since his removal it has not been possible to discern a single new government initiative that makes use of union co-operation.

(There is one apparent exception to this in the discussions with the TUC of the government's plans for making union affiliation to the Labour Party difficult. These resulted in an agreement to drop that part of the legislation imposing a system of voluntary 'contracting in' by individual members in exchange for some voluntary action by the unions to publicise the rights of individual members not to pay the 'political levy'. However, this has no implications for industrial relations policy. It results from the shared fear of the Conservative and Labour parties that if the Labour Party is weakened it may be replaced as the main opposition by the Liberal and Social Democratic Alliance.)

Although, as has been noted, many institutions embodying union participation remain, the direction of Conservative policy is now clearly set in the direction of 'labour exclusion', the eventual logic of which is that political exchange is reduced to a minimum, even collective bargaining is made difficult, and strike-breaking rather than conciliation is the hall-mark of government intervention. Such a policy is just possibly reconcilable with a conventional pluralist system, given the need for pluralist systems to reduce the political intensity of industrial relations action. It could be claimed that the government is trying to restore a pluralism more suitable to British institutions in place of the unsuccessful corporatist experiments of the previous 20 years, such a restoration requiring a less powerful and less politicised union movement if it is to be compatible with economic stability. The problem is that delegitimating unions and breaking down institutionalised conflict removes some of the characteristics of pluralism, while the intensity of the political attack on the unions is hardly compatible with a depoliticisation of industrial relations.

To put it another way: under neo-corporatism unions meet regularly and routinely with ministers, civil servants and employers' representatives in many different gremia. Under pluralism they meet employers across the bargaining table; meet ministers and civil servants in order to lobby them; and the government intervenes in conflict with mediation services. Under labour exclusion, or contestation, they meet the police on the picket lines. It is in this last direction that British industrial relations are gradually moving.

There remain government policies under E above. The rejection of 1970s discussions of co-determination is of course compatible with the adoption of labour exclusion policies and the rejection of corporatism, especially when it is recalled that in the British context national schemes for worker participation in management are certain to imply a strong role for unions. However, the government's interest in schemes for 'employee involvement' should not be written off as mere rhetoric. In several industries there are reports of employers taking the initiative in reintroducing joint consultation. This has some interesting implications for the possible future shape of industrial relations in Britain. The recession, together with the general lines of government policy, have given employers an opportunity to restructure industrial relations on lines more favourable to themselves and less favourable to the kind of shop-floor militancy that was so important in the 1960s and 1970s.

Some employers have in fact taken advantage of that very decentralisation of the union movement that provided such problems for neo-corporatism in order to construct a company level of relations, sometimes based on shop stewards, sometimes not (Brown, W., 1982; Department of Employment Gazette, 1981). The advantage of the company level for employers is that it induces *Betriebsegoismus* in the workforce, enabling national union organisations to be bypassed. This is especially effective at a time when many workers fear for the future of their companies; like some of the other developments discussed here, matters would look somewhat different during a period of economic expansion. Sometimes, of course, employers use consultation systems and sophisticated personnel management techniques to avoid the need to recognise unions altogether. It is not coincidental that the Prime Minister goes out of her way to praise the personnel and other policies developed by the large retail chain Marks and Spencer Ltd. The company has combined a refusal to recognise unions with welfare and consultation policies for employees that seem to progress considerably beyond simple old-fashioned paternalism. Several US multinationals, such as IBM, also manage to maintain a non-union strategy that is attracting the attention of many British managements who, a decade ago, would not have contemplated such possibilities.

Other employers, while accepting unionisation, are placing it in a framework unfamiliar to the great majority of British union officers and activists. Some of the most significant agreements on this basis have been signed between the Electrical, Electronic, Telecommunications and Plumbing Union (EETPU) and various employers in, significantly, the high-technology sector (see *IR-RR*, 1983). These have included some Japanese multinationals and also Inmos, the state-owned microprocessor firm. These agreements typically concede sole negotiating rights to the EETPU (including its white-collar section) and a management commitment to encourage union membership, though there is no closed shop. In exchange the union commits itself to no-strike clauses during the currency of agreements and acceptance of works-council arrangements for employee consultation that do not embody a union role.

So far all these new experiments are limited and small in number. But they demonstrate that present Conservative policy is not simply restricted to the goal of reducing union influence. It has some, as yet unassessable, potential for giving employers scope to try to change the character of the system in a variety of ways.

Some will simply bide their time, expecting union strength eventually to recover and risking no major deterioration in relations with them meanwhile - though even these are likely to be taking advantage of the changed position on the labour market and in politics to win back many of the concessions made to union influence during the 1970s. Others will develop advanced personnel policies that include a role for unions, but one dictated on management's terms, not one conforming to the traditional collective bargaining strategy favoured by the unions - a kind of 'Japanisation'. Those following more strictly the nods and winks emerging from the government will push instead for 'Americanisation', for the gradual reduction of the size of the unionised sector.

ACCOUNTING FOR THE CHANGE

In the past Conservative governments have been noted for their attempts at co-opting and incorporating union leaders, for trying to minimise conflict and for seeking friendly relations with organised labour. This has been most distinctive of post-war politics, but it can be traced back to the beginning of the century (Middlemas, 1978) and beyond (Brown, 1983: chs. V, VI). What has either enabled or necessitated a shift in this stance? Part of the complex answer which that question requires has to do with economic problems of managing a declining economy with a high level of public spending, but there are some aspects more specific to industrial relations issues. Traditional Conservative benignity towards organised labour was based on the following:

1. fear of social unrest and upheaval of the kind that had indeed occurred, in Britain but mainly elsewhere, when political confrontations between labour and capital were not moderated;

2. since the Second World War a belief that Conservatives could win elections in a mass democracy only if they could provide full employment; and full employment in turn implied union strength and hence a need to come to terms with unions in the interests of moderating wages pressure;
3. a view of the working class as loyal or potentially loyal to the labour movement, obliging a Conservative government to dispense with major displays of anti-union hostility;
4. belief that positive gains could come from co-operation with union leaders that would compensate for the compromises involved.

What has happened in Britain, and perhaps elsewhere, is that these circumstances no longer seem to hold; Conservatives have therefore ceased to pursue the policies implied by them. Let us consider the four points in turn:

1. Workers' industrial action has steadily become more sectional; many shop-floor struggles are over minor advantages for small groups. There is little reason for workers not involved to believe that these disparate conflicts are part of one big class struggle. This is especially true of decentralised bargaining under full employment, where the maxim that 'one man's wage increase is another man's price increase' has considerable force. On the other hand, larger struggles have tended to be in the public services, and those not involved experience these as, at best, inconveniences, at worst, evils. Far from threatening to confront Conservatives with a massed and militant working class, such conflicts are more likely to rally public opinion behind tough anti-union policies.

It is highly doubtful whether the bulk of the modern working class - among whom manual workers are in any case a declining minority - will be able to produce a politics of mass defiance. Those groups who still possess the sense of the community identity and autonomy required for it - for example, black minorities in the inner cities, coal miners - are, by the very distinctiveness that gives them their inner cohesion, isolated from the rest of the society. (Even then, it is notable that the urban riots of 1981 were one of the rare occasions for talks between the Prime Minister and the TUC, and that the government passed up several opportunities before it decided, in 1984, that the time was ripe for a clash with the miners.) Conservatives make a reasonable sociological gamble if they judge that the period when capitalism faced the constant threat of social disorder from the working masses is now safely past.

2. During the 1950s and 1960s it was a near-universal article of faith in British politics that no government could survive if it failed to deliver full employment; the relationship between unemployment levels and government popularity could be traced with some statistical precision (Goodhart and Bhansali, 1970). This may have changed. Some observers claim that there is no longer such a relationship (Crewe, 1984); though others insist that when account is taken of the special factor of the Falklands War the Conservative Government of 1979-83 remained as vulnerable as any to this force (Dunleavy and Husbands, 1985). What does seem to be the case is that, inflation having become such an overwhelming priority during the 1970s, Keynesian economics was thrown into disarray. Deflationary policies, whether or not dignified by particular economic theories, became virtually irresistible. At the time of the 1979 election public opinion in Britain placed a premium on combating inflation; by 1983 it saw unemployment as the over-riding issue but remained unconvinced of the viability of polities claiming to solve it. Full employment lost its place of predominance in economic policy, and with it went the need to co-operate with trade unions in the search for price stability.

It is unlikely that Conservatives ever expected unemployment to rise to quite such high levels, and they remain potentially highly vulnerable to it. To have the main Opposition party split and to win a minor war both within 18 months was luck of a kind that governments cannot expect to encounter more than once. However, the continuing effect of the Labour Party split will probably remain beyond the next general election. In that case the Conservative Government will have enjoyed nearly a decade free from the political constraint to make a priority of full employment that was imposed on all previous post-war Conservative Governments.

3. Evidence of the declining popularity of the unions and of the opportunities with which this presented the Conservative Government has been discussed above. This evidence has been widely known for several years, but the labour movement has neglected to do anything about it. During the 1970s union leaders could take encouragement from their rising membership figures and consider that it did not matter. Others of them perhaps saw their industrial 'muscle' as not being dependent on public support and therefore cared little about it.

But they also neglected to secure even their members' loyalty. This was concealed during the 1970s by the spread of shop-floor activism and the apparent willingness of large numbers of workers to engage in conflict. Union leaders, of left and right alike, buried themselves in their bureaucracies, busy with the neo-corporatist activities sponsored by both Conservative and Labour governments. Shop-floor activists secured a base of support by representing workers' immediate grievances and opportunistic pay demands, but then took advantage of the co-existence of that support with widespread apathy over longer-term and more political issues; they used their branches and shop-steward groups to assert positions on behalf of the workers for which the latter had very little sympathy. The relatively high number of Communist and other far-left groups among union activists (and some leaders) in contrast with the minimal support attracted by these groups within the working class is evidence of how potentially out of touch the unions' militants were becoming. Once the recession replaced workers' willingness to take opportunistic action by fear of unemployment, they ceased to have any use for the militants and deserted them. The gap between representatives and represented became obvious. Critics were able to point to the dubious methods by which officials were elected and policies approved within unions, which helped explain the gap. And the route was open for a Conservative trade-union policy that could attract widespread support among union members.

The fact that the Labour Party has been losing support among manual workers and union members is a further factor reducing Conservative fear of a monolithic working-class movement. And, as already mentioned, the manual working class is no longer that dominating majority of the adult population that it was in the first half of the century.

4. It is a matter of fine judgement for capitalist interests whether the political exchanges involved in tempting unions into neo-corporatism are worth while. Are the concessions that have to be granted worth the union restraint that is offered? Historically, at the moments when British capital needed some kind of national political exchange with labour, it did not require anything as developed as a fully fledged corporatism. Rich, imperial British capital could afford to distribute its part of the exchange in a relaxed way, while the admission of labour leaders into the gentlemanly, relatively informal norms of British public life was enough to extract from them the small amount of co-operation required. British

Conservative Industrial Relations Policy:

Conservative leaders, as the political spokesmen for capital, developed an easy confidence in their ability to make reasonably satisfactory exchanges when they needed them. The extraordinary degree of national co-operation achieved during the Second World War sustained this confidence long past the period when the British economic superiority that had initially fostered it had disintegrated.

By the 1970s all that had changed. A new generation of Conservative leaders, who had not been involved in war-time politics, had appeared. British capital was now in deep trouble; concessions to labour in a fully employed but declining economy had begun to hurt. In its turn, labour was less easily satisfied than in the past: its leaders demanded extensive legal support for union and worker rights and refused to accept a decline in the wage share to assist profitability. Meanwhile, the rank and file were more militant and resistant to the entreaties of their leaders when the latter were willing to co-operate.

Problems for the New Strategy

British industrial relations have moved a long way since 1979. The dilemma for capital's political strategy used to be: what combination of toughness and concessions through corporatism will best secure a deal that will stick with union leaders? After more than a full parliament of unemployment, union exclusion from political respectability, fairly successfully introduced (though hardly fully used) legislation hostile to union interests, declining union membership, a broken Labour Party and an increased Conservative parliamentary majority, the choices confronting capital seem to have improved considerably. At the same time, major doubts remain over the continued capacity of the system to support the new policies. These may be summarised briefly as follows:

(i) high unemployment cannot continue indefinitely. Even if the absolute level remains considerably higher than in previous decades, there must come periods of at least temporary improvement. Labour shortages will develop in some unionised sectors; redundancy and company bankruptcy will cease to be an immediate source of fear for many sections of the work force. Since fear has been the main weapon ensuring workers' moderation, a reduction in fear must be expected to lead to a revival of militancy. Further, grievances will have accumulated during the years of recession which workers will want to resolve; the 'explosions' of militancy could be severe. This, one must remember, has been the normal history of

French industrial relations: long periods in which labour remains weak and grievances fester, followed by sudden, massive if temporary explosions when either labour-market or political conditions improve; and it is partly a French model that the government and sections of capital are pursuing in their 'labour exclusion' strategy.

(ii) Although the shop-floor movement has had its strength broken, this must be seen in historical perspective. British unionism has long had a powerful, autonomous shop-floor base, starting with the 19th century craft unions; becoming, temporarily, a major force during and after the First World War; becoming more militant from the mid-1950s; extending into a wide range of new occupations since the late 1960s. High unemployment breaks it; but it returns. One should expect a similar pattern during the next economic up-turn.

(iii) If there is any validity in social-scientific theories concerning the function of the institutionalisation of conflict and the co-optation of labour leaders in limiting and mollifying industrial unrest, then one has to predict an eventual rise in conflict levels in a society which undergoes de-institutionalisation and a rejection of co-optation as ruling-class strategies. Changes in occupational structure and the increasing isolation of militant sectors may diminish the likelihood of this, but they are unlikely to have rendered them nugatory. The danger is not so much that conflicts will spread to embrace vast numbers in class conflict, but the damage that is done to public institutions and the norms regulating public life by the crude methods of conflict control that are used against dissident minorities in the absence of institutionalisation. The miners' strike of 1984 stands as a major example of this. When one industrial dispute produces changes in the position of police forces in polity and society and in the form and character of their deployment, precedents are set which may have implications going far beyond industrial relations. Even if elite and public opinion share the government's view of the miners' case, they may not accept the wider ramifications of the government's actions, which challenge many of the assumptions of characteristic 'British' institutions.

The Conservative government is engaged in a race against time. If the economy (and therefore worker and union confidence) recovers before any final transformation in the industrial relations system has been achieved, the government (and employers who have taken a 'labour exclusion' line) will be in great difficulties. There will be an accumulation of grievances alongside a deterioration in the institutional defences against the spreading of conflict. On the other hand, changes in occupational structure, in internal union politics, in the legal structure and in the overall level of unionisation may produce fundamental changes in the character of British industrial relations before an economic recovery raises labour's potential power. The unions would then emerge permanently weakened and structurally no longer able to raise major industrial or political challenges. The government could then afford a more relaxed, benign strategy. The problem for the government is that, for the latter to be possible, the recession will have to be prolonged. But that fact would itself carry grave political threats. In the past one might have argued with complete confidence that a government that continued indefinitely with a high level of unemployment could not possibly continue to win general elections. This is where the split in the non-Conservative opposition in Britain, combined with the country's electoral system, may be crucial to the government's chances of success.

REFERENCES

Brown, P.B., 1983: The Origins of Trade Union Power (Oxford: at the University Press)

Brown, W. (ed.), 1981: The Changing Contours of British Industrial Relations (Oxford: Blackwell)

Crewe, I., 1984: 'The shocks that could shake our certainties', The Guardian, January 13

Crouch, C.J., 1985: 'Corporatism in industrial relations: a formal model', in Grant, W. (ed.), The Political Economy of Corporatism (London: Macmillan)

Department of Employment, 1981: 'Developments in employee involvement', Department of Employment Gazette, February-June, September

Dunleavy, P. and Husbands, C.T., 1985: British Democracy at the Cross-Roads, (London: Allen and Unwin)

Goodhart, C. and Bhansali, R., 1970: 'Political economy', Political Studies, 18

IR-RR, 1983: 'Binding arbitration at Immos', Industrial Relations Review and Reports, July 12, pp. 8-11

Middlemas, K., 1978: Politics in an Industrial Society (London: Allen and Unwin)

Moran, M., 1974: The Union of Post-Office Workers: a Study in Political Sociology (London: Macmillan)

Conservative Industrial Relations Policy:

Nielsen, H.-J., 1984: 'Trade unions, politics and public opinion in Britain' (University of Copenhagen, Department of Political Science, mimeo.)

PART THREE

"Italy: The Permanent Impasse?"

Chapter 7

THE TRILATERAL AGREEMENT OF 1983: SOCIAL PACT OR POLITICAL TRUCE?

Mario Dal Co and Paolo Perulli

THE AGREEMENT OF JANUARY 22, 1983

One event in the Italian industrial relations scene of the early '80s stands out as particularly innovative and significant. After a long and disputed controversy, the government, unions and entrepreneurial organisations reached an agreement to modify numerous issues of economic policy, labour market regulation, income policy and collective bargaining (documented in: IRES-CGIL 1984, pp. 230-43). In a system like Italy's, characterised by a traditional absence of income policies reached by consent of the social partners, and a decentralized bargaining system, this trilateral agreement is heralded by many as a "turning point".

Numerous factors contribute to such a strong judgement. In the first place, the form and contents of the negotiation: trilateral and "neo-corporatist", negotiated between the government and peak-level interest organisations, characteristics of a prescriptive "framework-agreement" with respect to the structures and lower levels of bargaining, definition of common objectives among the partners (reduction of inflation and unemployment).

The agreement modifies the wage indexation system, reducing the effectiveness of the "scala mobile" as the union "contribution" to the fight against inflation. It also sets three-year wage increases that industry-wide contracts can forecast and puts an 18-month freeze on enterprise wage bargaining to avoid phenomena of wage-drifts.

The government pledges to "compensate" real wages with a fiscal manoeuvre aimed at eliminating the fiscal-drag, which during high inflation and with a very progressive fiscal system penalizes worker purchasing power. In addition, the government would maintain state-"administered" prices and tariffs within the limit programmed for inflation. In turn, the entrepreneurs reaped their share of benefits from the government: fiscalisation of the social contributions and more freedom in company hiring, hence greater flexibility on the labour market. This appearance of a trilateral agreement led many observers to speak of a turning point, an epochal watershed leading towards a new industrial relations system.

In actual fact, a more careful analysis of the context and contents of the agreement and the rationale of the social partners offers the possibility for another interpretation. According to this more pessimistic yet also more realistic point of view, conditions in Italy are such that they do not provide the grounds for political exchange consciously pursued by industrial relations partners with effect from the agreement. In other words, all the preconditions which are common to the "neo-corporatist formations" and those that characterize the establishment of forms of stable and systematic political agreements between the State and large interest organisations do not exist in the present situation. Thus it seems more pertinent to define the agreement as a trilateral compromise that was provisional, unstable and lacking in normative elements able to determine the future of industrial relations in Italy in neo-corporatist terms. Thus, the agreement represented a "break" in the crisis of the industrial relations system that was destined to reappear. To understand the meaning and dimensions of this crisis we must go back to the '70s, the period during which the crisis exploded.

THE INFLATIONARY PACT OF THE '70s

The major question of the recent phase of industrial relations in Italy is still how the union was able to consolidate the explosion of claims of the late '60s ("the hot autumn") in a highly conflictual industrial relations system which in the '70s showed considerable vitality in spite of the internal deterioration of several bargaining instruments characteristic of the system itself. One of the necessary conditions - pointed out by many - is room for decision-making provided by the political system, which the union initially claimed without much success: fights for housing, transport, services in the early '70s - and which later became real issues of negotiations: controversies with the government over social security, tariff, health and fiscal policies.

The Trilateral Agreement of 1983:

But the great capacity for mobilisation that came to the fore during the course of the decade is naturally not explained solely by the benefits offered by the expansion of bargaining, supported by the legislative evolution. The consolidation of the bargaining system on the three levels - company, industry, and interconfederal - was made possible not because the latter, closest to the heart of political exchange, led the others, but rather because it was helped by the unquestionable effectiveness of the former two. And it is this effectiveness - prolonged and indifferent to the more obvious changes of the political picture - that must be explained in more than just organisational terms, the correct but partial approach adopted by sociology up to now. This effectiveness is due basically to the response given by means of the economic and, in particular, monetary policy to the demands originating from industrial conflict.

In 1981, the first year of Italy's current economic recession the share of workers' income in added value was still higher - for the entire economy - than the already high 1970 level. The difference is almost 8 points, 3 of which are a result of the growth of the share of public administration in the added value in the years following the first oil crisis. In the industrial sector the share of workers' income in 1981 was practically the same as 1970. If we look at the years in between, the trend for the first half of the '70s shows a rise (reaching the maximum in 1975) followed by a slow descent in the second half of the decade. For industry - the sector most vulnerable to the effects of the recession - the end of the '70s marked a consolidation of the victories of the "hot autumn" in terms of income distribution. The '70s were characterised by counter-cyclical fluctuations of the labour share: it shrank during phases of expansion and expanded during recessions. This trend was the combined effect of the stability of employment, rigidity of real wages, and fluctuation of activity levels.

The union was able to stabilise employment with the help of the Workers' Statute on the one hand and the "Cassa Integrazione" (partial layoff payments) on the other. But it also stabilised real wages and even made their growth fairly <u>independent</u> of the economic cycle. In fact, in 1975 two interconfederal agreements were signed. The first instituted a new system of wage indexation, the second broadened the possibilities of recourse to the "Cassa Integrazione Straordinaria" (prolonged partial layoff payments). In this context, the shrinkage of the activity levels was paid by enterprise profits. The interventions aimed at reducing the social contributions and easing the fiscal pressure on the enterprises were positioned alongside a growing number of transfers to public enterprises. This provoked a rise in the public deficit with respect to income. However, the public deficit was partially balanced because inflation produced a heavy increase in the earnings deriving from direct taxation, in particular withholdings on workers' incomes. In the latter half of the '70s we find an increase in gross real wages, which was confiscated to a great extent by the State through the operation of fiscal drag.

In this period a kind of implicit political pact became evident which led to "national unity" governments supported by the Communist Party. The pact suggested that given the union's strong position in industrial relations, economic policy must assume a certain wage dynamics and employment stability as constraints and treat inflation, exchange rate and public deficit as its objectives. Thus, what Hicks had called the wage-standard was realised, i. e. a system in which the purchasing power of currency was tied to the level and dynamics of the nominal wage. The nominal wage in this period was certainly inflexible, but thanks to the "scala mobile" and national and enterprise bargaining, real wage was quite inflexible too. The only way to reduce or limit its growth was inflation. In fact, the "scala mobile" did not guarantee a total protection of average wages, and hence the rise of inflation produced an erosion - though modest - of real wages. In addition, the rise of inflation produced a more rapid growth of fiscal pressure than that of inflation itself. Data show that from 1977 to 1980 the increase in direct fiscal pressure on wages amply compensated the fiscalisation of the social contributions for the enterprises.

Thus the latter half of the '70s was a period of dynamic balance. We may summarise the situation as follows:

- the union's strength in the bargaining area may be attributed to historical-organisational factors and to the favourable conditions created by the economic policy;
- the basic rationale behind the monetary policy was the idea that to modify the power relationships on the bargaining level, the sacrifice in terms of employment and the cost in terms of conflict would be too great for a country like Italy, which has recently reached the phase of intermediate development and is characterised by strong territorial imbalance;

- the fiscal policy has strengthened the normative and social security system that constituted an important security network for the two social partners involved in the industrial conflict and for the union in particular. In return it showed a spectacular increase in the direct pressure from the fiscal drag, used to a large extent to reduce enterprise costs and, in the case of public enterprises, often to keep them operative in spite of very heavy losses.

THE CRISIS OF THE '80s

The 1975 agreement was the result of various factors. First, the accumulated strength of the union on the bargaining market. In spite of the intense - but short-lived - first recession, the union was able to reach an understanding on the political market which both protected and enlarged its social area. The new "scala mobile" system protected the "central" working class but also parts of weak labour which was on the fringes of the bargaining system. A second factor was the entrepreneurs' concern with freeing the enterprise from a distributive conflict that was particularly intense in the early '70s and introducing elements of "centralisation" in determining wage dynamics.

These elements of union compromise (helped by an entrepreneurial ideology of "alliance among the producers") became part of a political scenario in motion (growth of the Left, affirmation of the Communist Party, government of national solidarity). These factors brought about an original form of Keynesian intervention based on a particular mix of "scala mobile", devaluation, transfers to the enterprises, public spending to support profit margins, fiscal drag. Thus a system of mutual compensations was activated. And the result for the union was a substantial defense both of average wages and employment in the face of a considerable decline in productivity. For the enterprises, devaluation and an increase in transfers by the State are the way to maintain the limits of competitiveness; in addition there are the "other" labour market and the development of the informal economy. In this context and under these conditions we may consider this a phase of political exchange (though limited and incomplete) that is, in effect, a system of compensations.

On the basis of this logic of compensations, the union together with the entrepreneurs and government defined the agreements of 1977. Their defense of the "scala mobile" system was compensated by a series of "concessions" related to a more flexible use of the labour force. This compensation system proved unstable right from the start, and it gave way to a rapidly decreasing political output. It was not to be part of a systematic political exchange. The blocking of the political exchange at the end of the '70s occurred at a time of failure of the exchange between government structural reform policies and union bargaining moderation policies. Hence it may be argued that the wage restraint policies of the late '70s (including the 1979 contract renewals) were practised by the Italian union in a context less of exchange than of bargaining self-moderation and wage solidarity tied to the preservation of the "scala mobile". We might say, an Italian version of central wage governing models typical of other industrial relations systems.

1980 marked a change most notably with respect to the enterprises and the State. Heavy industrial restructuring got underway, leading to an appreciable drop in employment in 1981 and 1982. In spite of the recession, the restructuring gave way to a considerable growth of productivity. With the phase of national solidarity "over", the State started moving towards substantial deregulation (first with respect to economic and monetary policies, followed by industrial policies and, finally - the current phase - social policies). Deregulation in the sense of denationalisation, privatisation, etc. The conflict over the "scala mobile" was central to the change since 1980 (cancellation of the agreement by the Confindustria, i.e. the federation of private industry June 1982). The entrepreneurs have aimed at a considerable wage reduction but, most important, more flexible forms of remuneration and hence of management of the labour force. This line implies the decision to centralise bargaining. In fact, compared to the previous phase the same form of centralised bargaining has now become a necessity for the union rather than an occasion to confirm its power in the political arena. A centralised bargaining over the "scala mobile" penalises the union's decentralised bargaining function and creates passivity at the local and company union levels in a phase of intense industrial restructuring.

THE DYNAMICS THAT LED TO THE 1983 AGREEMENT

If the partners were moving along basically different lines how was an agreement reached? The answer is rather simple and "reasonable". The three social partners needed an agreement for reasons that were both similar and different. And the solution was, for all three, second best.

> In this sense the agreement may be interpreted as the release of tensions accumulated over the previous two years in industrial relations and on the political market. For the government it was a matter of re-establishing a consensus among the social partners that was indispensable to reaffirm its own authority. The threat to proceed by decree expressed by both the Spadolini and Fanfani governments (and, in 1984, by the Craxi government) only represented a signal of urgency to the partners (and, if anything, of its own weakness).

It is probable that had the government been able to decide autonomously it would have chosen a hard-line incomes policy. The first version of Fanfani's programme (November 1982) called for a minimum two-year wage truce, the neutralisation of the "scala mobile" with respect to increases in tariffs, indirect taxes, imported inflation and, on this basis, the pre-determination of the evolution of the "scala mobile". Room for manoeuvring in industry contract renewals would only have come through a further compression of the "scala mobile". But given the conditions in Italy in which union power was still strong (in terms both of resources of mobilisation and influence on the government and opposition parties), this type of line proved to be unfeasible. Hence the need to seek consensus, a naturally costly resource and the final choice of the government. It offered new resources to the partners, becoming part of complex redistributive exchanges. Unions were offered a review of the fiscal, social and tariff policy which compensates the neutralisation of the "scala mobile". Entrepreneurs were offered fiscalisation of social contributions and greater flexibility of the labour market. These additional resources, which were intended to transform the game from a zero sum into a positive sum one, made the agreement feasible.

But the established measures had limited value and duration. It was clear right from the start that they would be subject to renegotiation. In many cases they were statements of intent that were not binding or prescriptive. If anything the agreement indicated a way to work out the differences which hopefully would continue to be respected. As can be seen it was less than a neo-corporatist pact or a new social contract. A further and decisive indication of the instability of the agreement on the part of the government was represented by the precarious nature of the government coalitions and by their internal political fragmentation. Hence there was a plurality of political lines and initiatives within the government and a block in the phase of "implementation of the results". Moreover, there was (and is) no corporatist structure at the central or local level to handle any possible "common" objectives.

As far as the entrepreneurs were concerned, they seemed to be rather uninterested in neo-corporatist solutions during the course of the negotiations. Diffidence towards the government and agressiveness towards the union appeared to be their basic attitude. Any sign of a climate that was ripe for social partnership was denied by the type of industrial relations created in the enterprises, at least starting from the Fiat controversy. Industrial relations based on social partnership were (and are) basically limited to public industry. With the cancellation of the "scala mobile" the private entrepreneurs, though internally articulated, proposed several "unifying" objectives:

1. sharp reduction of the coverage of the "scala mobile";
2. sliding of collective contract renewals;
3. regulation of enterprise bargaining.

Clearly all these objectives converged towards a weakening of the union. The entrepreneurial strategy aimed at recovering margins of manoeuvrability in the enterprises to complete a phase of intense restructuring: the basic condition of such a strategy is the reduction and weakening of union bargaining power. In this sense the decision to enter into an agreement represented for Confindustria a simple truce, made necessary by the pressures exercised by the political power and by worker mobilisation and "spontaneous" strikes. Nevertheless, the results obtained with the agreement are rather significant for the entrepreneurs: an almost 20 per cent reduction in the coverage of the "scala mobile", an 18-month suspension of company wage bargaining, a partial "liberalisation" of hiring policies.

The limited prescriptiveness of the agreement may be seen from the further sliding of the contract renewals, whose wage increase had been defined in the agreement, and by the obvious differences of "interpretation" regarding the calculation of the "new" "scala mobile". In short, the motive that led the entrepreneurial associations to the agreement can in no way be confused with a precondition for future social contracts. Rather, we can predict that they will exercise a growing pressure for a review - for the worse - of numerous clauses of the agreement. Indeed a further weakening of the union is still the explicit objective of the entrepreneurs in the present economic and political phase.

Finally, an analysis of union bargaining behaviour confirms the shift away from neo-corporatist models. The most obvious is the shift away from their prerequisite of strong centralisation, concentration and strategic unification in managing union representativeness. The "strategy of EUR", a district of Rome, where in 1978 a congress was held by the three Italian union confederations which, among other things (cf. Carrieri/Donolo in this volume) aimed at a centralization of trade union politics, was only for some time and only partly realised.

During the course of the controversy, union behaviour was the result of a combination of basically different strategic lines - a combination rooted in the conclusion of the previous phase, characterised by the EUR strategy. In spite of everything the union organisations were harmonious in their approach to bargaining. The image of the representativeness and the culture of the bargaining did not differ among the organisations or, at any rate, did not go beyond a legitimate degree of "competition".

Tensions within the union (that were not cause for worry) concerned relations between the top and base, but the union managerial group gave a rather homogeneous interpretation of "general interest" that could easily be opposed to sectoral interest and corporatist-type pressures. Opposition to the confederations' strategy was limited though significant. On these bases, even though in the absence of a high degree of associative monopoly, unity and centralisation, which are features of neo-corporatist systems, union unity and premediation of interests represented in Italy the functional equivalents sufficient to guarantee an experience of social partnership.

The picture has changed rather radically over the last two years, not just because of union "tactics" but because of the prolonged development of the crisis. The very base of union representation seems to be in question. There appears to be verbal agreement on the crisis of the binomial representation-representativeness, but there is deep dissent on the possible ways out of such a crisis. In the face of a progressive breakdown and contrast among workers' groups, the type of social demands that the union must choose and its social project are in question. It is a matter of problems not only of income distribution and remunerative hierarchies, but of labour distribution among the employed, unemployed and temporary workers. It is a matter of problems regarding the protection and orientation of consumption and savings. It is a matter of appropriate models of social equity and of a response to the "new inequalities" induced by the crisis. On this basis there have been different strategic options during the course of recent years.

A first trend sees the defence of the central working class hit by restructuring and de-indexation policies (the "scala mobile" protects the lower middle incomes first and foremost) as the union's main task. This defensive attitude originates from the assumption that, with the adoption of the EUR strategy, the entrepreneurial and conservative forces defeated an entire line of workers' advance in the '70s.

The union must defend the rigidities regarding "work rules" (organisation of work and employment) and income distribution ("scala mobile"). The objective is to minimise the losses, i.e. a "resource" to administer while waiting for more favourable conditions that would allow a new advance. This tendency, with which a good number of those industrial categories that had resisted the austerity line and base sectors of the union organisation identify, experiences the entire controversy on the cost of labour as a terrain of "manipulated resistance". This resistance must be developed with respect to the entrepreneurs and the government and, first and foremost, with respect to those sectors of union leadership that exercise the most pressure for change (whatever kind) in the mechanisms of indexation as a union contribution to the increase of governability of the political system.

A second trend that could be classified innovative-reformist is instead much more attentive to the ongoing changes in the social composition of the working class. During the course of the '70s this tendency had tried to identify in the autonomous role of the union as political subject a basic condition for the reform of the state. In other words, the union produces political innovation in the state to the degree to which it maintains and increases its capacity of representation and adopts instruments of democratic participation and consensus. The institutionalisation of "market" relations between union and state is considered the presupposition of a delegitimisation and of a crisis of union representativeness. A strategy proposed as an alternative to political exchange is self-management of the various workers groups, but in relation to the control of enterprise policies and government economic policies.

Also during the course of the post-EUR phase there has been an attempt to reconstruct a union bargaining strategy oriented towards the extension of representation in the face of the ongoing productive restructuring processes. Hence, a union that wants to maintain characteristics of general representation and solidarity must give up the rigidity both in company bargaining and in the governing of the labour market. Instead of being a terrain of resistance or "concession", the controversy over the cost of labour is experienced as the occasion to introduce elements of reform in the institutes that regulate both wages and the labour market. As far as wages are concerned, there were proposals regarding the relationship between wages and fiscal pressure, wages and family income, wages and "professionalita" (skill requirements), wages and consumption. If we consider that suggestions for reform concerned relations between the State and enterprises we have a picture of reform policies for income redistribution. These can represent a perspective of a flexible income policy which goes beyond the mere re-proposal of "classic" income policies. On the one hand they protect an autonomous role for the union and its bargaining policy, on the other they ask for a profound reform of the State.

A <u>third</u> trend present in the controversy and in the more recent union debate concerns <u>political exchange</u>. The solution of the union crisis is entrusted to its capacity to promote forms of political exchange as an alternative to the free market and state regulation.

There is definitely a "paradox" here: political exchange was theorised and sought during the phase in which the political system was "blocked" and the composition of governments did not include a pro-Labour party like the Communist Party. Under such a condition (and there is no doubt that this is the situation in Italy starting from 1979) every hypothesis of political exchange is directed at a government that does not offer the necessary guarantees of stability and certainty. In addition, the problem of the effects of a political exchange strategy on the representativeness of the union was not explained. As a consequence of political exchange a reform of the bargaining structure towards centralisation should be pursued. Likewise the area of the exchange would be extended to include wages and working time through generalised forms of working time reductions. Similarly new social actors outside the traditional labour market were to be included by means of the proposal of forms of worker management and co-operation and the activation of a "solidarity fund". Thus the union's behaviour in the course of the controversy was the result of a mixture of these basically different strategic lines. This marks the shift in Italy from neo-corporatist models in which strong union centralisation and unification are requested.

The lack of unification among the different cultures and the political-strategical hypotheses in the union gave way to a complex internal pre-negotiation. Its outcome was uncertain (in so far as it is continuously subject to internal re-negotiations) and hardly convincing (with respect to both the partners and the representatives themselves).

AFTER THE AGREEMENT, THE BREAK

The developments of industrial relations and of the relationship between the union and political system after the agreement of 1983 confirm the hypotheses formulated up to this point. At the end of 1983 a new bargaining round developed between the new Socialist-led government and the social partners. The limited normative value of the trilateral agreement is evident at this point. Theoretically speaking the new bargaining round should have verified the inflation trend during 1983 and have established "who gained and who lost" as far as the positions in income distribution are concerned. In actual fact, the government pressed for further reduction of the "scala mobile", this time with less fiscal or other types of compensations for workers. The sole compensation was the commitment to hold prices and tariffs within a pre-established limit. Differences between the unions and within the CGIL transformed into an open break. Part of the union movement agreed with the government manoeuvres, counting on the fact that the resulting reduction in inflation would have positive effects on wages. Another part of the union movement considered unacceptable an agreement that did not offer certain guarantees of wage recovery and proposed a price and income freeze like the French experience of 1982.

The result was a vertical break of the CGIL (the confederation is divided between Communists and Socialists) on the one side and CISL and UIL on the other. At this point the government decided to intervene by decree, setting a quantitative limit on the "scala mobile" points. In this way the social partnership that marked the previous phase was ended, and a climate of political and social conflict whose outcome is uncertain was determined. The break of union unity in the early months of 1984 was determined by the growing differences in the strategies of representation within the union movement and to the change in the relationships between the union and political system.

We have already discussed the first point at length. The different union strategies have progressively eroded the margins of internal pre-mediation that characterised the previous phase and produced the agreement of 1983. The motives for this erosion may only be hypothesized, but one thing is certain: a basic precondition for social partnership has fallen. A new, obscure phase opens up in which the entire pyramid system of industrial relations could be questioned in so far as the division of the union could be reproduced at all levels, starting with the Shop Stewards Committee. The evolution of the relationships between the union and political system bears great weight on the reconstruction of this new scenario. The union's "invasion" of the political arena having ended, the political system takes the initiative and attempts to win back lost space. In this sense, the intervention by decree on a matter traditionally left to the autonomy of collective bargaining may be more than just an episode. It may well be the indication of a future trend of government reappropriation of decision-making autonomy.

Many ask for the recovery of "decision-making capacity". But it is certain that this could determine the end of any perspective of social partnership and political bargaining. In this case industrial relations in Italy would evolve towards the sum of government intervention and market power, and the union would be excluded in the end. An alternative might be the redefinition of rules of the game shared by all the partners, in particular with respect to political bargaining. Its limits would need to be precisely identified, the autonomy of the bargaining subjects strictly respected and the prerogatives of the political system, government and parliament clearly defined. But is such a union of corporatism and neopluralism possible?

REFERENCES

Altieri, G. et al., 1984: La vertenza sul costo del lavoro e le relazioni industriali, Milano

Baglioni, G. et al. (eds.), 1983: Prima e dopo l'accordo di gennaio, in: prospettiva sindacale, no. 47 - vol. XIV

Baglioni, G., E. Santi and C. Squarzon (eds.), 1982: Le relazioni sindacali in Italia, Rapporto CESOS 1981, Roma

The Trilateral Agreement of 1983:

Baglioni, G., E. Santi and C. Squarzon (eds.), 1983: Le relazioni sindacali in Italia, Rapporto CESOS 1982, Roma

Dal Co, M., 1983: I sistemi di relazioni industriali e la crisi economica, in: Democrazia e diritto, no. 6

Hicks, J. R., 1974: The Crisis of Keynesian Economics, Oxford

Leon, P., 1983: Crisi delle politiche keynesiane e politiche dell'offerta in Italia, in: Problemi del socialismo, no. 26, vol. XXIV

Perulli, P. and B. Trentin (eds.), 1983: Il sindacato nella recessione, Bari

Regini, M., 1983: Le condizioni dello scambio politico. Crescita e declino della concertazione in Italia e Gran Bretagna, in: Stato e mercato, no. 9

Chapter 8

COLLECTIVE AND POLITICAL BARGAINING

Gian Primo Cella and Tiziano Treu

OPEN PROBLEMS IN ITALIAN INDUSTRIAL RELATIONS

The general trends and development singled out at the beginning of the 1980s (recentralisation of industrial relations; prevalence of interindustrial bargaining, etc.) were amply confirmed by the important events that followed.

The year 1982 was decisive for interconfederal bargaining between the peak organisations of the three unions (CGIL, CISL, UIL) and the employers' associations. During the course of the year, marked by highs and lows and often contradictory events, the way was paved for the agreement of January 1983, one of the most - if not the most - significant examples of interconfederal agreement in post World War II industrial relations. A particular feature of this year concerns the characteristics of the bargaining process: lengthy, but with profound and frequent interruptions and rarely formalised (perhaps only at the end, during ministerial mediation); government interventions were numerous but always outside the realm of an institutionalised framework with contacts among the parties that were mostly indirect or made through the mass media.

The particularities of the bargaining process indicate the difficulties for a real interconfederal bargaining level to assert itself in our system, even in the presence of numerous elements that urge general bargaining solutions. These elements are:

(a) the persistent economic crisis with the related need to control the wage dynamics and labour market. In 1982 the inflation rate was 16.4 per cent and unemployment over 9 per cent;

(b) the need to modify the effects and dynamics of the 1975 agreement on the cost of living allowance;

(c) the government's repeated and declared willingness to intervene directly in the industrial relations area; and
(d) the widespread trends towards centralized bargaining.

Acting against interconfederal solutions we find:

(e) the noncentralisation of the social partners' organisation (trade unions and employers' association);
(f) the low formalisation and institutionalisation of Italian industrial relations;
(g) the complexity of the bargaining structure which remains firmly bipolar;
(h) the unreliability of the public institutions that should support numerous aspects of general bargaining solutions and make them work.

Such a discontinuous, informal, tormented yet tough bargaining process shows us the conflict operating between these favourable and unfavourable elements.

Given these numerous and opposing elements, we can see that there are many open problems in industrial relations at the start of 1982 that awaited some sort of temporary solution through interconfederal bargaining. A first series has to do with the dynamics and structure of wages and labour costs. Wage issues concern mainly indexation, especially related to the functioning of the 1975 agreement on the cost of living allowance and escalator clause (INDENNITÁ DI CONTINGENZA). The aspects under discussion in a time of heavy inflation (much heavier than could be predicted in the mid-'70s) were mainly two: the size of increases in the cost of living allowance, which is equal for all employees, not proportionate to skill wage (and which therefore considerably reduces wage differentials) and the effects on indexation of devaluations in the exchange rate abroad and the tax increase.

The problems related to the wage structure are evident and have long been discussed within the union movement and by the entrepreneurs: a general "cleansing" of the structure, better redefinition of its components (base, family, seniority, etc.) and also the relative bargaining competencies of the different union organisational structures.

Also under discussion in this context is the role of the government and government policies, especially the fiscal one, which can be decisive in realising interconfederal bargaining solutions. These issues are rather unusual for industrial relations: yet they are part of a trend towards the "fiscalisation" of industrial relations that concerns all advanced capitalist countries.

A second series of problems concerns the labour market: the functioning of the placement system, the possibilities of establishing territorial organs for managing the market, the norms for particular categories of workers, the forms of redefinition of the "Cassa Integrazione" (partial layoff payments) in connection with labour mobility.

A third type of issue concerns working hours, and reduction in work hours requested by the unions in order to defend employment in those sectors that are hit by crisis or involved in restructuring processes.

Another series of problems is related to the structure and functioning of industrial relations per se. For example, the needs to reform (or patch up) the bargaining structure (the relationships among the different bargaining levels), the control of conflictuality, especially micro-conflict, the use of more functional and effective procedures for resolving disputes.

The fact that the interconfederal level turned out to be the ideal site for dealing with these problems could hardly be contested, even though union leaders did not openly admit it. Perhaps only working hours issues could find effective solutions within the various national branch agreements. But they would have been included better in a set of rules valid for all categories. It seemed highly unlikely, however, that the interconfederal level could deal with all these problems through an agreement that determined a new industrial relations system. The agreement of January 1983 seemed possible but improbable a year before. Pressure on the top bargaining levels was great, but forecasts as to their effectiveness and potential were uncertain.

SOME PRINCIPLES OF METHOD

The importance of the agreement of January 22 1983 as an attempt to rationalise Italian industrial relations has been widely recognised even by many of its critics. It must be evaluated in the overall context of industrial relations, of which it is a particularly significant indicator. The elements of continuity and discontinuity must be analysed with respect to the previous state of the system and also to noteworthy foreign experiences. Finally, the agreement must be examined for the prospects it may hold for the system, although the real impact of the single clauses, especially those with delayed effectiveness, depends on numerous variables and has proven to be somewhat precarious.

The agreement includes several general principles that are important for characterising the industrial relations model. Each one, seen in itself and with respect to its potential significance, presents innovative aspects in terms of our recent experience, but the latter conditions the agreement to the point of hindering its application.

(a) A first feature of the agreement that is generally acknowledged consists in its being tripartite: this is quite explicit, not hidden as in the past, by "parallel consultations" between government and the single social partners. The mechanism goes beyond institutionalised consultation, considered inefficient for a consensual governing of the economy, yet it is far from a system of institutionalised co-management. The tripartism is not only formal but substantial. It means that the public subject - the executive - has intervened not only as an active mediator but as a partner in the exchange with full negotiating rights. Unlike the past, it was not even restricted to formulating negative sanctions in the case of no agreement among the partners; it has made its own resources available to favour the agreement. The government's commitments on contributions and fiscal and tariff matters in exchange for those asked of the social partners are not new. Nevertheless, the scope and finalisation of the manoeuvre were unprecedented.

The public resources invested were enormous and had a decisive role in the exchange. They compensated union acceptance of the slowdown in wage growth and entrepreneurial acceptance of the packet of contract renewals.

The triangularity of the agreement raises delicate institutional problems in the relationships between forms of social and political representation of interests. Beyond the strictly legal aspects - for which the possibility arose that the agreement could be broken for violation of its contents - its basic effectiveness is related to the fact that the overall balance of its parts was respected: those concerning programmatic and contractual regulation of the labour relationship and those concerning government political commitments.

(b) The main objective of the agreement, and the basic element of its triangularity, is the connection between collective bargaining - recognised as the fundamental instrument for governing industrial relations - and the framework of economic compatibilities assumed as the basis of the agreement, first and foremost the containment of inflation in maintaining the real income value. A similar agreement, which is the premise of every incomes policy, was operated in this case in protecting the autonomy of the partners, and it stimulates explicit union involvement in macro-economic responsibilities.

(c) The agreement increased the de facto centralisation (at least since 1975) of industrial relations in Italy as elsewhere. The centralisation corresponds in part to the macro-economic and political importance of the major issues under discussion. But it brings to light the need for articulating the different levels and for bargaining decentralisation. This need is not completely negated by the agreement, on the contrary it is partly inherent in its nature as a framework agreement. In the context of its directives, the agreement maintains areas of autonomy for decisions of the public and private partners at the various levels. The balance between centralised initiative and articulation of the methods of intervention proved to be a decisive point for the real significance of the agreement. However, it is one of the most delicate issues for governing industrial relations.

(d) The agreement paves the way for an initial proceduralisation of industrial relations. Until now our system has lived in a state of almost total informality: absence of legislative and bargaining rules in all its main aspects, i. e. bargaining structure, union representation at the various levels, worker participation, labour disputes and conflicts. The informality was useful and probably necessary during the tumultuous growth of the system (1968-73), but contra-indications are increasingly evident. It facilitates waste of resources and excess of conflicts, overlapping of competencies, irresponsibility (often mutual) of the actors, unpredictability and non-transparency of bargaining relations. To oppose this trend what may well be the most important directives of the agreement are procedural, and hence by definition their effectiveness depends on how they are handled. Procedural rules are envisioned for the conduct of micro-conflicts at the enterprise level and for the definition of the relationships among the different bargaining levels. But procedural directives - added to programmatic indications on the solutions to be sought - also concern the management of the labour market, sectoral industrial programming, and institution of the Solidarity Fund. It is no accident that union participation in governing economic processes is involved in various ways in all these issues. The indications are procedural, somewhat generic and flexible, and have been left mostly to bargaining initiative. If the informality that has prevailed up to now shows the effects of the fragile balance of our industrial relations, the reversal of the trend hypothesized by the agreement shows the effects of the persistent instability of the system and is in fact barely touched upon. It is also significant that there are no indications for the proceduralisation of other aspects of industrial relations, in particular the forms of union representation at the enterprise level.

With this characterisation in mind, it is clear how the January agreement was judged to be rich in innovative elements: a real turning point or the closing of a phase of Italian history.

In the logic of the agreement the triangularity, centralisation, proceduralisation of industrial relations and the link between contracts and economic policies with union involvement in governing the economy were all permanent not transitory features. They aimed to stabilise Italian industrial relations in a direction similar to that pursued by the more consolidated systems of central and northern Europe. In this sense they tended to reduce those particularities or anomalies that during the course of the '70s had put our system "midway" between the purely pluralistic and so-called neo-corporative models prevalent in other countries.

The tendency shown by the agreement was sufficiently clear with respect to the above-mentioned models. Some of what were generally considered characteristics of neo-corporative models or "concerted" economies were corroborated: centralisation of choices; triangular method with active government role and partial marginalisation of parliament; union involvement in economic choices, especially in incomes policies; growing institutionalisation and proceduralisation of collective social relationships.

Nevertheless, the characteristics outlined by the agreement of 22 January 1983 are still substantially different from the central European systems and from neo-corporatist models, particularly in their "strong" version. And the differences are even more evident if we consider the general situation of our system, which has actually reduced the effectiveness of the agreement to a great extent.

The centralisation of our system needed to control co-operation between the State and social partners has remained precarious, threatened by the traditional polarisation of the organisational and bargaining structures.

The role of the classic organs of representative democracy was not dimmed by the triangular agreement between the social partners and executive. Party pressure and interference with respect to the unions and union unity continued, causing persistent tension and instability. The instability grew because of the overall situation of the political system which continued to be fragile (see anticipated general elections of June 1983) and lacking in institutionalised and explicit links with the union movement.

Lastly, the agreement came at a time of economic decline. This reduces a certain amount of welfare resources distributed by the State to compensate the social partners for their self-denial in pursuing their own short-term economic objectives. This compensation is a well-known feature of the political exchange which had for a long time helped guarantee the respect of social agreements in other central and northern European countries (from Great Britain to Sweden), where it was tried out decades before in a phase of economic expansion. It goes without saying that in our country the capacity of the State to supply welfare services to this end is compromised by the unreliability and inefficiency (to say the least) of the public administrative machine. Hence Italy's social and political context explain the scope of the agreement, the practically exclusive reliance on the bargaining instrument (even though tripartite) to deal with such diverse subjects and the programmatic or indefinite nature of many of its directives.

The fact that such an ambitious objective as the definition of general rules for industrial relations and labour laws was pursued as a multilateral agreement is related to the historical characteristics of economic instability and the strong sociopolitical tensions of our country.

THE GUIDING DIRECTIVES

The guiding directives contained in the various points of the agreement are consistent with its general approach. However, their effectiveness differs considerably. Automatic legal effectiveness was given only to the regulations on the "cooling down" of the escalator clause (scala mobile), whereas the majority of the clauses had programmatic value inasmuch as they called for commitments by the government or parliament (for example, on fiscal and labour market issues) or by the social partners (for example, directives on future bargaining).

It is noteworthy that the main directives of the agreement apply to the private and public sectors. This is an unprecedented confirmation of the rapprochement of the two sectors - even more than that contained in the framework law on public employment reached after years of labour, thanks also to the impact of the agreement. This is another aspect of the attempt to make the industrial relations system more homogeneous with respect to the public sector - which has proved particularly resistant towards directives of "coherency" in labour relationships.

Among the guiding contents of the agreement one directive was particularly significant: the reform of the bargaining structure (an 18-months wage truce and, particularly, specialisation of enterprise bargaining in the sense that it was prohibited from negotiating issues already defined at the national level). This directive aimed to make the bargaining system more cohesive, thus enabling it to adapt to the re-entry from inflation and to the objective of greater productivity. The promise contained in the agreement to introduce conciliation and arbitration procedures into the national contracts to resolve disputes over the interpretation of the enterprise-level bargaining agreements is significant in this context.

Many found the indications on pay policies to be among the least innovative of the agreement. In actual fact, this was meant mostly to contain labour costs especially by means of the social redistribution of income. This redistribution is achieved through the social differentiation of fiscal charges and public tariffs as well as through family income support (family allowances) and the differential reduction of wages. However, the slowdown of the "scala mobile", with the preservation of its fixed value, already points towards its transformation into an indexed minimum wage equal for all workers. Indeed the issue of minimum wages is once again on the union agenda. Thus the agreement particularly protected those on the lowest wages, although there are rather general indications that professional skills are being more generously rewarded due to a widening of wage differentials and a reduction of automatic wage increases linked to seniority.

Several factors point towards active manpower policies. The agreement tends to combine different and converging objectives in a consistent logic. On the one hand it seeks greater flexibility and hence greater efficiency in the use of manpower in the enterprise and on the labour market. On the other, it aims at supporting employment: specifically with the directive on the reduction of working time and more generally with the reform of the institutional instruments of manpower (public placement service, mobility, solidarity contracts). The institutional formula that supports this part of the reform is the flexible but negotiated management of employment.

The exchange is consistent with the general approach of the agreement to favour a consensual solution with public support of the major problems of industrial relations, the premise being that this guarantees both the efficiency and certainty of mutual control. It is significant that the suggestions, reitereated in the recent debate, that the protective character of the Workers' Statute be altered on this matter were not accepted. Its aim was to lift only the most obsolete legislative rigidities which were actually counterproductive. Likewise the rather detailed solutions on absenteeism rely on the improvement of the public and collective instruments of control rather than on automatic punitive measures (such as the undifferentiated loss of wages in the case of brief illnesses). But the margins of consensus among the partners and the institutional framework proved to be rather limited on this issue.

A last directive of the agreement concerns union participation in industrial and enterprise politics and it consists of two instruments: the so called Solidarity Fund and joint controls of the social effects of restructuring and technological innovation on employment. The second instrument aims to reinforce the current rather ineffective bargaining experience of union rights to control and to information on enterprise policies. The formula echoes that of joint examination often used in the first part of the contracts.

It is noteworthy that, while the agreement envisions forms of triangular participation in the public organs for the labour market, the formula for the enterprise is not institutional participation-codetermination but that of rights to information and external union control. In other words, the issue of industrial democracy is treated in its "blandest" version, i.e. rights to disclosure of information and external union control.

The other instrument envisioned in the agreement - the Solidarity Fund - moves along a different line (but not in contrast with that of external control and information) of direct worker participation in capital formation. Several more precise indications were added by industrial collective bargaining, which sanctioned not only the collective-voluntary nature of the 0.5 per cent withholding from wages, but also union competence in defining the methods of constitution and use of the

Fund. The regulation of some basic aspects of the Fund is left to the law.

AN ASSESSMENT

The monetary and fiscal parts of the agreement were effected to a good extent: correction of fiscal drag in favour of the workers to compensate them for the slowdown of the "scala mobile", fiscalisation of social security contributions in favour of the enterprise to reduce the cost of labour. The public commitment to control tariffs and prices was not fully respected. This constituted a major reason for the failure to respect the inflationary ceiling, as monetary authorities themselves acknowledge. With respect to this objective, the most evident shifts in the wage trend were to be found in the public sector contracts. In the private sector, on the other hand, the directives on ceilings and issues for national bargaining were generally respected. So too were the directives regarding the blocking of enterprise bargaining. In both cases this occurred because of the structural crisis these bargaining levels are experiencing.

In contrast neither the directive to review the relationships between bargaining levels and to change wage policies were followed up. The round of national contracts renewals of 1983, among the most difficult since World War II, barely touched on the problem and discussion within the unions was laborious and uncertain.

The part of the agreement on the labour market was partially enacted. The norms of the agreement aimed at partly liberalising hiring and several directives on welfare and pensions were applied. Some measures to control absenteeism were implemented. The other commitments of reform assumed by the government were formulated with difficulty but not concluded: reforms on placement, "Cassa Integrazione" (partial layoff payments), labour mobility, part-time and temporary employment relationships, solidarity contracts.

The solution indicated by the agreement - flexible but "concerted" management of the labour force - is proceeding slowly. The pressure of the crisis has facilitated entrepreneurial attitudes to return to a unilateral management of the labour market. In a similar framework of institutional uncertainty and entrepreneurial hostility, the unions were often forced to passively resist change rather than deal with innovative social projects.

The directives on union participation in industrial and

enterprise politics have not been implemented at all. The two possible instruments - the Solidarity Fund for investments to support employment and the joint controls among the parties on the social effects of restructuring and social innovation on employment - have been on the agenda of the Ministry of Labour for some time. It is evident that the limits in implementing the January agreement were - like the agreement itself - triangular, i.e. distributed among the government and the social partners. In reality what is most striking is the fact that the non-fulfilment concerned mostly the reform of the fundamental traits of industrial relations, i.e. the central nucleus of the agreement. For a period of time the agreement did help to contain the instability of our industrial relations. But its greatest effect was to "fiscalise" the social conflict, that is reduce its effects at public expense, while the ambitious project to move our industrial relations system towards concerted stabilisation policies did not make substantial progress. Such shortcomings bore their weight in the event of early 1984.

COLLECTIVE AND POLITICAL BARGAINING OF FEBRUARY 1984

At the end of 1983 the need to control inflation still existed and was more pressing in view of a possible economic recovery provided by the international economic situation. The reduction of wage indexation acquired a decisive place in the government's anti-inflation policy. Thus a new round of collective and political bargaining was opened up aimed at a programmed reduction of inflation. The unions were asked to accept a lowering in the coverage of the escalator clause "scala mobile"; in return the government offered a series of measures, i.e. the blockage of the indexation for rents, the creation of new jobs for young people, particularly in public administration, the enactment of a law to favour the "solidarity contracts" (providing a partially state-financed work hour reduction). In the final phase of negotiations there was no consent from the CGIL, or better yet from its communist majority. Union unity was broken. Lacking consent from all the unions, the Craxi government issued a decree containing the main points of the agreement accepted by the other two confederations (CISL and UIL).

The decree on labour costs raised various types of problems: the organisation of industrial relations, constitutionality, state-union relations, political problems tout court.

The latter two are the most pressing and directly concern the methods of governing industrial relations. The question of constitutionality is also broadly connected. In actual fact, the strongest argument of those who hold the decree to be unconstitutional concerns the lack of unanimous consensus in the decision, i. e. of the communist component of the CGIL. It does not concern the content or the general possibility of a decree on labour costs. A 1977 decree on this matter, issued under the government of national unity was held to be lawful even by the jurists of the communist area.

We feel that the issue of constitutionality is unfounded for reasons similar to those alleged at the time by the Court and numerous jurists. It is dangerous to question the judgement regarding the constitutionality of a legislative intervention to unanimous union consent. Union consent is a condition of effectiveness of the law, but it does not constitute a necessary nor sufficient condition of legitimacy. Nevertheless, the problem of consensus for governing is crucial. Many saw in the February decree the failure, established in fact by decree, of a <u>concerted</u> method of governing industrial relations and have praised the rediscovered decision-making capacity of the public power.

The decree and the previous break in union unity are not contingent events. But it would be shortsighted to use the decree to draw hasty conclusions regarding the end of concertation. The decree is not the heart of the matter. It is wrong to dramatize or <u>think</u> that it constitutes the sign of a new way of governing industrial relations.

The events of these months indicate the political and social difficulties in governing industrial relations and in the organisation of consensus in post-industrial societies. Some of these difficulties are common to all advanced countries. They are linked to the changing social composition and the changing labour force in post-industrial society, to the way it is articulated, differentiated or fragmented. The flexibility of the productive techniques obscure the traditional professional identities upon which Western industrial trade unionism was based and mark a lowering of its representativeness. The new professional figures, the new, often partial jobs that are midway between autonomous and dependent, are difficult to govern not only for the unions but for every pluralistic government. Even centralised governments that run the strong systems of central and northern Europe have a hard time resisting the impact of the professional diversification and the resulting dispersion of interests.

In the case of Italy such social difficulties are aggravated by specific factors of an economic (the unbalanced and fragmented national development) and social (ideological lacerations and inequalities) nature. And to these we may add the internal tensions within the political system (instability and blocking of the alternation between majority and minority) and those between the political system and industrial relations.

The experience of recent years shows that social concertation does not necessarily require pro-labour governments. But it does require a balance between the internal components of the political and union systems and an interest in its preservation or steady improvement. Thus we can understand the possibility of social pacts with central governments in Spain before Gonzales, and the PCI's interest in using the agreements with the CGIL to lend credibility to its legitimisation and a progressive inclusion in the government area.

Politically speaking, the break of these months is due to the change in balance with the increased initiative of the socialist (or non-communist) components in the government and union with respect to the communists.

The symptoms were already seen in 1983, when the agreement was reached in extremis, with the "union" reasons for the agreement prevailing in the CGIL over the "political" reasons for the break. In 1984 the "detonator" of the socialist presidency was added to the deterioration of the political climate in the left and the fear of an upset in relations between the socialist PSI and communist PCI.

If this diagnosis is correct, it has implications for the dispute over "interventionism" or, better yet, over the methods of governing industrial relations. "Interventionism" or state decision-making is an ambiguous term. It can mean 'decide for the sake of deciding', to avoid the costs of mediation. But it also means to come out of an impasse, after having considered the alternatives, resolving mediations that would otherwise have been blocked, as was the case with the February 1984 decree.

The issue is the same for the advocates of concerted or bargained solutions. In fact, bargaining and concertation are not synonymous of unanimity. The government that has decided by decree in February 1984 has simply made a political choice of which it assumes the risks. And the same applies for the unions that supported the anti-inflationary manoeuvre.

The polemics on decision-making in this sense are out of place. In actual fact, the problem concerns the social alliances which constituted the government's decision: they are different from the traditional ones and challenge the hegemony of the communist area in the union movement.

The relationship between law and contract, which is an application of the relationship between State and the social partners, must be read in the same terms. Bargaining has never lived in a legislative and institutional vacuum. And this is even less so after the intensification of the relationships between society and state and between economy and politics found in all modern systems, even the most inclined toward "neo-laissez faire".

The term NEO-CONTRATTUALISMO ("neo-contractualism") used with reference to the events of 1983 meant that the instrument of bargaining was adopted rather than the law, but on a much wider terrain than the traditional wage/work relationship. This neo-contractualism serves to define the main macro-variables of industrial relations. Hence it operates in areas where an encounter with the State is inevitable: thus it is tripartite, with the State being the one to stake its own resources. So the traditional division of competencies between law and contract has changed everywhere in recent years. Besides the increase in bargained laws both the traditional principal that the contract can always break the law so long as this is done in favour of the workers and the opposite principle that the contract cannot accept terms and conditions less favourable than those fixed by law are requested. The legislative constraint to bargaining becomes necessary for the control of economic compatibilities when this control is not sufficiently guaranteed by the partners themselves.

This legislative intervention to set maximum limits to (wage) bargaining, will have to be reserved for exceptional cases, and properly justified, in order not to alter the still fundamental role of collective autonomy. But similar cases of binding interventions are found in systems with different political regimes and different union composition. Thus the power given to collective bargaining to regulate matters that were previously "guaranteed" by statute is explained by the need to make certain rules (especially on the labour market) more flexible and better suited to the changeability of economic and social situations. It is an aspect of deregulation, neither wild nor left to entrepreneurial power, but supported by collective bargaining control.

Analagously - and increasingly more often - the law entrusts bargaining with the task of completing directives on unusual matters, i. e. the redistribution of scarce resources among workers. For example, the "solidarity contracts" introduced by the recent decree, where bargaining has a decisive role in distributing the work hour reduction also with the possible reduction in wages. Bargaining has the same task in France with reference to the implementation of the 39 hour work-week reduction as established by law.

As can be seen, relationships between law and contract are complex and "interferences" are mutual. It is not correct to speak of an increased weight of the law in industrial relations. This is denied by most European experiences, and the Italian case is no exception. On the contrary, the Italian union has elements to protect it against a centralised evolution in the governing of industrial relations.

Moreover, the European experience questions the effectiveness of an authoritative control of industrial relations. The great success of social stabilisation in countries like the Federal Republic of Germany, Holland and Austria depends more on the quality of the political exchange among the three actors of industrial relations and on economic stability than on the institutional forms of regulating the exchange. Nor is the example of Spain and France, where decision-making has other traditions and the unions are historically far weaker than ours, totally pertinent here. A neo-laissez-faire evolution of industrial relations is a more likely prospect than that toward neo-interventionism. In this case we have international examples such as the USA and Great Britain. And Italy has its neo-laissez-faire orientations in the entrepreneurial and party areas. Recent events have led many to hope for a <u>return</u> of the social partners to their traditional (limited) roles.

These appeals raise the real problem of a clearer distinction of roles between industrial relations partners. But those originating from the communist area of the CGIL and the Confindustria have disturbing implications.

The call for certain sectors of the CGIL to return to bargaining and to increase the traditional wage claims leads the unions to defend the strong but declining areas of the working class. These claims may benefit increasingly smaller groups of workers (mostly unskilled). In the long run they would be ignored by the majority (in particular the growing area of skilled and "grey collar" employees) and would reduce union representativeness. The centrality of the working class is at an end, not because of a government decree but because of the productive transformations. And it cannot be restored by reiterating the claims or taking the road of union and political "opposition".

In fact the neo-laissez-faire doctrine and practice negate the capacity of the union and current collective instruments of industrial relations to represent the new work realities in industrial society. They tend to confine them to the representation of those mostly unskilled workers of the declining mass industry and branches of the traditional service sector.

This is not what is needed for a fair and effective governing of industrial relations. The road is more complex, i. e. new collective identities and new reasons for solidarity must be sought with more difficult processes to obtain consensus and not with the simple reappropriation of old tasks.

For this reason, the search for methods of concerted governing of industrial relations cannot consider itself over. Its abandonment or failure would probably lead in Italy to a stalemate, social division and deterioration of the system rather than to the choice between neo-intervention or neo-laissez-faire. The memory and dangers of impasse are clear within the Italian labour movement, particularly the communist part of it. Indeed the present communist opposition might be directed at showing that their consent is necessary to stabilise industrial relations and at ameliorating the terms of exchange more than at rejecting definitely the practice of concerted action.

The recent events, however, reveal serious problems within industrial relations. If the functioning of the system is to be improved and concerted governing made more feasible these problems must be faced.

A redefinition of responsibility appears necessary to reduce the overload of union tasks and of social pacts themselves. In Italy the overload depends to a great extent on institutional and government weaknesses. But it has affected both the unions and the system.

The greater solidity of certain middle and north European social pacts also depends on a better distribution of roles between unions and institutions. The latter serve to reduce the need for union actions to compensate for failures elsewhere. For example, the union bargains the fiscal drag for the dependent workers but unlike in Italy it does not need to do the same for other fiscal matters because the public power guarantees adequate taxation of other incomes (independent workers, professions, estates). The call for a greater distinction of roles must be understood in this sense, not as a return to mutual indifference. It is meant to relieve the union of undue responsibilities and make the state truly "authoritative" also with respect to the actors of industrial relations.

The success of a concerted solution of industrial relations problems depends on improving the effectiveness of the institutions' role as mediator and enactor of the social pacts. It is also the way to reduce the frequent direct incursions (that is, not mediated by the institutions) by the political parties in industrial relations. These incursions constitute one of the destabilising and anomalous factors of the Italian system.

Another aspect of role redefinition concerns state intervention in industrial relations. One possibility is to reduce the interventions into the detail of problems (such as labour costs) which should be resolved by the two sides of industry and, instead, to specify the rules of the game that must guide their behaviour. The rules of the game on the functioning of the labour market, industrial policy and economic programming are inadequate. Fixed points of reference upon which the partners can make better decisions are lacking. More precise rules are also necessary in the specific procedures of industrial relations: those of prevention and conduct of conflicts and those of union democracy.

HYPOTHESES FOR FUTURE DEVELOPMENT

Collective and political bargaining at the start of 1984 wound up in disagreement among the unions and with a government decree. It has had a profound traumatic effect on Italy's industrial relations system. In addition, it has contributed to heightening conflict in the political-institutional system on account of radical opposition of the Communist Party. This opposition was successful, through filibustering, in bringing about the fall in parliament of a first version of the decree. The government had to present a second version to the chambers of deputies which has just been approved (June 1984).

Whatever may happen, it is certain that the general outcome of the bargaining was not greater stability in the political system and industrial relations. If strong communist opposition to the government and dissent among the union central organisations persists it is unlikely that new attempts at a "social pact" or tripartite agreement explicitly aimed at wage regulation will be successful in the near future.

We have already observed how the Italian experience

shows that a declared pro-labour government is not necessary for the success of this type of agreement. However, a continuous balance between the political system and industrial relations system was necessary so that the exclusion of the major labour party from the government was compensated by its full participation in the formation of union and labour policies. Now this balance has been broken, and the first condition is not at hand. In addition, the other important condition, valid also for the Italian experience, is lacking.

The competition by CISL and UIL vis-à-vis CGIL is growing. The monopoly of representation enjoyed by the two confederations that have acted as main partners of the government in the decisions of February 1984 is not strong enough to guarantee the success of a concerted action without CGIL consent (unless the relative representativeness of the three confederations change drastically, particularly among the new but unorganised groups of service workers).

At this point it is difficult to forecast what the future developments of industrial relations in Italy will be, especially in the absence of real possibilities for change within the political system. As a contribution to the discussion we will conclude this paper by indicating three possible hypotheses of development for the immediate future.

The <u>first</u> may be defined as exogenous to industrial relations. According to this hypothesis, the economic recovery and the successful reduction of the inflation rate make the need for tripartite agreements for governing industrial relations less urgent. Tensions are reduced. The unions can continue to bargain unitarily at the enterprise, national and even interconfederal level (with entrepreneurial organisations). But they would no longer aim at general regulation of the system - or would not be able to reach agreements on such a regulation. In the short term it is a hypothesis that does not necessarily require neo-laissez-faire choices. It may simply go along with an impasse situation among the unions. But the problems will all reappear at the first signs of economic difficulties; and the danger of lack of general choices will increase as well.

The <u>second</u> hypothesis envisions the <u>reduction of the overload</u> of demands and responsibilities on the industrial relations system. According to this hypothesis, the areas of centralised bargaining would be distinguished more clearly (those between the unions and government and those between unions and entrepreneurs), so as not to overlap the tensions and occasions of conflict. Bargaining would remain tripartite but not formally so; its contents would be different, though related, and they could have different timing. Greater effectiveness of the public institutions in their own tasks is required for this hypothesis. This separation of areas could be coupled with greater proceduralisation of industrial relations so that centralised bargaining would be left mainly with tasks of defining rules and basic compatibilities and decentralised bargaining those of regulating the merit of industrial relations problems. Central control on fundamental choices would go together with more flexible industrial relations at decentralised levels. This is a trend which can be traced also in other European systems and corresponds to the need to make concerted action less centrally oriented and more adaptable to the changing needs of the market.

But this adaptation of concerted industrial relations policies would still require a re-establishment of a minimum of unity within the Italian labour movement and with the political system (or a drastic change in the relative bargaining power between the communist and non-communist sectors of the labour movement).

The third hypothesis acknowledges the break in the balance between the political system and the system of union relations. Consequently it implies a readaptation of industrial relations and of its relationships with politics. The centralised agreement is replaced by state legislative action which, especially through decrees, generalises the outcomes of the negotiations in which only a part of labour unions participate. The hypothesis would repeat the events of February/May 1984. It could be transformed into a kind of temporary delegation to the government (partially supported by social partners) for the control of industrial relations. It is difficult to forecast what might happen to the decentralised bargaining levels, but it is possible that the divisions among the unions spread.

We feel the third hypothesis is unlikely because of its destabilising effects. The best solution might well be the second hypothesis, but again we do not know how likely that is. The most probable hypothesis for the future may be the first, but it certainly will not solve the general problems of governing industrial relations in Italy.

REFERENCES

Baglioni G., "Costanti e varianti in tema di scambio politico", Giornale di diritto del lavoro e di relazioni industriali,

n. 20, 1983, 839-877

Baglioni G. et al., "Per analizzare l'accordo del 14 febbraio", Prospettiva sindacale, n. 51, 1984, 135-177

Carrieri M. and Donolo C., "Oltre l'orizzonte neo-corporatista", Stato e Mercato, n. 9, 1983, 475-503

Cella G. P. and Treu T. (eds.), Relazioni industriali. Manuale per l'analisi dell'esperienza italiana, Il Mulino, Bologna, 1984, 2nd. edition

Cella G. P., "Democrazia e centralizzazione", Il Progetto, n. 21, 1984, 110-114

C. E. S. O. S., Le relazioni sindacali in Italia, Annual Report, 1982/83, Edizioni Lavoro, Roma, 1984

"I rinnovi contrattuali 1983 nell'industria", Contrattazione, n. 4, 1983

Treu T. (ed.), Il patto contro l'inflazione, Edizioni Lavoro, Roma, 1984

Chapter 9

THE POLITICAL SYSTEM AS A PROBLEM FOR THE TRADE UNIONS IN ITALY: 1975-1983

Mimmo Carrieri and Carlo Donolo

ITALIAN TRADE UNIONS AND POLITICS

In this chapter we offer a schematic reconstruction of the evolution of some aspects of the Italian political system in terms of the political-institutional conditions under which union political action is carried out. In particular we consider what problems and opportunities have been presented to the union movement by some crucial components of the political system. We focus on the second half of the '70s through the early '80s, not only because they are the most recent years, but also because they bring to light all the unsolved or unsolvable problems of union political action.

The previous phase (1968-75), characterised by mass mobilisation and militant unionism, is less interesting from this point of view. The union was fully recognised as a political actor, it learned to operate in two areas (industrial relations and the political system), and it carried out functions of substitution and stimulation with respect to the parties. But, most important, it operated in its most significant aspects either as a social movement or as the effective organiser of industrial conflict. In this way it somehow avoided the political problems of the subsequent phase. In this period, between the "hot autumn" and the agreement on the "scala mobile"[1], the so-called "fusion" between civil and political society was getting under way (cf. Farneti 1983 and Pasquino 1983). But the political system had to adapt itself to the fact that demands for concerted decision-making and reforms were now coming from society. There were no previous experiences of concertation but the systematic confrontation between union and government in a bargaining framework became an established practice. In general the union's political role was recognised and it was accepted as representing the workers. But the union organisations presented themselves more as the solution to the distortions of the political system than as instruments for protecting interests (especially those rooted in industrial relations) in the political arena. The union probably reached the culmination of its political potential in this phase, in the sense of attaining the maximum offensive power. This can be seen, for example, in the unions' role in the fall of a government. The union became a part of the political market, but it did not itself enjoy suitable means for constructing productive mechanisms of political exchange with the other political actors.

In this period, therefore, the union movement became a candidate for the role of the main interlocutor in the aggregation and synthesis of interests. This occurred because the other political actors proved inadequate and there was also an unprecedented level of social mobilisation. The union movement entered an area previously occupied exclusively by the political powers and became a strong substitute for party action on the left as well as right. These conditions favoured the creation of organisation interests distinct from those of the parties. However, no decision-making system was affirmed as an alternative to the classic parliamentary one. For no new institutions were created (since the proposals to establish organs of triangular agreement were rejected); and the increased importance of the union had the (temporary) effect of reinforcing the bargaining power of the entire left in Parliament. Thus, although the expansion of the unions' tasks caused problems in its relations with the traditional political actors, it did not encounter any great obstacles at the start in as much as it also increased opportunities for everyone. But the results of the interaction between union behaviour and that of the other actors were neither innovative nor univocal because their horizons were so different. The union did not solve the problems it itself raised; the movement atrophied and the first disappointments arose. "Citizenship" rights within the political system were broadened to the point of covering a large share of the weaker groups, but in a way that was often disorderly and took the form of charity rather than welfare rights.

With this background in mind we can consider the subsequent phase: 1975-1983. An analysis of this period is complicated by the fact that it includes two distinct moments: one, lasting from 1976 to 1978, in which it seems that the union was about to reap the political fruits of its economic and social action, and the other from 1978 to the present day, in which relations between the union and political system have become increasingly difficult. Nevertheless, the two phases must be analysed together in order to understand the political conditions of union action today and in the near future.

In this analysis we will not consider the political system and the union in terms of their overall interrelations, assuming them to be compact and unitary universes (cf. Pizzorno 1978; Regini 1981; Trentin 1977; Cella 1978). Generally speaking, the literature of political science has not paid much attention to the interaction between the cycles of action of the party system and institutions on the one side and the union organisations on the other; nor to their reciprocal influence which determines adaptations and retroaction in their respective behaviours. With some exceptions, analyses of the political system even during the '70s stayed within the boundaries of political-institutional relations. From other points of view, the interaction between the union and political-institutional systems was seen as a process of basically simple arithmetical sums, underestimating both the polycentric nature of the political system and the growing differentiation within the union movement and the fragmentation of union action itself[2]. In actual fact, the two poles of interaction would need to be analytically disaggregated. This would help to reveal the joint operating of the unitary federation, single confederations, and, thirdly, social strata which lie behind the union; and also to understand more fully the various theoretically significant features of the process.

For simplicity's sake, however, we will still assume in general that the union is a unitary and univocal subject, whereas we will analyse the evolution of the political system in terms of the various dimensions we consider significant for our argument. This can be justified by our concern to discover how the numerous shadows of the political system are cast onto the area of union action. Among the various topics we will consider the following:

(i) the evolution of the party system,
(ii) the evolution of the political formulae,
(iii) the evolution of government policies, and
(iv) the intensification of the fiscal and administrative crisis.

Each of these aspects has interacted and interfered with union practices, strategic orientations, and the union's capacity to act. Even though union interaction was certainly not passive, on the whole - and particularly for the most recent phase - we can assume that these different political moments had an impact on the union and not vice-versa. For just a brief period (from 1975-78) the union movement as a whole could have played all its political cards to demand, and contribute to producing, a different sort of evolution from the one that the internal dynamics of the political system itself produced. This did not happen or, at any rate, it did not occur with the energy, clarity and timeliness required. Although the progressive deterioration of union unity is definitely an important explanation, other obstacles and contradictions are to be sought within the culture and strategies of the single confederations which have always had less understanding of the specific problems of the political system. The complexity, and, indeed, the growing confusion in union party relations had a negative impact; so did the chronic inadequacies of the State regarding the administrative and welfare systems. The so-called "EUR policy" was the biggest effort by Italian unionism to become political[3]. But the specific nature of the problem that was supposed to be solved politically in this way, i. e. the anomalous position of the permanent exclusion of PCI from the supposedly symmetrical alternation of parties, weighed negatively in the end. In the face of the initial difficulties the interconfederal drift substantially reinforced the prepolitical elements, often masked by hyperpolitical elements, which are widespread in Italian unionism. These elements are reflected in the union's inability to reckon directly with the deficits of democracy and the ineffectiveness of the political system. The final effect of heterogeneous party affiliations (particularly the resulting tensions in the union movement and its inability to assume a privileged and cooperative relationship with the leftist forces) is a dilemma for the union movement. It leads either to a union that depends on inter-party dynamics without having any influence in the party system or to one that is continuously tempted to reconquer an autonomy in society (as is sometimes the case with the CISL) which is only a pretence in the relationship with the party system.

To understand what follows we must keep two points in mind:

(a) Throughout the period from 1970 to 1983 the relationship between the union and the political system may be considered in the light of the problem, posed by the political left and the union movement, of overcoming the deficit existing in political will and/or performances by the political system. This deficit results from the position of the DC as the prevailing centre in the goernment coalitions and from the limited efficiency of the public administration. Italy therefore differs substantially from countries in which union action integrates government decisions, because now it becomes essential, at least functionally speaking, to change the partisan character of the choices of the central apparatus of political mediation. Compared to other nations, the prevalence of bargaining as opposed to co-operative behaviour - or better yet a mixed, fluctuating game of conflict and co-operation - thus depended on an objective (and insufficiently stressed) reason: the union movement's need to operate in the context of the very limited stability and effectiveness of Italy's political-administrative system.

(b) The characteristics of a blocked political system in which there were not alternations of government and electoral preferences were not determined solely by the effectiveness and results of the government coalitions. This fact has an ambiguous effect on union behaviour: on the one hand it means increased difficulties in maximizing the benefits demanded by the union from centre-dominated governments; on the other hand it represents a further political resource for the union which could put itself (and in some cases actually did so) in direct competition with the political left or some of its components for the representation of the workers.

DEVELOPMENTS OF THE PARTY SYSTEM AND THE ROLE OF THE TRADE UNIONS

We have now touched upon our first topic: the evolution of the party system (cf. Farneti 1983 and Pasquino 1982). We may summarise the evolution for the period under question as the shift from the problem of what the left will be and do (or the problem of democratic rotation) to that of who will be at the centre of the party system. With the electoral successes of the PCI in 1975 and 1976 the possibility emerged of a normalisation of democracy in Italy. By means of a renewed national solidarity pact the PCI was fully legitimised to lead an alternative alliance to that centered on the DC. And it was generally felt that the push for reform expressed by the social movements of those years together with the fight against right- and leftwing extremism would soon lead Italy's blocked democracy to alternate between a moderate and progressive pole. Naturally, the union, having been a great organiser of social conflict in the early '70s and in many cases the only effective and completely legitimised channel to convey demands, was involved directly in this process. Thus a relationship of natural continuity between union strengthening within industrial relations and activation of a reform policy was established. In this sense a friendly government would have been the logical outlet of an entire cycle of struggles. But it appears that the union did not consider the problem of the political formulae suited to its economic and social programme until the mid-'70s. The intent may have been to wrench the reforms from a reluctant or fading executive rather than to obtain them by co-operating with a friendly government. With the PCI's electoral victories of 1975-1976 the possible political formula suitable for effecting a popular reform policy became a union problem. As already mentioned, this occurred immediately afterwards with the national solidarity pact and EUR policy.

The instruments chosen by the union in this phase were not always suitable for enhancing its resources. The agreement on the "scala mobile" (1975), which represented a self-containment of demands handled by the confederal centre reduced the resources for effective bargaining with management and government by favouring automatic wage adjustments. Concentrating more power in the confederations did not widen the resources available to the union movement at the centre of the institutional system, because the long-term agreement on the "scala mobile" weakened the union's bargaining power. If we add to this the fact that the EUR policy involved the union in unilaterally imposing a wage policy while awaiting ameliorative state interventions, we can see that directing action towards the political system is not a guarantee of greater effectiveness in State behaviour. While party-union interdependence was potentially heightened (with the PCI's rapprochement with the government), the impossibility of changing the Italian reality emerged: we see the first identity crisis as (parts of) the union saw a threat to the political role it had previously won. In other words, there was no effective interaction between the union and political system. There was even resistance to establishing mechanisms of concertation. Union action continued to prefer direct confrontation with the executive and ran on tracks parallel to those of the parties.

In this phase the balance of the relationships swung in favour of the political system, which pretended to determine the objectives to be reached and with which the union ought to comply (austerity, economic recovery, new development). The union was obliged to anticipate government programmes, even when they were not clear or had not been negotiated. Hence governments were inclined to use their freedom of manoeuvre given them by the traditional decision-making system that was never questioned by the unions. On the contrary, they supported governmental and parliamentary activity in meetings with the delegates of the majority (which included the PCI). But this support confirmed the union's exclusion from macro-political decision-making and the recovery of a primary role on the part of the parties. The political exchange intended by the union and the political left remained implicit, with no clearly defined shape and mutual responsibility. It became a union gamble on the success of the new political framework. In this sense union consent was not bargained; it was a ready resource for the political system which was not obliged to give definite compensations. And, in addition, the unstable equilibrium among the parties of national unity was great enough to immobilise the union's strength and its threat potential because of the organisations' fear of putting the existing situation in crisis.

The best results of this phase of passive union co-operation included the containment of inflation with instruments of economic stabilisation that did not penalise the most heavily protected labour force (for one of the most interesting reviews of this period cf. Salvati 1982). The effects on social and labour issues are more diversified. The union intervened more actively, participating in the creation of legal provisions and contributing with continuing bargaining procedures to their subsequent improvement. Results were definitely inferior in respect of new productive initiatives (the law on industrial reorganisation) and active labour market policies (the law on employment of young people). On another front employment was defended and wages guaranteed, but the instruments of protection did not lead to new initiatives in the public institutions as had happened earlier with the "Cassa Integrazione" (partial wage layoff payments). But the failure of these reformist plans generated some of the unintended consequences of the following period: union action was dispersed in fragmented actions adapting itself to the method imposed by the political system, and it pursued the maximum benefit possible in every area; the diversification of the forms of protection opened the way to numerous claims that undermined the very bases of union representation.

Although the material on the subject is meagre, we can see that the EUR policy effected a basic innovation: it introduced neo-corporatist elements with the help of a friendly government in the form of a collaboration between the two major parties. The union - not without internal conflicts -

committed itself heavily to this "political" road, i.e. to co-produce a new political formula and a new level of governability. But it immediately came under pressure from two directions: the social crisis and the spectre of the two societies[4], on the one hand, and, on the other, the growing division in the left, paradoxically induced by the historic compromise from which emerged a strategic refounding of the PSI between 1977 and 1979. In addition the second oil crisis and the 1979 elections later did away with the material basis for this strategy. In short, the union first and foremost paid the price of the hidden ailment of the Italian political system - the division of the left and the anomalous status given to the PCI. In the period after 1979 the union was completely on the defensive and could only hope to exploit to the utmost the one solid acquisition of the "corporatist" period: the 1975 agreement on the "scala mobile" (and its delayed completion, the 1978 pension reform). Nevertheless, both these resources soon became the real or presumed cause of the issues of crisis imposed on the union: inflation and the fiscal crisis. Thus the questions to which we have no answer:

> Could or should the union have done more to avert the structural deficits in the functioning of the party system?
> Should it have considered the problem of the bias of the political formulas in a different light as a union that wants to be a political actor and not return to its unlikely old job?

While the union found itself in an increasingly difficult position in industrial relations and is jointly blamed for inflation, public expenditure deficits, and low labour productivity - a traumatic redefinition of the image of the union movement which just a short time before had seemed almost the hero that could save the parties from their incurable ailments - the idea of a <u>centre</u> in the party system was raised again. The party capable of building this centre will be the one to govern and the DC-PSI challenge on this front becomes stronger. The analyses based on "centripetal pluralism" (Farneti 1983) are valid here. But it must be understood that the appeal of the centre is meant in a strategic sense (its occupier defines the type of coalitions which are possible and forces the other parties to follow suit). And this applies not so much in the sense that the "centre" is related to the prevalance of the "catch-all" party-form and consequent moderate policies. The new centrality pursued by the PSI and DC (and also by the

PRI) leads to the targeting of a specific electoral base and to convergence among strategies for keeping governing capabilities at the centre of attention. These centripetal strategies are clearly a response to the lack of party-political alternation and the failure to consolidate a sufficiently homogeneous progressive pole through a national solidarity pact. There is a shift from the forced co-operation between the DC and PCI to competition among the parties to occupy the centre. This shift in the internal logic of the party system entailed the loss of a sure political reference for the union. This situation culminated in the agreement of January 1983 (cf. Cella/Treu and Dal Co/Perulli in this volume), when each of the three major parties tried to "use" the union for its own strategy. In this sense "centripetal pluralism" serves to immunise the governments - and the supporting party coalitions - from the need for the consensual support of the union (cf. Carrieri/Donolo 1983 a). The union is either superfluous in the political game or it must transform itself into a resource of governability, not in the sense of participating in wage bargaining or policies, rather as a <u>means</u> of government policies. In the "centre"-oriented political game the union is politically degraded; sometimes it appears simply as one interest group among others, and this is perhaps the real bargaining concession, Italian-style.

Many felt that the union, which in previous periods was able to solve political problems either by activating or joining up with a reform policy, could serve the political system by not questioning it and helping to maintain its balance. But this gives the union a more limited role. It is no longer a subject committed to rationalise the distortions of the system; it is a part of the system, called upon by the other actors in turn to support their own objectives. But it is not so important to note that the union is structured more and more by the games of the political system of which it is a component and that it either competes or joins forces with other partners. More important is the fact that the union was pushed in this direction, without taking account of the lack of rules of competitive pluralism in such a fragmented political system. It is not surprising that union consent may have been seen, by some, or maybe all, parties, as a means to keep the political system operational or to correct the impracticability of plans for institutional simplification. Parliament's veto power could have been reduced, at least in the short-term, not through movement towards a presidential system or a much strengthened executive, but through aiming to involve the union movement in a minicorporatism. What is more surprising is the fact that the union did not explicitly ask to participate in a redefined organisational network and a clearly designed institutional system. It is even more surprising that its line of behaviour favours and even aggravates the increasing vices of the political system so that the union risks contributing to the entropy of the political system rather than healing it.

This scenario is undoubtedly conditioned to a great extent by specific crises and problems. The most innovative plans for forms of control and industrial democracy (such as the enterprise plan and the solidarity fund) were inconclusive, and defensive policies prevailed, especially concerning the employment problem. The issues induced by the lack of development have become central. First and foremost was the anti-inflation pact (cf. Dal Co/Perulli in this volume), the first initiative taken in a long time by the public powers. But this was based on a demand for a reduction in the cost of labour without visible compensations for the union (except for an unlikely reduction in inflation); and in this case the union was presented as directly responsible for the problems under discussion. Hence, in 1983, the first government of the new legislature, led by Craxi, the Socialist leader, involved the union in proposals for welfare reductions to reduce the public deficit and thereby unloaded some of the resulting problems onto the union leadership.

As it has become more problematic for the union to wield power in industrial relations, its demands - often contradictory - are directed at the political system. It has greater need for public resources and for the state, whereas the latter suffers from the crisis of its instruments of macroregulation. The union - with some exceptions - aims at drawing benefits from the state apparatus and this in turn means that they are bound to more complex and unfavourable social selection criteria; it becomes more dependent on the political centre while the latter's regulative capacities and the need for union consent for maintaining the political system are reduced (cf. Carrieri/Donolo 1983 b). But in this framework the union does not pose the question of explicit institutional rules for the representation of interests. In a political phase dominated by the confused search for new rules and the difficulty of defining and affirming them, the union does not really deny that the search for solutions on this matter lies with the parties, and that its role is to support current crisis policies. Party government prevails because it controls the union role, but it is limited by its reduced capacity to improve the performances of the system. On the contrary: the instability of the coalitions seems to worsen because of the broadened competition to win the centre of the political system. The agreement on the "scala mobile" of January 1983, which marked the end of this period, did not reverse the trend. It was the highpoint of formalised, explicitely tripartite concertation reached in Italy, though the initiative and determining role in the choice of issues belonged to the government and the entrepreneurs as the strategic importance of union consent was reduced. The agreement led the way to the affirmation of a concerted method mainly directed by the political system imposed upon the union and obstructed by the Confindustria (the employers' organisation). However, the agreement was unable to introduce new neo-corporatist-type institutions because the relationship between tripartite and political-parliamentary decision-making remained undefined and contested. The agreement solved some problems but it did not create stable procedures nor rules of the game recognised once and for all (cf. IRES-CGIL 1983; Prospettiva sindacale 1983).

POLITICAL FORMULAS AND TRADE UNION POLICY

The question of the political formulas makes our argument clearer, and the following analysis is strictly complementary to that above. In the time span considered there was a shift from a "historic compromise/national solidarity" for an austerity policy to a split between "governability", in its DC and socialist variants, and the "alternative". The different formulas adhere to the different dynamics in the party system. In the view of the union there are great differences.

The first formula called for a political union willing - in exchange for full, even institutional, recognition - to contribute, by corporatist-type mechanisms to help prevent the economy and society from collapsing. It was not asked to reduce, but to redefine all the objectives within a coherent reconversion policy of the productive apparatus including a mixture of guarantee systems and wage policies. Obviously, in this role the union would have experienced all the tensions of representing and aggregating interests already tried in other similar national contexts. Nevertheless, this burden seemed to concern only the initial phase of the new formula. With the subsequent relaunch of accumulation and the upturn in employment, the union would have had much to offer its own base. Even with so many anomalies, it was basically a matter of the "social democratisation" of the union and the left, i.e. of an Italian variant of the tripartite government developed in other societies. It is also evident, now, that these strategies were based on a quasi-catastrophist analysis of the socio-economic crisis and on the idea that the mechanism for growth was still intrinsically healthy or treatable with a surplus of political will. Both assumptions were unfounded, but we can still see the confirmation of the strong historical tie between neo-corporatist proposals and the goal of growth; or, from the opposite point of view, the high instability of a neo-corporatism called upon to handle the crisis.

Starting from 1979 and the liquidation of the historic compromise another issue came to the fore: occupation of the centre and governability. While "austerity" is still conceived as a compact series of material policies (a list like the PCI's medium-term programme), "governability", having become a value in itself, has contents that are much more abstract and formal. It is concerned with governing several macro-economic variables which have an exaggerated symbolic value, with stabilising the centre ground of politics, and with the political management capacities of the executive. It involves specific institutional and constitutional proposals and it refers to imperatives of the economic and political-institutional system. Whereas "austerity" implied the supremacy of party politics, and hence of parliament, governability as a formula reinforces the centripetal game between the parties of the government coalition. For it implies that one of the parties (the PSI), by acting more decisively, could partially release the executive from the constraints of inter-party politics. From this point of view, the present Craxi government is not a repeat of Spadolini's governments (1981-82). With the hypertrophic role of the "centre" party, a curious therapy for the ills of the DC as the "natural" party of government is attempted. The emphasis on an abstract governability may reflect increasing seriousness of the crisis such that the latter can no longer be cured by a reform policy but only by redesigning the rules of the political game itself. Or it may depend on the dissolution of the rather problematic bond established in the area of national solidarity between the supremacy of politics and the need to enact programming-oriented material policies. Nevertheless, it is evident that governability in this sense means, there is no longer any political space for the union other than to accept a more limited role within a programme of "governability" defined by the executive.

In the previous phase the risk for the unions was that of being used to solve a problem of the party system; in the more recent one of being used to solve a problem of the government. This process is overshadowed by the recurring attempts to enhance neo-corporatist opportunities (January agreement of 1983) or to focus on a wage policy (stopping the "scala mobile") in which it seems that the union is still an essential part. But the fact is that in the concept of governability, the union's area of action is considerably reduced and its effort to gain political recognition is a constant one. The union remains a political subject, but "under protection".

The tangle between industrial relations and the political system was not resolved by the agreement of January 1983, and the situation remained indefinite during the course of a new bargaining round on labour costs started by the government at the end of 1983 and concluded with the Craxi decree in February 1984 which cut three points off the "scala mobile". The attempt to produce "breaks" in the previous rules encountered new difficulties: not only did some social and political groups step up their opposition, but there were no clear ideas on the "new rules" of the game for conducting the bargaining, defining the union's forms of political access and enacting the institutional reforms. The decree had the consent only of the CISL and UIL, and was opposed by the CGIL and PCI. The attempt to modify the decision-making process in industrial relations gave rise to a movement of social opposition, culminating in the demonstration of one million people on 24 March 1984, which joined - something unheard of in recent years - the leftwing political opposition in Parliament, particularly the PCI. Thus the instability of the 1983 agreement was confirmed. It neither defined nor maintained clear instruments for subsequent relations among the actors; it precedes but not predetermines the dynamics of future bargaining.

POLITICAL FLUCTUATION AND ITS CONSEQUENCES FOR THE TRADE UNIONS

An analysis of the policies attempted from 1976 to the present day confirms that the union's room for action is narrowing and its political role is shrinking. There was an initial attempt to face the economic and social crisis with a consensual wage policy enriched by programming policies, e.g., a law for industrial reorganisation and a law for youth employment. Subsequently, politics have been increasingly directed towards the "solution" of two problems: labour costs and the public deficit. In both cases the union is held responsible. It is no longer seen as a subject that collaborates in the solution for these problems, but is blamed for them. The "scala mobile" and the welfare system are actually attacked both by the entrepreneurs and by the successive governments after the failure of the historic compromise. Interestingly enough the "scala mobile" and the welfare regulations were the union's two strongpoints in the recession which helped to defend the quality of working life. But now we clearly have to observe a shift from a period of leftwing policies to a period of moderate-restrictive policies. The greatest effect on the unions in this shift was realised not so much through the political attack on their general strategy but through the move from consensual incomes policies supported by "active" programming policies to fiscal and budgetary policies. This has severely limited the area of union political action. The union's consent to cuts is no longer so useful to the union movement; indeed, if anything, its role in managing the undesired social consequences of the cuts and rationalisations would serve instead the objective of "governability". Our reconstruction of this shift is undoubtedly incomplete since it does not consider the impact of union errors and delays on the failure of the first phase. But here we are only interested in seeing how the functioning of the political system causes problems for the union.

In actual fact the restriction policy is more often preached than practiced, but the union is still obliged to accept the political agenda entailed in these issues and the limits this poses on its effectiveness. The redefinition of the terms of the Italian crisis as a "fiscal" crisis and a crisis of the welfare system reveals several major inadequacies in the political culture of the Italian union, providing a further weapon in the hands of its opponents. In the long run this may be useful if the union finally faces issues such as wage distribution and life chances in less economistic terms. For now it must pay, since it has no serious alternative proposals on welfare and wage guarantees. On the other hand, the employment problem that was still important - even in the fight against inflation - from 1975 to 1978, has practically disappeared from the political scene - even though the debate on active labour market policies has recently started up again and the CGIL has relaunched an initiative on the subject. Employment is the most concrete issue, and it is no accident that it carries no weight in an abstract framework "governability". Here more than in any other area we can measure the scope of the oscillation that occurred from the early '70s to the early '80s.

The supremacy of politics, which has always characterised the culture of the left and the union (except for the conspicuous exceptions and inhibitions of certain members of the CISL) had been questioned from 1968-75 because of the social nature of the crisis, the numerous forms of social mobilisation and the fact that in many respects unionism itself tended to assume characteristics of a social movement. The subsequent phase seems a rather visible rejection of a poor attempt to politicise society. During both phases of "historic compromise" and "governability" interparty "hyperpolitics" once again came to dominate; and in the union movement the characteristics of a movement were also reduced in favour of those of an interest organisation. The paradox of the EUR policy may be defined as the attempt to solve a problem of the parties by using a union that is political because it is fully legitimised on the social level. In recent years the traditional meaning of the supremacy of politics has changed to mean the symbolic-strategic communication among actors in one arena. The union also participates in this type of interaction though a closer analysis would reveal a strange mixture of symbolic-strategic and material-exchange forms of politics (cf. Manghi 1976).

All this is a rather simple explanation of why the neglect of the union and government decision-making was characteristic of both union culture and practice. Only in a more recent phase have the problems of the administration found an audience in the union, and with this comes an increased awareness that implementation should follow the formulation of a political action. That the union experienced the fiscal and welfare crises mainly in quantitative terms would be normal if the unions had not previously elaborated an approach to the problems that provided room for active politics and the introduction of elements of programming that are not limited to putting numbers in order (as with the elaborations on sectoral programmes or the proposals on industrial and economic democracy), and if it had not always been acutely aware of the inadequacy of a quantitative and centralised macro-regulation to spark a process of growth. As mentioned, <u>policies</u> of this type were obtained during the period of national solidarity. But there is still no analysis of the failure of such policies that goes to the roots of the ills: why the union contents itself with the <u>formulation</u> of such policies is unable to implement them. The union's conspicuous failures in this field (sometimes remedies proposed by the union to make the administrative machine more effective, e.g. participation and decentralisation, proved to be worse than the ills they were supposed to cure) have helped to provoke the formula of "governability". As a result of the entire period, if the union wants to influence the real processes it must reckon with the problems of the administrative machine. This task is conditioned by two factors: the actual dependence of many union options on the functioning of certain systems of social guarantee and transfer and the way in which the union organises workers' interests in the public sector. These are issues for the near future, if we are willing to admit that the shadows cast by the current organisation of the administration are among the most dangerous factors of corruption and paralysis also in union political action.

CONCLUDING REMARKS

We have seen that different elements of the political system - the party system, the growth and decline of political formulas, the displacement that occurred between politics and policies, the inefficiency or ineffectiveness of public administration action - are a heavy burden on political union action in Italy.

Union political action was unable to effectively intervene on any of these elements, and it was even blamed for many external conditions of the political-administrative system.

Can we, after a decade of intense relations between the union and political system, affirm that party government was questioned and new decision-making mechanisms intervened? Until now - and this includes the agreement of January 1983 - negotiations were multilateral rather than triangular, with considerable interference and overlapping by the parties in every phase of decision-making, so that an autonomous neo-corporatist-type decision-making circuit did not appear. It may be more exact to argue that the characteristics of the Italian system are those of a party-dominated pluralism with strong articulation and internal conflicts. In fact, we may say - also with reference to other countries - that functional type decision-making mechanisms have a significant role in decision-making as long as there are accepted procedures and an understanding with the corresponding partners or the consensual definition of areas of intervention among the different political actors. This is why the affirmation of a more direct decision making power of the union caused conflicts and presents itself more as a variant of competition among the parties than as an autonomous institutional plan. Just as the union let itself be used as the bridgehead of the political legitimisation of the left in the early '70s, in the last legislature parts of the unions and parties moved together to simplify the decision-making processes in favour of the executive. In this way the union contributed to the increasingly problematic nature of the situation. The unregulated, often factional, competition among the political actors has become an additional worry for the political system. The problems that arose in the union as a result of the crisis and the blockage of the political system have become factors of instability of the political framework and of the institutions.

Although we have not considered many other economic and social variables here, our analysis indicates that the union - by means of the purgatory of national solidarity and governability - faces at least three critical situations which concern its capacity of action and its identity as well:

- a crisis of representation deriving from the pretensions of the political system in its confrontations with the union movement and from more restrictive boundaries imposed upon the union;
- a crisis of effectiveness, rooted in the character of its own culture and from inadequate organisational resources, as well as from the crisis of administration and welfare in the state system;
- more generally, a crisis of orientation, especially of the CGIL, less so of the CISL (which had already partly adapted to the new social and cultural context of the '80s); this derives from the uncertainty and the growing inconsistencies regarding the desirable image of society (cf. Accornero 1983).

Generally, these and other difficulties facing the union today are explained by economic development, new characteristics of society, and the peculiarities of union organisation and history. Our task in this paper, however, has been to show how these problems can be understood from characteristics of the political system.

NOTES

1. The expression "hot autumn" is commonly used to indicate the resumption of worker struggles starting in the large northern factories in 1969. The agreement

on the "scala mobile" of 1975, co-signed by the three union confederations and the Confindustria rationalised and universalised the automatic protection mechanism of real wages and, in this sense, was somewhat the culminating symbol of the "civil" victories of the Italian union at the end of a phase of high industrial and social conflict.

2. For thirty years Italian trade unionism has been based on three confederal or central organisations: the socialist- and communist- oriented CGIL; the Social- Catholic CISL; the laic and social democratic UIL. In the early '70s a unitary federation was established among the three organisations but it was unable to achieve organic unity. The behaviours, and also the political cultures, expressed by the three organisations changed progressively over the course of the most serious crisis, culminating in the paralysis and declared death of the Unitary Federation in the occasion of the decree on the cost of labour in February 1984. An archipelago of autonomous unions from the central organisation followed from this. On the other hand, the high fragmentation of the political system is evident (cf. Dal Co and Perulli in this volume) even considering just the party system: two large popular parties with mass appeal (DC and PCI), a medium-size party fluctuating between the left and centre and without a defined electoral base (PSI), a large number of smaller parties occupying the entire political spectrum and all with considerable blackmailing power.

3. On the wave of the electoral successes of the left in the 1975 regional elections and the 1976 political elections, and on the basis of an association between the DC and PCI theorized in the strategy of Aldo Moro, the DC leader, and in the "historic compromise" of Enrico Berlinguer, Secretary of the PCI, the Unitary Federation launched a proposal for economic programming and incomes policy (meant to heal Italy's crisis-struck economy and relaunch development) which got its name from the Roman district where it was officially proclaimed. Another aspect of the EUR-strategy was the objective of union centralisation (cf. Dal Co/Perulli in this volume).

4. In the 1977 non-worker youth-movement several theses and strategies of '68 were emphasised as forms of a self-organisation of a marginal counter-society

turned against the world of those guaranteed by political and union protection (cf. Asor Rosa 1977).

REFERENCES

Accornero, A. 1983: Sindacato e nuovi problemi sociali della tutela e della rappresentanza, in: Perulli/Trentin 1983

Asor Rosa, A. 1977: Le due società. Einaudi, Torino

Carrieri, M. and C. Donolo 1983 a: Oltre l'orrizzonte neo-corporatista, in: Stato e Mercato, no. 9. 1983

Carrieri, M. and C. Donolo 1983 b: Il negoziato politico nella recessione, in: Perulli/Trentin 1983

Cella, G. P. 1978: L'azione sindacale nella crisi italiana, in: L. Graziano and S. Tarrow, (eds.), La crisi italiana, Einaudi, Torino

Donolo, C. 1980: Social Change and Transformation of the State in Italy, in: R. Scase, (ed.), The State in Western Europe, Croom Helm, London

Farneti, P. 1983: Il sistema dei partiti in Italia, 1946-1975, Il Mulino, Bologna

IRES-CGIL 1983: La vertenza sul costo del lavoro e le relazioni industriali, Angeli, Milano

Manghi, B. 1976: Declinare crescendo, Il Mulino, Bologna

Pasquino, G. 1982: Degenerazioni di partiti e riforme istituzionali, Laterza, Bari

Pasquino, G. 1983: Partiti, società civile, istituzioni e il caso italiano, in: Stato e Mercato, No. 8, 1983

Perulli, P. and B. Trentin, (eds.), 1983: Il sindacato nella recessione, De Donato, Bari

Pizzorno, A. 1978: Political Exchange and Collective Identity in Industrial Conflict, in: C. Crouch and A. Pizzorno, (eds.), The Resurgence of Class Conflict in Western Europe since 1968, vol. 2, Macmillan, London

Prospettiva Sindacale 1983: Prima e dopo l'accordo di gennaio, no. 47, vol. XIV, March 1983 (special issue)

Regini, M. 1981: I dilemmi del sindacato, Il Mulino, Bologna

Salvati, M. 1982: Col senno di poi. Politica ed economia tra l'unità nazionale e il nuovo centro-sinistra, in: Quaderni Piacentini, No. 6, 1982

Trentin, B. 1977: Da sfruttati a produttori, De Donato, Bari

PART FOUR

"West Germany: The Disconcerted Impasse?"

Chapter 10

ECONOMIC DEVELOPMENT AND TRADE UNION COLLECTIVE BARGAINING POLICY SINCE THE MIDDLE OF THE 1970s

Otto Jacobi

The period of rapid economic growth which lasted up into the 1970s was also one of social prosperity. Continuously rising wages, the reduction of working-time and the expansion of the social security system raised the living standards of wage and salary-earners to an unprecedented level.

The trade unions, which made only occasional use of their potential to conduct labour disputes, gradually developed a collective bargaining policy whose aim was to enable wage and salary-earners to participate in economic progress. The strategic motive underlying this policy, however, was not to endanger the system-immanent (pre-)conditions of the growth process. The securing of economic growth demanded not only a high investment rate, but also - above all, in view of the great international dependence of the West German economy - the strengthening of the competitiveness of West German goods and services on the world market. Economic growth - even if for different motives - was the dominant economic policy objective of the state, capital and the trade unions, between whom a _de facto_ 'growth alliance' originated. Since then, beginning with the world-wide recession of 1974-75, the economic environment for trade union collective bargaining policy has changed fundamentally:

- Economic growth has not only decelerated, but has periodically come to a halt. The productive capacity of the German economy has become more modest and has objectively curtailed both the ability of the state and employers to make concessions and the scope for trade union action.
- The dominant macro-economic problem is not compensating for a short-fall in demand through state intervention, but rather the restructuring of the

production apparatus through investment in modern technologies. Therefore the classic trade union line of argument - justifying wage demands by reference to the stimulatory effects of increased mass purchasing-power on growth and unemployment - is no longer as convincing as it used to be.

- Weak growth and the continuing implementation of labour-saving technologies have led to the growth of mass unemployment. The societal balance of power has shifted to the detriment of wage and salary-earners and their trade union organisations.

The German trade unions are therefore confronted with radically-changed economic conditions and since autumn 1982 with a new conservative-liberal government. Up until now, the trade unions have concentrated on safeguarding the level of individual and collective welfare achieved for the working class during the period of prosperity. The trade unions have been relatively successful in safeguarding the social status of those who are in employment but they could not improve the chances for the unemployed of being reintegrated into the work process. They also could not check the massive cuts of social services. Generally speaking, the trade unions have adopted a policy of voluntary moderation and even in those cases where they launched strikes as for the reduction of working time, they showed an immense readiness to compromise.

ECONOMIC DEVELOPMENT AND ECONOMIC POLICY

In the following table (1), macro-economic data are assembled for two periods, which are comparable in so far as the 'base-years' represent the respective 'bottoms' of the first and second post-war recessions and, after interim phases of economic growth, growth came to a standstill again at the end of both periods.

The data portray well the change in the trend of economic development in the Federal Republic. Since the middle of the 1970s, economic growth has clearly slowed down. Notably, the development of industrial production (which, in the first period, increased at an above-average rate) is now strengthening the recession rather than promoting growth. A characteristic feature of economic development in the Federal Republic is the increase in international economic interdependence. This tendency continued, even if more weakly than before, during the years of world-wide recession. Compared

Table 1: Data on the development of the West German Economy

	1967-1974	1975-1982
	- Increase in % -	
Real gross domestic product	35	17
Industrial production	42	12
Export volume	106	46
Consumer prices	42	35
Income per employed wage and salary-earner:		
nominal gross	100	48
real gross	50	10
nominal net	79	41
real net	33	5
Unemployment rate (%, average)[1]	1.3	4.8

1. Proportion of the unemployed among dependent economically active persons (employed wage and salary-earners plus unemployed).

Sources: Sachverstaendigenrat zur Begutachtung der gesamtwirtschaftlichen Entwicklung, annual report 1983/84: Deutsche Bundesbank, report for the year 1983

with real GDP, the volume of exports grew at an above-average pace, with the result that the export rate increased from 20.5 per cent (1967) to 26.6 per cent (1975) and 33 per cent in 1982. This makes clear the extent to which the economic situation in the Federal Republic is dependent on the competitiveness of German industry on the world market. In this high degree of international economic interdependence lies the reason, too, for the two long dominant objectives of economic policy. The basis of the competitive strength of German industry on the world market is not so much a price-competitive supply of goods, but rather a broad supply of particular, technologically highly-advanced industrial goods. The 'advancing' economies, in particular Japan, have in many instances been able to close technological 'gaps', with the consequence that West German industry could not maintain its once leading position on some international goods markets. Therefore, it is an objective of state economic policy, pursued in agreement with the organisations of capital and labour and through the introduction of modern technologies, permanently to reproduce the competitive advantages deriving from technological superiority. The interests of the Federal Republic compel it to oppose all movements and tendencies towards protectionism.

The most lasting change affected the labour market. In place of full employment and an excess demand for labour, mass unemployment exists. While the number of unemployed totalled about 1 million, on average, in the years from 1975 to 1981, the beginning of a new recession was accompanied by an increase in the number of unemployed to an average of 2.3 million for 1983 - an unemployment rate of 9.1 per cent.

The reduction in employment took place almost exclusively in the producing sector of the German economy and affected preponderantly the group of manual workers (Arbeiter). In the period from 1970 until 1982, the number of employees in the producing sector fell from 12.2 to 10.2 million.

Consequently, the structure of employment in the economy as a whole has changed: the proportion of manual workers in the total number of wage and salary-earners fell from 56 per cent to 48 per cent, while the proportion of white-collar workers and 'permanent' civil servants increased from 44 per cent to 52 per cent. For some years, it has become increasingly clear that the absorptive capacity of the service and public sectors, which had served to stabilise employment, is dwindling, as, in these areas of the economy, too, the introduction of labour-saving technologies is being pushed ahead.

The effects of weak growth and unemployment on the incomes of wage and salary-earners are clearly visible. While the growth of real gross wages between 1967 and 1974 exceeded overall economic growth, the trend since then has been in the opposite direction. The redistribution of income in favour of wage and salary-earners - above all in the early 1970s - was succeeded by a reversal of the trend in the distribution of income in favour of incomes from profit. The development of real net incomes (which determine the real living standards of wage and salary-earners) proves that the still marked growth in earnings levels in the first period has now given way to stagnation. A further feature is that the burden of tax and social security contributions on wage and salary-earners' incomes has grown further. Thus, the growth in net incomes has clearly proceeded more slowly than that in gross incomes.

This change in the trend of economic development precipitated a change of course in economic policy in favour of neo-monetarist and supply-oriented policy strategies. The trail-breaker in this regard was the reserve bank (Bundesbank), which is autonomous and independent of the government in its monetary and credit policy decisions. The reserve bank - and, with it, the majority of scientific commentators - saw in the increased (even if, in international comparison, still low) level of inflation since the beginning of the 1970s a development which, in the long term, endangered the productive capacity of the economy. The reasons for the acceleration in the tempo of inflation were seen to be the increased cost of labour and the expansion of state expenditures, which had been brought about by the Social Democratic reform policy in the area of social policy in particular. The reserve bank's objective - even at the expense of a stabilisation crisis - was to break the mentality which this reform policy was thought to have produced and which, it was claimed, had led to excessive demands being made on the state. Through a potential-oriented money supply policy, that is, through tight and 'dear' money, the mechanism by which rising labour costs were passed on in rising prices and these, in turn, precipitated new wage increases was to be blocked - under conscious acceptance of the increased employment risk which this involved. In short: unemployment became an economic policy instrument to control the movement of wages.

The federal government supported this policy to combat inflation, but saw itself confronted, on the other hand, with the problem of growing unemployment, which had not been brought about, but had persistently been strengthened, by the policy of the reserve bank. Up until its collapse in autumn 1982, the Social-Liberal government sought to pursue a combination of a demand- and supply-oriented fiscal policy; the former Federal Chancellor described his economic policy as a "middle path between the two extremes of Keynesian economics and monetarist policy" (Schmidt 1983, p. 25). It must, however, be emphasised that the Keynesian elements of state fiscal policy increasingly receded into the background. The responsibility for this development lay in the assessment of both economic policy agencies of the state (the federal government and the reserve bank), as well as of the overwhelming majority of scientific advisors, that the chief economic problem was not of a conjunctural, but rather of a structural, character. Not the closing of a shortfall in demand, but rather the promotion of entrepreneurial investments as a pre-condition for safeguarding international competitiveness was and is seen as the order of the day. In calculations made by the former Social Democratic Finance Minister, it was outlined that, through an expansionary Keynesian stimulation of demand, about 500,000 jobs might be created (Matthoefer 1982).

Priority had therefore to be given to the technological modernisation of the production apparatus, from which, in the long term, employment possibilities were anticipated through the emergence of new goods markets.

The priority attached to investments corresponded with the government's and reserve bank's objective of improving the ability of entrepreneurs to invest by reducing their overall costs. Accordingly, the state's concept for managing the crisis had major consequences for wage policy and the distribution of income:

(a) The objective in terms of the distribution of income was a reversal of the trend in income-distribution by means of a correction of distributional relations in favour of profit incomes. The formula developed in the period of prosperity, whereby wages were adjusted in line with both the increase in productivity and the rate of inflation (in distributional terms, a 'status-quo' formula) was superseded by the demand on the trade unions to content themselves with increases corresponding to the rate of inflation. Since the new recession set in in 1981, only wage increases below the rate of price increases have been described as reconcilable with the economic situation.

(b) For the public sector, where the state is itself an employer and party to collective bargaining, a special variant of incomes policy was developed. The government argued that the trade unions here were under a particular obligation to exercise restraint in their income demands, as a high degree of employment security exists for public-service employees. Accordingly, the public-sector employers attempted in collective bargaining to implement a 'deduction' for the comparatively high job security, in order to keep incomes increases under the level for those agreed in the private sector.

(c) Another component was the demand on the trade unions not to take tax increases or increases in social security contributions as a reason for seeking (compensating) wage increases. If the trade unions were to attempt to keep wage and salary-earners free from such burdens and to displace them on to capital incomes, then this would lead to an undesirable shifting 'to-and-fro' of the burden - which must have had the effect of either stimulating inflation or reducing employment.

(d) In opposition to the objectives concerning a reduction of income differences contained in trade union collective bargaining policy, the argument was brought forward that wage and salary-earners' incentive and will to work would be reduced if the differences in pay for activities requiring different qualifications and skills were to be reduced. Rather, a sufficiently broad differentiation of wages was necessary, in order to allow the allocation function of wages to operate and to increase the flexibility of wage and salary-earners as regards sectoral, regional and occupational mobility. Moreover, with regard to the disproportionate increase in low incomes, it was objected that jobs for less well-qualified workers would thus be made unprofitable and that these workers would therefore fall victim to an accelerated labour-saving process of rationalisation.

(e) With the continuation of high unemployment, reference has been made more and more often to the "undesirable side-effects" of improvements in social policy. The improvements which were mentioned included sick pay, regulations preventing the dismissal of older workers, and increased wages for apprentices. The material compensation for unemployment, which is regarded as relatively high, has been viewed as especially disadvantageous for wage and labour-market flexibility and mobility.

The new conservative-liberal government could, without much ado, continue the economic policy of the preceding social-liberal administration. In the fields of economic, social and modernisation policy there are apparent continuities and there has been no change of strategy as regards the general principle. It is rather the cumulative effect of an austerity policy being continued with more determination, applied more rigidly and without any protective social or political compensation which is expected to bring about the conservative "Wende" step by step and via many detailed measures.

TRADE UNION WAGE POLICY

State economic policy, especially monetary and credit policies of the reserve bank, met with the opposition of the trade unions, because of the priority which was acceded to combatting inflation and to entrepreneurs' investment propensity over full employment (Jacobi 1979). In order not to be weakened still further by long-term unemployment, the trade unions centred their Keynesian-inspired economic policy demands around conjunctural programmes to promote growth and employment. In the economic policy programme laid out by the DGB (the trade union federation) in 1977, the allocation of absolute priority to the re-attainment of full employment was demanded. In this connection the trade unions supported a more expansionary spending practice on the part of the state, higher state indebtedness and an expansion of employment in the public sector. They justified their wage demands with the purchasing-power argument. From the strengthening of internal demand through a suitably high increase in wage and salary incomes, they expected an impulse to demand which would stimulate growth and employment.

The goals pursued by the trade unions in collective bargaining can be summarised in two points:

- The chief target of trade union wage policy was the safeguarding and improvement of the material living standards of employed wage and salary-earners. Correspondingly, the trade unions emphasised in their justification of their wage demands the necessity of compensation for inflation and the participation of wage and salary-earners in the increase in productivity. Also the demand for a redistribution of income in favour of the dependently-employed belonged to the unions' wage policy concept. While, despite the under-employment, these distribution policy components were not given up, they turned more and more into mere verbal gestures.
- While income-equalisation considerations became increasingly significant, they did not, however, lend any decisive impulse to trade union wage policy. Such wage policy demands were directed equally at an inter-sectoral and intra-sectoral reduction of wage differences. While, in the case of the former, what was involved was usually the need to 'catch up' on the part of those branches and trade unions which had 'lagged behind' in collective bargaining, intra-sectoral wage-equalisation was of much greater significance, as all the trade unions were confronted with the problem of overlapping, criss-crossing differentiations in wages. What was involved here were above all the differences in incomes between manual workers and white-collar workers, men and women, and between individual skill categories.

The contradiction between the economic and wage policy conceptions of the trade unions and the state did not result in intensified wage and distributional conflicts. Whereas the unions were able to exploit the favourable conjunctural and employment situation for income-distribution objectives in the early 1970s, their pro-cyclical pattern of wage-policy behaviour was reflected in the years of under-employment in an excessive adaptation to a problem situation shaped by world recession and structural change. Contradictory behaviour underlay trade union policy in the second half of the 1970s. Thus, the discrepancy between their economic- and wage-policy principles and their collective bargaining practice can not fail to be noticed. The trade unions could not - in any branch of the economy - implement their objective of obtaining improvements in income which could have unleashed an expansion of real mass demand to support economic growth. The unions' restraint in wage policy cannot be sufficiently explained by their weakened bargaining position and by the fact that the state - not least on account of trade union interventions - supplemented its dominant economic policy line with programmes to support the economic conjuncture. Rather, the contradiction in the positions of the trade unions, which is manifested in the relationship between a Keynesian-oriented economic programme and the modernisation of the economy through structural change (which was held to be inevitable), is of central significance for the comprehension of trade union wages policy. Whereas the economic policy demands are based on the assumption of an insufficiency of demand, agreement to the modernisation strategy as a perspective for economic development involves recognition of the priority of investments. Obviously, the assessment in trade union policy that it is imperative not to block structural change from the wages side has won more and more weight. The restraint of the unions in the pursuit of their collective bargaining objectives thus becomes explicable. It is not merely the result of an inability to implement their wishes. It also corresponds to the thinking that, through advance concessions in wage policy, a contribution could be made to the safeguarding of the international competitiveness of the West German economy. The extent to which the trade unions' ideas on incomes policy have begun to resemble those of the state is revealed by the following points:

(a) The practice of trade union wage policy shows that the trade unions have not been able to implement their objective of maintaining the 'status quo' in distribution policy and have been less and less able to achieve their wage policy goal of improving living standards. The fact that they have not engaged in strike action to achieve their collective bargaining objectives is characteristic of their co-operation in wages policy. The traditional pace-maker in collective bargaining, the IG Metall, has not carried out a wage strike to try to implement its distributional goals. As a rule, the trade unions withdrew their initial demands in wage negotiations and sought merely compensation for inflation. From the following table (2), it can be seen that real income could be improved only marginally between 1975 and 1979 and that reductions in income began to be experienced from 1980 onwards.

Table 2: Real net income and the real wage level of wage and salary-earners

Year	Wages and salaries per employed wage and salary-earner	Real wage level of wage and salary-earners
	- annual changes in % -	
1975	1.1	-1.8
1976	-0.1	-1.6
1977	2.0	-0.2
1978	3.7	-0.9
1979	2.0	0.4
1980	-0.3	1.9
1981	-1.3	-0.2
1982	-1.9	-1.4
1983	-1.2	-2.3

Source: Sachverstaendigenrat zur Begutachtung der gesamtwirtschaftlichen Entwicklung, annual report 1983/84

In terms of income-distribution, a shift in favour of profit incomes can be observed. The adjusted wage share (which is relevant in distributional terms), which rose from 61.4 per cent (1969) to 66.3 per cent (1974), has since fallen to 63.2 per cent (1983). Another indicator as regards the distribution of income is the position of real wages, which remains unchanged if the real income of wage and salary-earners increases so that the overall level of wage costs and distributional relations (the division of the national income) remain constant. On average, the position of real wages improved at an annual rate of 1.5 per cent from 1969 to 1974; since 1975, in contrast, reductions have occurred almost regularly. The success in the redistribution of income achieved by the trade unions in the early 1970s has not yet been rolled back completely (which is what the government and the reserve bank believe to be necessary).

However, as the collective bargaining round in 1983 showed, it must be supposed that the unions will be less and less able to resist further reductions. In 1983 the average gross yearly earnings amounted to 34,000 DM per employee in round figures; after taxes on wages and social insurance contributions of 30 per cent the take-home pay amounted to 24,000 DM.

(b) For the manual and white-collar workers and 'permanent' civil servants in the public service, the wage increase rates agreed in the past several years have been lower than those in the private sector of the economy. The trade union protest against the 'deduction' implemented by the public-sector employer remained verbal; in none of the collective bargaining rounds did the trade unions resort to strikes or similar measures.

(c) The trade unions have also acquiesced in the state's expectation that rising taxes and social security contributions should not be drawn into collective bargaining conflicts. In their view, considerations of principle prevent such impositions on wage incomes being corrected by means of collective bargaining: collective bargaining policy should not intervene to compensate for increased taxes and social security contributions when the latter contribute to social reforms and improved social security. It could not alter things, when the state spent money "in the wrong place and for the wrong purposes", for this was not an issue for collective bargaining, but a "question of our ability to implement our political objectives vis-à-vis governments and Parliament" (IG Metall 1975).

(d) In so far as trade union wage demands were connected with the intention of reducing income differences between different groups of wage and salary-earners, it must be concluded that such demands almost regularly fell victim to the trade unions' preparedness to compromise. However, neither the employers nor the state have succeeded in increasing wage differences between the individual branches of the economy. The collective bargaining outcome in the metalworking industry still has the function of a 'model agreement', which, with the exception of the public service, is carried over, with minor modifications, into the other areas of the economy.

(e) With regard to the protection of the employees in case of illness, retirement, inability to work and unemployment, cut-backs had to be accepted. On the one hand, through higher contributions and - as in the case of illness - through a certain degree of "own participation" (i. e., self-financing), wage and salary-earners were drawn more strongly than hitherto into financing the costs of the social security system. On the other hand, benefits - especially those for unemployment - were cut. In this way, wage and salary-earners - especially women and foreign workers - are to be forced off the labour market and the pressure on job-seekers to accept worse-paid jobs is to be increased. However, the trade unions succeeded in defending two social policy achievements won in earlier collective bargaining conflicts: protection against dismissal for older workers and the continuation of the payment of (normal) wages for workers in case of illness.

Trade Union Policy Regarding Working-time

The cutting of working-time has always been a central component of trade union programmes and policy. The demands of the trade unions regarding working-time can be summarised in a systematic overview, arranged according to leisure-time policy, health and humanisation policy, egalitarian and employment policy objectives.

The extension of leisure-time as an independent justification for the shortening of working-time - which was the dominant motive in the trade union campaign for the introduction of the 40-hour week in the 1950s and 1960s - has receded more and more into the background. Instead, under the impact of continuing mass unemployment, employment policy objectives became increasingly important in the second half of the 1970s. The demand for the introduction of the 35-hour week as the standard working-time to be laid down in collective agreements was associated with the view that a quantitative employment effect could thus be achieved which would force enterprises to recruit new staff or to continue to employ staff whom they would otherwise have dismissed. In addition, health and humanisation policy objectives influenced the working-time demands of the trade unions. From the point of view of the protection of health, priority must be awarded to the extension of holidays: here the trade unions can refer to medical findings, according to which the protective and regenerative effects considered desirable in terms of health policy can be expected above all from large 'blocks' of leisure-time. In the interests of humanising work, the trade unions demanded reductions in working-time, in the form of longer breaks and 'recovery-times' or additional holidays and 'free shifts' for older workers and groups of employees (above all shift workers) subjected to particularly severe physical and nerve-related burdens. A further goal of trade union working-time policy was the ironing-out of differences in working-time among employees. They sought, on the one hand, an ironing-out of differences in weekly and annual working-time between different sectors and, on the other, the levelling-out of working-times of different length for different groups of employees within the same branch.

A comparison with the actual development of working-time shows that the improvements obtained by the trade unions fell far short of their collective bargaining objectives. In comparison to the 1960s, the process of reducing annual working-time (annual holidays and weekly working-time taken together) as laid down in collective agreements has slowed considerably since the beginning of the 1970s. Whereas from 1960 to 1970 the yearly working time per employee had been reduced by collective bargaining agreements by 10.6 per cent there was only a reduction of 6.7 per cent for the period from 1970 to 1982. The trade unions did not engage in strike activity for their wage policy but there were several strikes in support of their demands for a reduction of working time. The most important results are summarised, according to weekly working time, holidays and improvements in working-time for particular groups of employees, in the following paragraphs:

(a) The most outstanding result is that the 40-hour week which was introduced in the mid 60s (first in the printing and in the engineering industry) as the standard working time, will be reduced in 1985 to 38.5 hours. In the last few years, almost all the trade unions have declared the introduction of the 35-hour week to be one of their primary objectives in collective bargaining. However, only the IG Metall and the IG Druck (Printers' Union) have made this demand into a topic for negotiation and strike. The other unions held back from putting this demand into practice in collective bargaining by remarking that this was a long-term objective or that they themselves could not serve as pace-makers.

The issue of the 35-hour week led to a strike with wide-ranging consequences in the steel industry in 1978. With the demand for a progressive introduction of the 35-hour week, the IG Metall opened a working-time and employment policy offensive. As the employers had stipulated in a so-called 'taboo-catalogue' that any movement below the 40-hour week was to be categorically rejected, both collective bargaining parties were aware that they were conducting this conflict on behalf of all trade unions and employers' organisations. Its outcome would necessarily affect other sectors of the economy.

The labour dispute ended after six weeks with the IG Metall giving up its collective bargaining objective and, instead, making do with the progressive extension of annual holidays up to 30 days. No stabilising effect on employment could be achieved with this agreement. The agreement must therefore be evaluated as a defeat, in a model power conflict, not only for the IG Metall, but for the entire trade union movement. No other trade union attempted to take up and continue the working-time offensive begun, for employment policy motives, in the steel sector.

In the beginning of 1984 the IG Metall launched a further campaign which was again solely motivated by employment policy considerations and which demanded the introduction of a 35-hour week. This time it risked the conflict in the metal working industry which constitutes, with its more than 3.5 million employees and its large sectors mechanical industry, electrical engineering and car industry, the core of the West German economy. (At the same time the IG Druck - the printer's union - were on strike for a reduction of weekly working time.) The strike was to become the biggest industrial dispute in West German history and it lasted for 7 weeks in the metal working industry. 57,000 striking employees, 155,000 who were locked out and 315,000 who were affected indirectly, were involved in the conflict. The latter were affected by - what is called in German trade union jargon - "a cold lock out" as many companies stopped production on the grounds that supplies were either lacking or could not be delivered to or from the strike areas. This argument sometimes served as a pretense but was true in most cases. The car industry which came almost to a complete standstill was most affected by the strike. It is to be expected that the loss of economic growth for the whole economy amounts to 1 per cent; one has to consider, however, that the stoppage of production caused by the dispute could mostly be counterbalanced. The IG Metall spent 600 million DM during the strike - mostly on strike pay for employees who were on strike or locked out -, the employers spent 1,000 million DM mostly on payments to companies suffering from the effects of the strike.

This confrontation had been foreseeable for two reasons. On the one hand the employers adhered to the positions laid down in their "catalogue of taboos" which rejected any reduction of weekly working time. On the other hand the conservative-liberal government interfered in the conflict in a manner which had been unknown in the social-liberal era. For this it exploited an internal split within the unions affiliated to the DGB as one group propagated the 35-hour week and the other a reduction of life working time by a pre-retirement scheme. The government not only rejected the 35-hour week "as stupid and silly" (Chancellor Kohl) and economically irresponsible but also passed a law providing financial means for pre-retirement.

The fact that a strike ballot found 80 per cent of its members in favour of a strike which was subsequently carried out with a lot of discipline must, in these circumstances, be regarded as a success for the IG Metall. The strike was settled by arbitration (the arbitrator, Georg Leber, is a conservative Social Democrat and a committed catholic who was a president of the building union, then a minister of transport and later a secretary of defence). The most important points of the arbitration agreement are:

- an increase of wages by 3.3 per cent for 1984 and by 2.0 per cent for 1985;
- voluntary pre-retirement from the age of 58 onwards with continuing payment of 65 to 70 per cent of the last wage;
- from 1985 on a reduction of the average weekly working time to 38.5 hours; in order to prevent a loss of income a pay rise of 3.9 per cent was agreed;
- through agreements between management and works council the working time of individual sections of the company and/or of individual groups of employees can be fixed within a margin of 37 to 40 hours.

The essential part of the agreement is the compromise on working time. The IG Metall succeeded in bringing down the principle of a 40-hour week which had been maintained by the employers until the end but on the other hand it had to concede the plant-specific flexibilisation of working hours, which permits to separate the machine time from the working time of the groups of machine operators. Although the agreement is completely insufficient from the angle of employment policy, the collective bargaining dispute cannot be regarded as a defeat for the trade unions. This is because the IG Metall could assert its fighting strength and could thus make a first step towards a 35-hour week in spite of political and economic conditions which were adverse to its interests.

(b) It can be taken for granted that an annual holiday length of 20 days (equal to 4 weeks) existed in almost all regions of the economy in the early 1970s. In the years up until 1979, in connection with wage agreements, repeated improvements in holiday regulations of one to two days were implemented. The most important holiday agreements came about in 1979. The agreement reached in the steel industry - to increase annual holidays for all employees in stages up to 30 days - was carried over into the metal-working, chemical and printing industries. Similar agreements were concluded later in other areas of the economy.

(c) The IG Metall was able, by means of a limited strike in the region of Baden-Wurttemberg in 1973, to push through selective reductions in working-time for groups of employees with difficult working conditions. For the first time, the union succeeded in agreeing 'minimum rest-periods' within the framework of the prevailing 40-hour week. A rest-period of five minutes per working-hour was set down for all assembly-line, piece- and bonus workers. The unions have subsequently succeeded only in exceptional cases in having comparable regulations carried over into other collective-bargaining regions of the IG Metall and other areas of the economy.

The result is, that a holiday period of 6 weeks has been reached for the mid-80s for more or less all employees, regardless of age and professional status. Additional holidays or 'free shifts' could be achieved - with continued payment of normal wages or salaries - for older workers and for shift workers in the steel and printing industries. Comparable agreements were reached in only a few other areas - as, for example, in 1980, after a short strike, for postal employees.

(d) New forms of cuts in working-time have originated with the agreement of "pre-retirement sabbaticals" for older workers. The aim of such measures is to offer older workers a flexible transition into retirement, with full or normal compensation for the loss in wages which would otherwise be involved, before they reach the legal retirement age. In 1978, for the first time, an agreement was reached in the cigarette industry, whereby older workers were given the possibility of reducing their weekly working-time, with full wage-compensation, to 20 hours or of retiring early on 75 per cent of their gross earnings. Up until now, such collective agreements have extended above all into the various branches of the foodstuffs industry.

In 1984 a reduction of life working time by voluntary pre-retirement of employees from the ages of 58 to 64 was introduced in some sectors of the economy. This scheme had been propagated by some trade unions and had the support of the conservative-liberal government. The regulations lay down that, on the basis of collective bargaining agreements, the employers pay a considerably reduced "wage" to their employees who are willing to retire (about 50 per cent of their former effective earnings plus contributions to the old age pension and health insurance). For the companies such pre-retirement schemes are not so expensive as the costs are taken into account in the collective wage agreement for the other employees and because they permit a replacement of inefficient older by efficient younger employees. In addition, the government grants an employment subsidy in the event of replacements for jobs which have thus become vacant. The effect on the employment situation is after all limited as the number of employees eligible for retirement is not very large and the majority of employees will not make use of pre-retirement because it involves a considerable loss of income and it is expected that there will only be partial replacements.

When the cuts in working-time are measured against the trade unions' working-time aspirations, then it can be maintained that the overall not inconsiderable extension of the length of holidays took account of leisure-time and health considerations to a high degree. It has now become possible for the majority of wage and salary-earners to divide their annual holiday entitlements into two holidays of three weeks each - which, according to medical findings, is particularly beneficial for wage and salary-earners' health. In view of the small number of wage and salary-earners who benefited from selective measures to reduce working-time, the trade unions cannot point to any notable success in terms of 'humanising' working life. In contrast, in their efforts to smooth out intra- and inter-sectoral differences in working-time, the unions were highly successful. It can be assumed that a holiday entitlement of 30 days will have been achieved for all wage and salary-earners, almost everywhere in the economy, by the middle of the 1980s. The traditional differentiation in holiday entitlements according to age, income and status will have been largely eradicated. The trade unions experienced their greatest failure in their attempt through cuts in working-time to contribute to a stabilisation of employment. As effects on employment can be expected above all from a reduction in weekly working-time it must be assumed that trade union working-time policy has not extended employment possibilities for wage- and salary-earners.

Qualitative Collective Bargaining Policy

The trade unions succeeded with some qualitatively new objectives in setting a few noteworthy accents in the development of collective bargaining since the middle of the 1970s. Their dominant feature is that demands for the prevention of the negative social consequences of enterprise rationalisation policies - which up until then had been neglected - have been added to the traditionally dominant demands concerning wages and working-time. All in all, a more critical attitude on the part of the unions towards the social effects of technological progress can be observed. Certainly, it cannot be said that the traditional confidence of organised workers in technical progress has given way to pessimism, but it cannot be overlooked that sensitivity regarding the application of modern production, administration and 'control' technologies has grown.

This judgement must be qualified, however, with the remark that only two trade unions, the IG Druck and the IG Metall, were prepared to turn such new demands into issues for negotiation with employers. The explosiveness of such demands was manifested by two bitterly-fought strikes (1978), which were inflamed by employers' lock-outs. Both unions achieved partial successes, but had also to give up a substantial part of their initial demands.

- In the printing industry, union demands concerned employment risks - specifically in the area of print-setting (Mueller-Jentsch 1979). The introduction of the 'new technology' replaced the traditional lead-setting with photographic setting through the application of electronically-directed 'text-systems'. This endangered the basis of the occupational existence of a highly-qualified group of skilled workers which also formed one of the core groups of the IG Druck und Papier and had exercised a major influence on its structure and politics in the past. The union demands for rules relating to manning, protection of earnings, rest-periods and for a reduction in weekly working-time for employees working on screen terminals were inspired by job- and income-protection and by organisational objectives. On the one hand, they were directed against the threats to the jobs and incomes of the setters; on the other, against the dangers for the existence and strength of the trade union. At the same time, the union's demands implied far-reaching intervention in employers' personnel and investment policies. After a long and toughly-led strike, the IG Druck was able to achieve some new kinds of collective bargaining agreements (far-reaching protection provisions, temporary manning rules for the work on terminals and job- and earnings-protection over a period of years for skilled employees). As it was waging a defensive struggle against the present consequences of a development which, in the medium-term, could not be halted, it had, however, to give up the idea of exerting a determining influence on the application of modern technologies and the new jobs to which they give rise.

- In the metal-working industry in 1978, the IG Metall demanded individual and collective safeguards against occupational 'demotions' caused by changes in jobs brought about by rationalisation in the collective-bargaining region of North Wurttemberg/North Baden (Hildebrandt 1979; Dzielak 1979). This demand derived from the fact that, through rationalisation measures affecting technology and the organisation of work, jobs had arisen involving activities which, on the basis of work-evaluation analyses incorporated into earlier collective agreements, were to be lower-paid. The employers could demote the employees affected by such changes in their jobs into lower categories. In order to protect the latter from such measures, the IG Metall wanted to obtain an agreement which ruled out individual demotions. To prevent enterprises from being able to achieve a lower factory wage-level by dismissing employees in higher wage categories and making recruitments in the lower categories, the union demanded collective safeguards to try to preserve the existing categorisation pattern. The individual and, in particular, the collective safeguards against demotion would have involved far-reaching interventions in the freedom of action of employers regarding personnel policy and determining pay-scales. With the protection sought against demotions - and here lies its short-coming - no employment policy effects could be achieved. This was rather a defensive measure, which was vigorously pursued in so far as far-reaching demands were made concerning income-protection, against the consequences of enterprises' rationalisation policies for the wage structure. With the agreement that demotions may not exceed two wage categories and, in the case where a demotion has been made, previous earnings are temporarily guaranteed, the IG Metall obtained new kinds of collective bargaining regulations and therefore a partial success. But it was not able to push through a complete ban on individual demotions or so much as the rudiments of collective safeguards against demotions.

It must be conceded to the trade unions that they have reacted with conceptually new collective bargaining demands to the increased number of ways in which the interests of wage and salary-earners are harmed by the present rationalisation drive. It may be supposed that qualitative goals will become more significant in collective bargaining if the process of rationalisation, with its negative consequences for employment and working conditions, begins to affect not only the marginalised groups of employees, but also, more strongly than hitherto, the group of skilled workers, which represents the heart of the 'core' company work forces in industry and the core of the membership of the trade unions.

STRIKES AND LOCK-OUTS

The Federal Republic of Germany has always had a comparatively low frequency of strikes. In the last years, periods of major strikes have almost regularly been followed by periods of an almost total absence of labour disputes. This pattern has not changed since the mid-seventies.

Table 3: Strikes and lock-outs

Year(s)	Workers involved	Days lost
	(annual average, '000s)	
1967-1974	170	865
1975-1982	143	699
	(annual, '000s)	
1975	36	69
1976	169	534
1977	34	24
1978	487	4,281
1979	77	483
1980	45	128
1981	253	58
1982	40	15
1983	94	41
1984*	approx. 600	approx. 6,000

*Trade Union figures

The strike behaviour can be attributed to the fact that the trade unions' readiness for co-operation, which was developed in the long phase of economic expansion, has been maintained up to the present in spite of the 10 years of mass unem-

Table 4: Major labour disputes since 1975

Year	Economic branch	No. of workers involved Strikers	locked-out	Demand
1976	Printing industry	60, 000	70, 000	Wage increase
1978	Ports	20, 000		Wage increase
1978	Printing industry	20, 000	50, 000	Job- and earnings- protection
1978	Metal-working	90, 000	145, 000	Earnings-protection
1978/79	Steel industry	45, 000	35, 000	35-hour week
1980	Post office	25, 000		Additional leisure-time for shift-workers
1984*	Printing industry	45, 000		35-hour week
1984*	Metal-working	57, 000	155, 000 315, 000 (affected by 'cold lock-outs')	35-hour week

* Trade union figures

ployment. For the trade unions the strikes in the Federal Republic are very much characterised by their ability of standing the hardness test of the employers by demonstrating their members' continuous commitment and the fighting strength of the organisation.

This survey of the major labour disputes since 1975 marks two prevailing tendencies. First, it is remarkable that the major issues have almost exclusively been non-monetary in character. Second, the table shows how extensively employers exercised their right to lock out and have thus adopted a method of industrial action which has effectively improved their resilience against trade union demands.

The labour dispute in 1984, for a reduction of weekly working time, was certainly embedded in the tradition of industrial relations in the Federal Republic. As the employers and the government had believed they could inflict a genuine defeat on the trade unions, the traditional trade union pacemaker, the IG Metall, first had to prove its fighting strength before all participants could agree to a compromise formula and thus paved the way for a renewal of co-operative relations. The fact that the IG Metall could secure its position as the legitimate representative of the employees and has maintained its position as the established partner on the bargaining market, will be an essential determinant for the development of industrial relations.

REFERENCES

Brandt, G., O. Jacobi, W. Mueller-Jentsch 1982: Anpassung an die Krise, Gewerkschaften in den siebziger Jahren, Frankfurt/New York

Crouch, C., 1979: The Politics of Industrial Relations, Manchester

Deutsche Bundesbank, report for the year 1983, Frankfurt

Dzielak, W., Hindrichs, W., Martens, H., 1979: Den Besitzstand sichern, Frankfurt

Hildebrandt, E., 1979: Der Tarifkampf in der metallverarbeitenden Industrie 1978, in: Jacobi, O., Mueller-Jentsch, W., Schmidt, E. (Hg.), Arbeiterinteressen gegen Sozialpartnerschaft, Kritisches Gewerkschaftsjahrbuch 1978/79, Berlin

Jacobi, O., 1979: Gewerkschaftliche Lohnpolitik unter dem Druck antikeynesianischer Wirtschaftspolitik, in: Bergmann, J. (Hg.), Beitraege zur Soziologie der Gewerkschaften, Frankfurt

IG Metall, 1975: Der Gewerkschafter 12/1975, Frankfurt

Matthoefer, H., 1982: Wir muessen fast zwei Millionen neue Arbeitsplaetze schaffen, in: Frankfurter Rundschau vom 2. 1. 1982, Frankfurt

Mueller-Jentsch, W., 1979: Der Arbeitskampf in der Druckindustrie 1978, in: Jacobi, O., Mueller-Jentsch, W., Schmidt, E. (Hg.), Arbeiterinteressen gegen Sozialpartnerschaft, Kritisches Gewerkschaftsjahrbuch 1978/79, Berlin

Sachverstaendigenrat zur Begutachtung der gesamtwirtschaftlichen Entwicklung, 1983: Jahresgutachten 1983/84, Bonn

Schiller, K., 1968: Konjunkturpolitik auf dem Wege zu einer Affluent Society, in: Schwedler, R., Foehrenbach, W. (Hg.), Jahre der Wende, Karlsruhe

Schmidt, H., 1983: Die Weltwirtschaft ist unser Schicksal, in: Die Zeit vom 25. 2. 1983, Hamburg; (The World Economy at Stake, The Economist, February 26, London)

Chapter 11

LABOUR LAW AND INDUSTRIAL RELATIONS

Ulrich Mueckenberger

JURIDIFICATION

Should anyone really have been in doubt as to the high degree of state law and judicial regulation of industrial relations in the Federal Republic of Germany, the fight of the metal workers for a 35-hour week in the spring of 1984 proved the point brilliantly. In the current manner of industrial action, the metal workers' strike began as a selective strike confined to Baden-Wuerttemberg and Hessen, and, as is also the tendency today, the battlefield was rapidly broadened by retaliatory lock-outs. All the doctrines developed by the courts to deal with this type of industrial dispute were continuously reaffirmed during this conflict:

- The employers adhered precisely to the ratios of locked-out employees to workers on strike as prescribed in the 1980 ruling of the Federal Labour Court (dealt with in more detail below). Attempts by the metal workers' union to have the lock-outs stopped in Hessen, where the constitution forbids lock-outs, failed even on appeal in the Labour Court of Hessen. This court based its ruling on rulings of the Federal Labour Court. If the Labour Court of Hessen had ruled that the lock-outs were unacceptable, the case would certainly have gone to the Federal Constitutional Court for a final decision.
- Any selective strike which affects key factories within the area covered by a collective agreement will eventually - and this intention is clearly stated - cause shut-downs in factories outside that region. The question is whether the employees at the plants thus affected (who are not involved in the dispute

themselves) are entitled to continued payment of their wages or not. Although §615 of the German Civil Code (Buergerliches Gesetzbuch) clearly comes down on the side of the employees in this respect, labour courts have rejected this since a leading ruling of 1923 (Colneric 1984, pp. 315 ff). Consequently, even today, in 1984, employees laid off as a result of strike action did not receive any pay.

- As a rule, employees affected by a temporary shutdown are paid "wage substitutes" from the unemployment insurance fund. However, the Employment Promotion Act (Arbeitsfoerderungsgesetz, §116) states that unemployment insurance funds have to adopt a neutral stance in industrial disputes, and must not act in such a way as to affect the bargaining balance by making financial payments. In 1984, then, the argument was resumed as to whether employees affected by, but not participating in, industrial disputes are entitled to payments from the unemployment insurance fund or not (Bley 1982, pp. 308 ff). Social insurance courts dealing with these cases in Hessen and Bremen ruled that such payments should be made and confirmed this ruling in appeal. The employers once more immediately appealed to the Federal Constitutional Court, and this court would have made a final ruling on the matter, had the strike not been called off shortly before the date of the hearing.

Those were particularly spectacular legal events of the 1984 dispute. But the courts also heard numerous other less dramatic cases relating to the dispute, usually concerning individual companies and the actual situation induced by the strike. For example, courts had to decide whether the Employees' Council (Betriebsrat) can still exercise its statutory rights in a factory which has been temporarily closed down by a strike. They also ruled on whether members of the Employees' Council have a right of access to company premises during a strike. They defined the width of the passage to be left open by pickets for those wishing to go to work. Numerous other practical aspects of the strike were also ruled on by the courts.

All the rulings quoted so far passed a special forensic procedure for urgent matters, and were made in the form of temporary injunctions. As a rule, the courts do not tend to be involved until the actual dispute is settled. Then they are called in to settle the extent and the distribution of the damages incurred. In this normal situation which the law provides for, they do not have a preventive, controlling role, but a reactive, assessing role. Temporary injunctions, however, as they were applied in the dispute of 1984, tended to draw the courts into the dispute before it was settled. Thus the courts really became actors in the dispute.

The 1984 dispute is a convincing empirical example of the high degree of juridification of industrial relations in Western Germany today. But it is more difficult to demonstrate the process whereby this system of legal regulation developed. Inevitably, different assessments must be made according to sphere and form of regulation. I should like to do this, for the development of the past decade and a half, with the emphasis on collective labour law (Mueckenberger and Welteke 1975: Mueckenberger 1980 b). But first I will sketch the background to this account.

The law regulating industrial relations operates in three main areas (Korsch 1922; Mueckenberger 1984). The first of these is legal protection of the individual employee against the dangers inherent in the production process and against risks stemming from temporary or permanent inability to work. These regulations are contained in the system of individual labour (particularly in employment contract law) and in factory legislation and social welfare law (particularly social security legislation) (cf. Daeubler 1979; Bley 1982). The second area mainly covers collective bargaining on wages, hours and other conditions of work between collective parties on both sides of industrial conflict. The relevant regulations are contained in the main sectors of collective labour law, particularly laws on collective bargaining, conciliation, arbitration and industrial disputes (cf. Daeubler 1982; Soellner 1981). The third area regulates the actual deployment of labour in the plant and company via joint (labour and capital) consultation and bargaining committees on plant and company level. In the Federal Republic of Germany, these regulations constitute a subdivision of collective labour law, namely Works Constitution Law and Company Co-determination Law (Betriebsverfassungs- und Mitbestimmungsrecht) (Daeubler and Soellner, ibid).

Within each of these areas there are two main forms of regulation. The first of these is designed to fix precisely defined quantitative or qualitative standards which must neither be failed nor exceeded. The legal system refers to this form of regulation as "substantive law". The second form does not fix standards, it simply lays down procedural frameworks within which a particular standard is to be agreed on or modified. This form is referred to as "procedural regulation" (Clegg 1980; pp. 1-2).

The first of the three areas defined above falls within the domain of substantive law, although it undoubtedly incorporates numerous procedural provisions. The second two areas, on the other hand, fall within the domain of procedural law. Historically, the development of distinct industrial relations laws in all capitalist industrial states began with the laying down of substantive individual rights of the contract of employment and the protection of the labour force through factory legislation. Then, as both parties in the industrial conflict formed collective bodies capable of bargaining and confrontation, law shifted to procedural regulation of collective bargaining and of participation/co-determination at plant as well as at company level (Blanke et al., 1975, vol. I). Although this in no respect meant that individual substantive regulation no longer had any relevance or potential for further development, the character of industrial relations is now largely shaped by their procedural, collective framework.

Against this background, the following theses can be suggested:

1. The assertion that the industrial relations system of the Federal Republic of Germany is characterised by a high degree of juridification refers in particular to the procedural aspect of collective bargaining and of participation at plant and company level. In this respect, the Federal Republic of Germany is markedly different from its continental neighbours and Great Britain. In the areas of individual labour and social security law, the differences are far less pronounced, as numerous historical and current examples could testify. This is why I shall restrict my remarks here to industrial relations law.

2. Throughout the history of collective bargaining and industrial dispute law in the Federal Republic of Germany, there has been a constant tendency towards suppression and prevention of labour disputes by means of legal regulation. Two things are characteristic of this development, which I shall describe in more detail later. Firstly, this suppression has largely been achieved by court rulings. There have been no substantial legislative interventions in industrial disputes and collective bargaining throughout the history of the Federal Republic of Germany, and the recent change to a conservative

government seems unlikely to alter this. Secondly, suppression of labour disputes by labour court decisions not only dominated the two decades of conservative government after the Federal Republic of Germany emerged (1949), but it also continued throughout the Social Democratic governed period of reform in the 1970s - despite the fact that this period involved intensive legislative activity in the fields of labour and social security law.

3. The sphere of collective labour law was mainly modified with respect to plant and company participation during the SPD-FDP coalition. The rights of participation of Employees' Councils, and co-determination in large companies were greatly extended. Court rulings have largely followed this legislative lead. And although there are currently substantial restrictions on participation in industrial matters, by means of labour court rulings, it would appear that even under conservative rule the basic framework of extensive participation at plant and company level is not being challenged.

THE LAW ON INDUSTRIAL CONFLICT IN THE FEDERAL REPUBLIC

There is not really any substantive law in the area of collective bargaining in the Federal Republic of Germany. The constitution (Article 9, para. 3) guarantees "free collective bargaining" (Tarifautonomie). Thus the Collective Agreements Law (Tarifvertragsgesetz) only provides procedural means for the conclusion, validity and extention of the applicability of collective agreements, but does not lay down substantive standards (Daeubler and Hege 1981). As a rule, the Federal Labour Court has also tended to give priority to the parties to collective agreements with regard to substantive standards. Admittedly there have been two important occasions where the Federal Labour Court altered its line, disapproving of particular clauses in collective agreements. This was at a time when the first signs of economic crisis were emerging in the country. An industrial dispute with the objective of achieving positive discrimination of union members against non-union members (1967) was held to be a tort, thus making the union liable for compensation. This was also the case in 1968 with a dispute in which a union tried to secure employees against pay losses due to the "wage drift" i.e. extra payments on plant level exceeding the payment provided for by the regional or national agreement (Daeubler 1982, pp. 100ff, 126ff). In view of the constitutional guarantee of free collective bargaining rights, however, court intervention in substantive clauses of collective agreements is not frequent.

But today the concept of free collective bargaining actually only has limited validity. For the courts have made increasingly narrow procedural limits in labour disputes. Thus by imposing procedural restrictions, the courts have automatically gained control of the substantive results of collective agreements.

The Federal Labour Court aims at industrial peace and relatively broad acceptance by both parties to industrial disputes. To see which mechanisms it employs to this end, I will consider some fundamental elements of its industrial dispute rulings. Since the law on industrial conflict in Western Germany developed out of case law, going back to the period immediately after World War II, my reconstruction begins at that point.

1. The first large industrial dispute in which the judiciary played a recognised role was the printers' strike in the newspaper industry in 1952. At issue was the conservative Works Constitution Bill, which ignored major union rights and demands. The Union of Printers and Paperworkers organised an industry-wide 2-day strike on 28 and 29 May 1952, in order to demonstrate against the passage of the Bill. Since the Federal Labour Court had not yet been set up (it came into being in 1955), it was the Labour Court of each individual state (Land) which mainly had to deal with the judicial consequences of this strike. The large majority of these State Labour Courts ruled that the printers' strike was political, and thus declared it illegal. The distinction of most of the courts as to whether the strike was a matter of labour law - and thus in principle admissible - or a political act - and thus in principle inadmissible - was not based on the substantive issue at stake: such as, for example, whether employees' working conditions were to be improved (= legal), or whether the strike was intended to challenge the ruling government (= illegal) (e.g. Landesarbeitsgericht, Berlin 1953). Instead, the courts applied a formal criterion, namely against whom the strike was directed (e.g. Landesarbeitsgericht, Frankfurt 1969). If it was directed against an institution of the state, it was deemed to be a politically motivated strike, contravening the principles of the democratic constitution. Only in cases where the strike was considered to be directed against an employer, and was in principle aimed at a collective agreement, was it deemed to be a matter of industrial relations law and therefore admissible.

This attitude of the State Labour Courts contradicted Article 9, para. 3 of the Federal Constitution, which states: "Every person and every profession has the right to form associations in order to preserve and promote their working and economic conditions." Thus the constitution emphasises the material objective pursued by the strike. And if this criterion had been applied, the strike in protest against the Works Constitution Bill would quite certainly have been pronounced legitimate in the eyes of the constitution. Instead of this, the State Labour Courts laid down a formal criterion, namely against whom the strike was deemed to be directed. This meant that the courts were already placing themselves above the constitution.

Thus the judiciary depoliticised the relationship between labour and capital. Political disputes between labour and capital could now no longer be pursued by means of strikes, and certainly not by means of full-scale strikes. Not too long ago, in 1979, this court decision was confirmed in a dramatic ruling by the State Labour Court in Munich. The radio and television workers' union had called television workers out on a short protest stoppage against the proposed closure of a broadcasting station. A temporary injunction was issued by the Munich Labour Court to prevent the stoppage. The ruling of the court confirmed the 25-year-old rulings of the various State Labour Courts on the printers' strike (Mueckenberger 1980a).

If we now consider the extent to which the working and economic conditions of employees are regulated or influenced by the state (pensions, unemployment and insurance benefits, health, education, local and regional infrastructure, etc.), we begin to have some picture of the breadth of the implications of this early court ruling. Any strike demonstrating in respect of these matters is addressing the state, then, and as such is political and therefore inadmissible. Thus an increasingly large part of working and economic conditions of workers is no longer within the scope of their influence or "industrial muscle".

2. After 1952 there was a second change in the attitude of the State Labour Courts, the effects of which are still evident today. Following the newspaper printers' strike, Professor Nipperdey was asked by the Employers' Association to present his legal opinion on the strike. He argued that any strike could be treated in principle as an intervention in the "established and practised enterprise." This meant that a strike always constituted a tort (civil wrong); and that the

employer was entitled to compensation for the losses caused by the strike. Only if this tort could be legitimised on grounds of "social adequacy" (Sozialadaequanz) would there be no liability for indemnity. Almost all the State Labour Courts classified the printers' strike of 1952 in the manner suggested by Nipperdey, and found the union liable for damages.

Granting priority to entrepreneurial interests over the basic rights of trades union freedom is another dramatic contravention of the constitution. The constitution guarantees the right to form trades unions, yet the courts now held that strike action could only be justified and permitted in exceptional cases. Subsequent rulings by the Federal Labour Court followed this lead. Nipperdey surfaced again here, having been involved in all forms of political justice in Germany in the past: the Weimar Republic, the Nazi Third Reich, the Second World War, and now the decisive formative years of the Federal Republic. By this time Nipperdey was no longer acting as the legal expert of the Employers' Association, but was president of the newly formed Federal Labour Court and chairman of the Great Senate responsible for key decisions of the Federal Labour Court. So it was under Nipperdey that on 28 January 1955, the leading decision on industrial conflict law was issued, which, although modified, in principle still legally regulates labour disputes today (Bundesarbeitsgericht, hereafter BAG, 1955). At that time, the Federal Labour Court took the concept of "social adequacy" and endowed it with precise legal contours which gradually became more defined in the ensuing years. The key sentence, which reveals the philosophy of the court, states: "Industrial action is generally undesirable to the economy, but is permissible within certain limits."

I should like to sketch briefly the basic features of this ruling, in order to clarify the mechanisms applied to reach it:

(a) Striking was declared to be a tort or civil wrong, i.e. an act which made the perpetrator liable for damages, unless the damage caused to the employer could be justified. The criterion for justification has been, with modifications, the principle of social adequacy.

(b) What is "social adequacy"? Only a strike which is directed against the employer and has as its professed objective a goal which could be achieved by a collective agreement is deemed to be justified as "socially adequate." This in effect confirms the depoliticisation of strike action.

(c) The Federal Labour Court ruled that striking was a *collective* act in view of its social relevance. Up until that point, the law on industrial conflict had followed the principles of labour *contract* law: legally, the right to strike was only granted to employees who handed in due notice of termination of their employment (Erd 1978: pp. 131 ff). Now the Federal Labour Court proclaimed that strikes should no longer be judged according to individual law but according to collective law. Since then, the only criterion for the legality of a strike as a whole has been the decision of the union to strike, and the legality of that decision.

The legal assessment of striking as a collective act is clearly ambivalent. It provides employees with an advantage in that they have the legal right to strike without having to hand in their notice and without being bound by the restrictions applying to the handing in of notice. But the 1955 ruling surreptitiously deprived individual employees of the right to strike. The problem of "wild-cat" strikes did not arise until the instrument of strike was taken out of the hands of the individual employee and placed in the collective hands of the unions.

The collectivisation of strike action has had its consequences. It has meant that in plants or areas with little or no union representation, strikes are practically outlawed. And even in disputes concerning industrial production policies, or fights against the whims of management, striking is illegal because these disputes are not regulable by *collective* agreement. These are all consequences of the third key point of 1955 which still affect the situation today.

(d) And finally, the Federal Labour Court stated that industrial disputes had to be treated according to the doctrine of "parity of weapons." Labour and capital were to be treated *formally* (i. e. notwithstanding their different *substantial/ material* conditions and power) as equal. This granted not only the right of employees to strike, but also the right of employers to lock employees out. Thus the weapon of lock-out, which had been the subject of much argument in the immediate post-war years, and was even banned in the state constitution of Hessen, was legalised by the country's supreme labour court. The court actually held the effects of a lock-out to be much more extensive than those of a strike: a strike only *suspends* the contract of employment temporarily, whereas a lock-out usually *terminates* the contract. This means that locked out employees have to be re-employed, with new employment contracts, at the end of the lock-out; and this naturally permits disciplinary measures and selective non-re-employment. The courts have still not completely ruled out the employers' weapon of the terminating lock-out, although there have been some modifications since 1955.

The leading decision of 1955 created a flexible regulatory system for industrial disputes, which offered broad scope for the representation of societal interests. This is the aspect which is still relevant today, namely the reinterpretation of industrial disputes. Instead of being regarded as narrow conflicts between the two collective bargaining parties, they now became affairs of state affecting global steering and income policies. Thus the state delegated the right of industrial dispute to employees and employers, but only on the understanding that they would not abuse it to the detriment of the "common good", an attitude which the 1955 ruling touched on in its reference to "damage to the national economy".

From then on, the Federal Labour Court continued to apply the clause of social adequacy to further restrict the acceptability of industrial dispute. It even went so far as to state that events occurring within unions could be viewed as industrial disputes and as such infringed the unions' peace obligation. After the metal workers' strike in Schleswig Holstein in 1956/57, the court ruled that even a strike ballot by the workforce, i. e. an autonomous measure of the unions, could be interpreted as part of the industrial action because of its effect on the general public, and could thus constitute a breach of the obligation to keep the peace (BAG 1958). Then in 1963 the court explicitly forbade wildcat strikes, a measure which was already implied in the ruling of 1955. It defined the unions as a "responsible factor in law and order" which had to keep watch over the dangerous instrument of strike activity (BAG 1963). This was yet another attempt to bring "order" into the sphere of industrial conflict by judicial means, and thus to pacify it. Other measures taken towards restricting strikes were to forbid the collective agreement clauses mentioned at the beginning of this section (BAG 1967 and 1968), thus imposing a type of "precensorship" of admissible matters of dispute within the collective agreement and industrial action.

3. When the SPD-FDP coalition began under Willy Brandt, this industrial dispute law, which was pure case law, not legislative law, entered a marked crisis of legitimacy. At the beginning of the '70s, a strong union movement became apparent against this industrial dispute law. In 1973, the metalworkers' union held a conference entitled "Strike and

lock-out", which received considerable public attention. Statements were received from many sources, including the chemical workers' union, the printing and paperworkers' union and the Federal Executive Committee of the German Trades Union Association (DGB), in opposition to the jurisdiction of the labour courts. As it later transpired, most of the opposition was only temporary.

Too much faith was invested in the Federal Labour Court, which planned a new ruling of principle on strike and lock-out. Of course this faith was betrayed. The ruling of 21.4.1971 did not break with previous rulings; it simply updated and modified its original form (BAG 1971). It contained three basic principles which still dictate the shape of industrial dispute law today:

(a) A new doctrine began a victory march through industrial dispute law, namely the concept of "commensurability" (Verhaeltnismaessigkeit). According to this concept, there has to be a reasonable balance between the objective and the means of industrial dispute applied to achieve it. The court justified this concept by stating that an industrial dispute is a tool which guarantees the functionability of the collective bargaining process. In contrast, Article 9, para. 3 of the constitution provides that the right to strike is to be construed as a freedom of expression and action granted to employees. But the Federal Labour Court interpreted it as a means for stabilising the system.

(b) In line with the concept of commensurability, the court began to weigh certain effects of industrial dispute against each other, and to make differentiations between the sanctions ensuing from an industrial dispute. This is why terminating lock-outs were held to be illegal for certain groups of the workforce and in the early stages of an industrial dispute. Thus the normal procedure would be suspending lock-out. But the court also emphasised the fact that when an industrial dispute reaches a particular pitch, or if illegal actions occur, it becomes admissible to switch to terminating lock-out with the above-mentioned consequences, because this would then be "commensurate".

Making suspending lock-out the normal procedure was certainly a step in the right direction for the employees. But it also definitely concurred with capitalist personnel policies. For capital, the instrument of suspending lock-out has two equally desirable effects. It exerts pressure on the opposite party yet still guarantees capital the continuing existence of the workforce (particularly important in the case of certain skilled workers who cannot easily be replaced).

(c) The 1971 ruling of the Federal Labour Court meant a shift from the paradigm of "formal parity of weapons" between capital and labour (as contained in the 1955 ruling), to one of "material parity". No longer were the weapons of both sides regarded as formally equal. Now the question had become one of whether the effects of pressure and counter-pressure, offensive and defensive, were materially equal, so that there could be said to be parity of weapons. Thus even at that stage, the courts felt that ideally there should be equilibrium in industrial dispute, neutralising the opposing forces and resulting in a deadlock, so that the dispute could not be won by either party, and compromise would be the only solution.

The nature of rulings on industrial disputes has not fundamentally changed since then. The logic is not to forbid industrial dispute or certain forms of it: such a means of restricting strikes is always risky since it can actually escalate the conflict. What it does is to regulate the form of the dispute in precise detail. Since it is the courts who make this definition, using extremely vague legal doctrines such as "social adequacy" and "commensurability", it is difficult for those involved to predict the outcome of court rulings. This means that any industrial dispute runs the risk of incurring unexpected sanctions. And since, after all, as mentioned initially, the instrument of temporary injunction is being applied with increasing frequency, the whole practice of judicial regulation threatens to become a flexible means of censoring industrial dispute while collective bargaining is in force.

4. There was no fundamental change in this approach to industrial dispute jurisdiction during the time of the SPD-FDP coalition government; nor has there been since then. In other Western European countries, the advent of prolonged economic crisis, continuing mass unemployment, and conservative policies - particularly in Great Britain - has brought large-scale attempts to apply legislative means to force industrial dispute into a predictable, legally binding procedural straight-jacket. There is no such legislative activity in the Federal Republic of Germany. The straight-jacket already exists: it was already provided in essence in the court ruling of 1955. It appears to have been effective against union opposition in the early 70s as well, since there has been relatively little activity in terms of suggested alternatives to the prevailing jurisdiction on industrial disputes.

Three more recent rulings illustrate this continuing line:

(a) After the selective strikes and large-scale retaliatory lock-outs of 1978, a series of rulings was made by the Federal Labour Court on 10 June 1980 (BAG 1980 a; and Mueckenberger 1980 b). The unions had pinned great hopes on these rulings, but again they were disappointed. The rulings did not find the lock-outs illegal (as hoped by the unions), and nor did they declare that in general they suspended rather than terminated the contract of employment (which again the unions had hoped for). Instead of this, a very precise system was developed to differentiate admissible lock-outs. The court thus quantified the concept of "commensurability" which it itself had inaugurated. So, for example, if selective strike action is taken by less than 25 per cent of workers within a collective agreement area, the employer has the right to lock out up to 25 per cent of the remaining workforce. If selective strike action is taken by more than 25 per cent of workers, the employer can raise the number of those involved in the dispute to 50 per cent by means of lock-outs. The court reasoned that this apportionment of admissible lock-out percentages was in accordance with its concept of "material parity". Selective strikes affecting only a few key plants of the collective agreement area were held to disturb this parity, and parity can - according to the courts - only be re-established by lock-outs.

As soon as an industrial conflict becomes governed by rules of battle laid down in precise numerical terms, it ceases to be an activity which is subject to the autonomous will of the collective bargaining parties. It becomes instead a ritual act directed by the state. The two parties in the conflict are set up opposite each other and the court applies its assessment until the balance is redressed and the forces on both sides are neutralised and "material parity" renders the industrial dispute superfluous. This is the basis on which industrial peace is re-established, under the direction and management of the courts.

(b) In a series of rulings linked to this, the Federal Labour Court on 22. 12. 1980 reallocated the liability for payment of wages for workers indirectly affected by selective strikes (this was alluded to above, in the description of the 1984 strike) (BAG 1980 b). As already mentioned, the practice since 1923 (Reichsgericht 1923: BAG 1957) had been that in factory shut-downs resulting from industrial dispute, the employees lose their wages if the shut-down is due to a <u>strike</u>, and the employer is bound to pay employees' wages if the shut-down is the result of a <u>lock-out</u>. Now, in 1980, the Federal Labour Court ruled that the responsibility for wages lost as an indirect consequence of industrial action, i. e. wage losses suffered by employees in collective agreement areas not directly involved in the dispute but affected by it, should pass in full to the employees, regardless of whether loss of wages was due to a strike or a lock-out. In justifying this new ruling, the court stated that the unions remained responsible for lock-outs provoked by confined selective strikes. That explained why the full risk had to be carried by the employees and the unions, at least if indirect effects of the strike disturbed the balance of forces wielded by those directly involved in the dispute.

This ruling serves two purposes. The greater the wage loss suffered by employees indirectly affected by strike action, the heavier the financial burden on the union strike fund and/or the greater the material pressure in the unions to end the strike as soon as possible. Since the decision to effect lock-outs lies with the employers' associations, they are able to restrict the unions' room for political and financial manoeuvre whenever it appears appropriate to them.

(c) In 1976, the Federal Labour Court declared that brief union protest strikes were admissible after expiry of the unions' obligation to maintain the peace (BAG 1976: and Erd 1978, pp. 209 ff). This may sound surprising at first, for the legitimacy of protest strikes during the course of negotiations had previously been a controversial subject. The court justified its ruling by stating that short protest strikes were in effect a means of "flexing industrial muscle", and thus had the effect of jolting bogged-down negotiations back into life, thus in turn helping to prevent potentially long-term strikes at an early stage. Thus what may initially appear to contradict the court's efforts to reduce industrial conflict is, on closer analysis, directed precisely towards this end. In a manner of speaking, the courts would like to see the "symbolic gesture" of a state of mobilisation take the place of actual industrial action. It considers it necessary to have a safety valve to indicate <u>preparedness</u> for conflict, in order to render <u>the conflict itself</u> unnecessary.

Another ruling on union protest strikes is expected in the near future. Considering the ruling of 10. 6. 80, it is to be expected that protest strikes will also become part of this strictly defined doctrine of "commensurability". It is not inconceivable that the court will define the limits of a protest strike in terms of minutes or hours, or a certain number of strikers. That would then reduce the unions' "early warning system" to yet another legal ritual.

5. Since the changeover to conservative rule in 1982, there has been no legislative initiative in industrial dispute law, and no marked shift in the nature of court rulings. Even in the 1984 dispute over the 35-hour week - certainly one of the longest and most important disputes in the history of the Federal Republic of Germany - no serious initiatives of this type were heard. The only suggestion which was made came from the liberal economist wing of the FDP. They proposed that prior to a strike, not only union members but all members of the workforce whom the strike could potentially affect, be forced into a ballot. This suggestion is, however, unlikely to find much support.

One reason for the period of legislative and judicial peace in the field of industrial dispute law has already been named. There is no need to force industrial relations law in the Federal Republic of Germany into a straight-jacket - it has already been so confined for three decades. If the 1984 dispute proved anything at all, it proved that the straight-jacket is effective. It was quite strong enough to withstand the "heaviest strain in the whole history of the Federal Republic of Germany". The metalworkers' dispute is a perfect example of the application - and by implication, the acceptance - of the limits laid down by the judiciary. At no point have there been notable, escalating attempts at "deregulation" or "politicisation". One could almost say that this was an industrial dispute of the cashiers and the lawyers of the unions. The fact that the outcome of the dispute fell so far short of expectations fully proves the astuteness of the Federal Labour Court's prediction. It was demonstrated in this dispute that if the _forms_ of industrial dispute are regimented and ritualised, the _outcome_ of the dispute can be controlled far more effectively than it could ever be if there were an undifferentiated blanket _ban_ on industrial action. This regimentation and ritualisation of forms of industrial conflict, however, is no different from what was characterised as the procedural regulation of industrial conflict at the beginning of this paper.

Procedural law of industrial conflict does not necessarily have to be mandatory. But since it is also not to be expected that those involved in the conflict will agree on a ruling which does not coincide with it, case law then practically develops the force of statutory compulsory law. And the fact that this method of procedural regulation looks back over such firmly established tradition and recognition is probably the strongest reason why it will persist in the future.

CO-DETERMINATION AT PLANT AND COMPANY LEVEL

Throughout the history of the Federal Republic of Germany, procedural law in the fields of collective agreements and industrial dispute has been and remains relatively uniformly restrictive. Reactions to changes in economic, political and technical aspects of industrial relations have at most been indirect. It is certainly not mere chance that, as mentioned above, the attempt to make a collective agreement safeguarding the "wage drift" was defeated by a court ruling in 1968, immediately following the country's "minicrisis" of 1966/67 (Mueckenberger and Welteke 1975). The connection between the function of collective labour law and state incomes policy, which influenced judicial practice, also became apparent. And finally the whole body of restrictive industrial dispute rulings increases the interest of the employer and the system in maintaining the continuity of the production process (which was illustrated in the previous section, particularly in the shift from terminating to suspending lock-out tactics). But the fundamental line of industrial dispute rulings has remained unbroken.

Works constitution and company co-determination law, on the other hand, have been subject to far more active legislative and judicial change since the early 1970s. The foundations of plant and company co-determination were laid in the early years of consolidation of the Federal Republic of Germany (Schmidt 1970). Very few of the demands for reform which existed immediately after the war were able to survive the Adenauer era. The 1951 Coal, Iron and Steel Industries Co-Determination Act was the only model of equal co-determination (paritaetische Mitbestimmung). And the 1952 Works Constitution Act fell far short of both the Employees' Council Acts immediately after the war, and the demands of the unions. It divided the Employees' Councils and the unions, and banished the unions from the plant. The legal form of representation of interests was different in the private and public sectors. Employees' plant bargaining committees had only peripheral rights of participation in economic affairs.

For almost 20 years there was no activity in this area of collective industrial law. But then the period of the SPD-FDP coalition saw major changes. A revised Works Constitution Act came into force in 1972. Although it retained the fundamental principles of the 1952 law, major aspects came a long way towards meeting union demands on participation

(Zachert 1979). Greater rights of participation in regulating hours and wages were granted, Employees' Councils had more opportunity to influence personnel policies and the ergonomics of the workplace, and the competence of conciliation boards for settling industrial disputes was considerably increased. The scope of participation was particularly extended on the social and personnel level, but on the economic level the 1972 reform did no more than extend information and consultation rights.

A new act on co-determination at company level was introduced in 1976 (Nagel 1980). In German law, the major feature of co-determination at company level is employee representation on the supervisory board of corporations, with defined numbers of seats and votes. The unions have always demanded equal co-determination rights at board level ("parity of capital and labour"). Since the reform of 1976, there have been three different forms of co-determination at this level:

- In companies in the coal, iron and steel sector, employees and employers are equally (paritaetisch) represented on the supervisory board. The chair, and thus also the casting vote on this committee, is controlled by both parties. Co-determination in this sector also means that the personnel director, who is responsible for personnel and social welfare matters, has to be trusted by the unions.
- Corporations with a normal workforce of more than 2,000 are subject to the 1976 Co-Determination Act. Equal numbers of employees and employers make up the supervisory board. But there is no parity, since managerial staff representatives are counted as employees, and the chair and casting vote are held by an employer, who can overrule the representatives of the employees in the event of a deadlock.
- In other corporations, employees have a one-third representation (seats and votes) on the supervisory board.

Thus the 1976 reform brought a not inconsiderable change to the whole of industry, which, with the exception of the coal, iron and steel sector, had until that time only been granted the last of these three types of co-determination. Although it still did not provide absolute equality of co-determination on the supervisory board, by increasing the representation of the employees, it increased pressure on the employer to reach agreement, since if capital constantly had to resort to the power of the casting vote, the efficiency of the supervisory board as a functional organ of the company would be severely restricted.

Analysis of the activities of the courts in these areas of regulation again reinforces the impression that, compared with earlier years, there has been considerable discontinuity since the beginning of the 1970s. In all major matters concerning details of the 1972 Works Constitution Act, there has been a judicial tug-of-war, too complex to describe here. But the jurisdiction of the Federal Labour Court has not in principle dissociated itself from the attitude of the reformed law extending participation. It has applied the "progressive" concepts of the act in individual cases arising in social and personnel matters and rights of the Employees' Council to information and consultation. Admittedly, decisions of the Federal Labour Court have become more restrictive again recently. For example, in 1983, the court refused to grant Employees' Councils a general injunction against an employer who introduces measures which contravene the Works Constitution Act (BAG 1983 a). This considerably restricts plant-level implementation of the law. Towards the end of 1983, the court made a very restricted interpretation of the participation rights of Employees' Councils in the matter of installing screens (BAG 1983 b). However, it is still impossible to say whether these restrictive rulings constitute a new trend in court attitudes.

The 1976 Co-Determination Act was not disregarded by the judiciary as had been feared by many in the initial period after it was introduced. Leading German corporations brought a much-publicised case against the act to the Federal Constitution Court, and in 1979 the court ruled that the law was unreservedly constitutional (Bundesverfassungsgericht 1979). The court referred in particular to the positive effect of equal co-determination in dealing with industrial and technological change in the coal, iron and steel industry, and expressed the hope that this positive experience might be repeated in large industrial sectors currently in turmoil. The highest constitutional court thus upheld the act as a whole, as in 1982 the supreme civil court had made a series of rulings against attempts to evade parts of it (Bundesgerichtshof 1982). Attempts of individual corporations to change the legally prescribed balance of the supervisory board in their favour, by creating and changing autonomous rules, were defined as contrary to the 1976 Co-Determination Act and were therefore inadmissible. Although application of the 1976 Co-Determination Act has repeatedly been associated with attempts to undermine it, we are not witnessing general restrictive practice or a change in jurisdiction policies in line with current political changes.

What, then, is the explanation for this positive attitude towards employees in the areas of plant and company level participation since the beginning of the 70s, which has clearly not been obstructed by recent political changes? Without underestimating the force of changes in the political climate, I nevertheless ascribe it primarily to the specific nature of the acts governing plant and company level participation. This is indicated by the quote from the co-determination ruling of the Federal Constitution Court. In a phase of rapid economic and social change and crisis-induced restructuring, plants and companies are under pressure to innovate and adapt. The traditional methods of authoritarian factory regulation cannot counteract this pressure. Expert opinion has long since come to agree that the massive modernisation programme which decimated mining in the Ruhr in 1968 could never have been executed so smoothly had it not been for the form of participation and co-determination already established in the coal, iron and steel industry. Interpretations by both the left and right endow the co-determination model in this industrial sector with the necessary power to adapt and integrate. The difference is that one side interprets this as a loss of union identity, and even "corruption" of its full-time officials, whereas the other sees it as a successful approach to modernisation by participation.

Both plant constitutional law and the law governing co-determination at company level are <u>mandatory procedural laws</u>. Neither the 1972 Works Constitution Act nor the 1976 Co-Determination Act contains substantive standards for the working and social conditions of employees. Both merely lay down procedural conditions. They determine in legal terms clearly defined areas which will be the subject of negotiations. They define the negotiating parties themselves, and the forums at which negotiations can take place. And they define the mode of reaching a decision if consensus cannot be achieved by negotiation. But by laying down the means whereby a decision is to be reached, other means are automatically legally excluded. Thus for example, since the 1972 Works Constitution Act grants the conciliation board the right to decide on a local industrial conflict (§76), it follows that it expressly forbids the Employees' Council from having recourse to open conflict, i.e. strike activity, as a means of decision making (§74).

Mandatory procedural regulation in industrial conflict on plant and company level is an extremely ambivalent arrangement. It provides employees and their representatives with a guarantee that certain procedures will be followed. Without them, the procedure would not be guaranteed or would have to be contested every time. But at the same time, mandatory procedural regulation is a restriction. It only leaves room for substantive results which can be achieved by means of negotiation and co-operation between capital and labour. If acceptable substantive results can only be obtained by "flexing industrial muscle", taking recourse to the social balance of power, and open conflict, then mandatory procedural regulation becomes a dangerous functional system acting against employees and their representatives. Presumably this is one of the reasons for increased legal recognition of employees' participation over the past $1\frac{1}{2}$ years.

COURT RULINGS

[1]Reichsgericht 1923: 6.2.1923, Amtliche Entscheidungssammlung des Reichsgericht in Zivilsachen Band 106, S. 272 ff.

[2]Landesarbeitsgericht Frankfurt 1953: 20.2.1953, Recht der Arbeit 1953, S. 195.

Landesarbeitsgericht Berlin 1954: 17.8.1954, Neue Juristische Wochenschrift 1954, S. 142.

[3]Bundesarbeitsgericht 1955: 28.1.1955, Arbeitsrechtliche Praxis Nr. 1 zu Art. 9 GG - Arbeitskampf -.

Bundesarbeitsgericht 1957: 8.2.1957, Arbeitsrechtliche Praxis Nr. 2 zu § 615 BGB - Betriebsrisiko -.

Bundesarbeitsgericht 1958: 31.10.1958, Arbeitsrechtliche Praxis Nr. 2 zu § 1 Tarifvertragsgesetz

Bundesarbeitsgericht 1963: 20.12.1963, Arbeitsrechtliche Praxis Nr. 32 und 33 zu Art. 9 GG - Arbeitskampf -.

Bundesarbeitsgericht 1967: 29.11.1967, Arbeitsrechtliche Praxis Nr. 13 zu Art. 9 GG.

Bundesarbeitsgericht 1968: 14.12.1968, Arbeitsrechtliche Praxis Nr. 7 zu § 4 Tarifvertragsgesetz - Effektivklausel -.

Bundesarbeitsgericht 1971: 10.4.1971, Arbeitsrechtliche Praxis Nr. 43 zu Art. 9 GG - Arbeitskampf -.

Bundesarbeitsgericht 1976: 17.12.1976, Arbeitsrechtliche Praxis Nr. 51 zu Art. 9 GG - Arbeitskampf -.

[4]Bundesverfassungsgericht 1979: 1.3.1979, Amtliche Entscheidungssammlung Bd. 50, S. 290 ff.

Bundesarbeitsgericht 1980 a: 10. 6. 1980, Arbeitsrechtliche Praxis Nr. 64 - 66 zu Art. 9 GG - Arbeitskampf -.

Bundesarbeitsgericht 1980 b: 22. 12. 1980, Amtliche Entscheidungssammlung Bd. 34, S. 331 ff., 355 ff.

[5]Bundesgerichtshof 1982: 25. 2. 1982, Amtliche Entscheidungssammlung des Bundesgerichtshofs in Zivilsachen Bd. 83, S. 106 ff. 145 ff., 163 ff.

Bundesarbeitsgericht 1983 a: 22. 2. 1983, Betriebsberater 1983, S. 1724 ff.

Bundesarbeitsgericht 1983 b: 6. 12. 1983, not yet published, (see: Presseinformation Nr. 24/83).

1. Supreme Court of the Third Reich
2. Regional Labour Court
3. Federal Labour Court
4. Federal Constitutional Court
5. Federal Supreme Court

REFERENCES

Blanke, T., et al. (Hrsg.), 1975: Kollektives Arbeitsrecht. Quellentexte zur Geschichte des Arbeitsrechts in Deutschland, 2 Baende, Reinbek

Bley, H., 1982: Sozialrecht, 4. Auflage, Frankfurt

Clegg, H. A., 1980: The Changing System of Industrial Relations in Great Britain, Oxford

Colneric, N., 1984, in: W. Daeubler (Hrsg.), Arbeitskampfrecht, Baden-Baden

Daeubler, W., 1979 und 1982: Das Arbeitsrecht, 2 Baende, Reinbek

Daeubler, W. und Hege, H., 1981: Tarifvertragsrecht, Baden-Baden

Erd, R., 1978: Verrechtlichung industrieller Konflikte, Frankfurt/New York

Korsch, K., 1922: Arbeitsrecht fuer Betriebsraete, Berlin

Mueckenberger, U., 1980 a: Der Demonstrationsstreik, in: Kritische Justiz 13, S. 258 ff

Mueckenberger, U., 1980 b: Der Arbeitskampf als staatlich inszeniertes Ritual, in: Blaetter fuer Steuerrecht, Sozialversicherung und Arbeitsrecht 35, S. 241 ff., 257 ff

Mueckenberger, U., 1984: Arbeiterbewegung und Arbeitsrecht, in: Eyferth, H., et al. (Hrsg.), Handbuch zur Sozialarbeit/Sozialpaedagogik, Neuwied und Darmstadt,

S. 122 ff
Mueckenberger, U., und M. Welteke, 1975: Krisenzyklen, Einkommenspolitik und Arbeitsrechtsentwicklung in der BRD, in: Kritische Justiz 8, S. 1 ff
Nagel, B., 1980: Unternehmensmitbestimmung, Koeln
Schmidt, E., 1970, Die verhinderte Neuordnung 1945 - 1952, Frankfurt
Soellner, A., 1981: Arbeitsrecht, 7. Aufl., Stuttgart
Zachert, U., 1979: Betriebliche Mitbestimmung, Koeln

Chapter 12

INSTITUTIONAL STRATEGIES FOR TRADE UNION PARTICIPATION: AN ASSESSMENT OF THE INCORPORATION THESIS

Hans Kastendiek, Hella Kastendiek, Hugo Reister

THESES ON THE "INCORPORATION OF TRADE UNIONS"

In West Germany, more than in most other West European countries, many mechanisms of co-operation have developed between the state, capital and trade unions. Among the features of these mechanisms we can note that:

(i) they are found in the factory, the enterprise, the sector, and macro-economic steering as well as locally, regionally and nationally;
(ii) they embrace economic and social policy and many other policy fields;
(iii) they are institutionalised and legalised to varying extents but also operate in an informal and non-regulated way;
(iv) they are based on bilateral relations between the state, capital and trade unions, which are often combined into trilateral and tripartite arrangements; and
(v) they are not only materially based in such phenomena as distribution policy but also have roots in social ideologies and behaviour patterns which involve the acceptance of a basic social consensus (or what is held to be one).

This close relationship between the state and trade unions led to the thesis of an "incorporation of unions into the state". For W. Mueller-Jentsch (1976) these tendencies are "associated with the growth in the economic functions of the State" and a Keynesian growth and full employment policy. As

> capital, protected by property guarantees, remains under private control, and the trade unions' legal status

> as a party to free collective bargaining can hardly be disputed, state economic policy can realise its objectives only by influencing the decisions of entrepreneurs and trade unions.

In this process, trade union wage policy in particular is functionalised through "state incomes policies into a conjuncture-political instrument of the state." Other authors who also argue in this way even speak of a 'statisation' (Verstaatlichung) of the trade unions (e. g. E. Schmidt 1976).

Similar theses have emerged from the corporatism debate on the increasing interconnection of political and socio-economic relations and the corresponding institutional interpenetration. Corporatism in its present form originated through the consensual establishment of negotiating structures and co-operative relations among the state, capital and trade unions. The continuation of these structures and relations, in particular through institutionalisation and legalisation, changed the mechanisms of economic and social policy-making and curtailed the participants' scope for action. In West Germany, the corporatism thesis was formulated most sharply by J. Esser and W. Fach (1979). Their analysis of crisis policies in the steel industry revealed a crisis cartel "in which the entrepreneurs of the steel industry, the responsible state institutions and the union involved came together informally" and formed a "corporatist bloc". This thesis was later extended to the "Modell Deutschland" as a whole. This term originated as an electoral slogan of the SPD and was transformed into an analytical and critical concept for assessing the highly-structured relationships among the state, enterprises and trade unions in West Germany (e. g. Esser 1982).

In our view such theses do not capture the complexity of the relationship among the state, capital and trade unions. Are the unions incorporated "into the state" or locked into economic steering processes? Is union wage policy subject to state influence or is it accepted as a constraint on the state's policy-making? What exactly does "statisation" of the unions mean? This label might be justified if it describes the unions' orientation towards the state or the fixation with the state in union politics and the manifold interpenetrations of this politics with state and party institutions. But this cannot justify one in speaking of an "<u>incorporation</u> of trade unions <u>into the state</u>". Certainly, the unions have assumed "the status of a quasi-public body through the allocation to them of public tasks and responsibilities" (Mueller-Jentsch, 1976). However, they could hardly be said to have become a part of the state apparatus, quite apart from the fact that the state would then have "incorporated" their socio-economic functions as well. In addition the concepts of a "crisis cartel" and a "corporatist bloc" are precarious. They assume a solidity of co-operative relations, a common political orientation, and a far-reaching institutional interpenetration which does not exist. Talk of a corporatist bloc is the result of generalising observations about problem sectors and enterprises. The authors observed co-operative strategies to solve crises and noted how these strategies were oriented towards the interest of core work forces and disadvantaged the peripheral work force. As important as these analyses are for our subject-area, however, it would be misleading to apply their findings to the political organisation of society as a whole. Yet this is what the authors have done: the principal characteristic of the German Model is, in their view, a bloc policy pursued by the core of society within the framework of, and as a consequence of, a coalition between the state, capital and trade unions.

In our opinion the concept of "incorporation" must be specified in the light of the societal constellation of present-day capitalist democracies. First, incorporation should not be equated with the obvious complex of interrelations between societal organisations and institutions into which the unions, no matter how asymmetrically, are drawn. The mechanisms listed above provide a framework for a possible incorporation but do not prove that it has occurred. Second, incorporation should not be discussed in terms of an absorption of one organisation or institution into another. The complex of interrelations cannot be comprehended as a "statisation of society, of the interest organisations, of the trade unions" or, conversely, as a "socialisation of the state", so that it has become a "pressure-group state", or even, indeed, a "trade union state". It can be situated neither in the political system nor in a system of interest articulation. It can more fittingly be seen as part of the political organisation of society. Third, this complex contains structures which can be called corporative and it also serves as the point of reference for corporative strategies. It is quite wrong to say that this complex of relationships has solidified, in its entirety, into a neo-corporatist system.

What might already have emerged, or is perhaps emerg-

> ing, however, is a network of corporative structures _within_ the existing political organisation of society. Such structures have evidently been formed in various areas of society, in many policy fields, and on different levels of the organisation of domination. (The task of analysis is to show) how they are connected with one another, how they complement and support one another, and whether, from them, a socio-political formation has resulted which goes beyond the normal patterns of integration in capitalist society (Hans Kastendiek 1980: 96).

Fourth, those structures and strategies can be conceived as corporative which involve functional or vocational groups becoming institutions for the implementation and intermediation of socio-politico authority. Trade unions are bound into a corporative network both as organisations between capital and labour and as mediating institutions between the state and/or political system, on the one hand, and wage- and salary-earners, on the other (this essential of corporatism has been described very clearly by Crouch 1983).

We can now formulate _our thesis_: one can talk of an "incorporation of the trade unions" when, as intermediary organisations between capital and labour as well as between wage- and salary-earners and the state/the political system, they are bound by manifold institutional, legal, political, economic, ideological and habitual mechanisms into a complex of relationships and institutions among the state, capital and trade unions which curtails their scope for action, but is nevertheless the essential point of reference for their politics.

Our thesis avoids two assertions: _first_, it leaves room for the perception of _non_-corporative structures and strategies. The weakness of some theoretical approaches lies in the fact that their prognoses of an increasing stabilisation of "liberal corporatism" have been disproven again and again, especially as governments, capital and trade unions have frequently switched to non-corporatist strategies. But the scope for such switches is typically over-estimated. A concrete policy is mostly a mixture of different strategies. The instability or even dissolution of a corporative structure can certainly change the "network of corporative structures", but can hardly render it completely inoperative. Typically the network is only re-structured and continues to express or displace conflict. In analysing the politics of West German trade unions, this should lead to scepticism about recurrent interpretations which already see evidence of an emergent autonomy for the unions from political restraints. Second, our thesis does not imply that the unions appear only as the object of integrative strategies. The unions themselves either demand, or enter consciously into, corporative structures, because they see them as means of implementing their political objectives.

To examine our incorporation thesis we have chosen the area of macro-economic co-determination because it makes especially clear trade union strategies in the complex of relationships among the state, capital and unions. G. Leminsky sees this area as:

> the totality of procedures and institutions through which the unions - above the level of the enterprise and beyond the traditional scope of free collective bargaining - seek to improve the living conditions and possibilities for self-development of wage- and salary-earners (1971: 602).

In this area we shall investigate three cases which dominated trade union discussions in the late sixties and in the seventies: (i) incomes policy and the Concerted Action, (ii) the Commission for Economic and Social Change, (iii) trade union demands for Economic and Social Councils.

Incomes policy and, for the Federal Republic, the Concerted Action stand (stood) in the centre of most incorporation theses. The other cases have been relatively neglected. For the Commission did not get very much public attention and the demands for Economic and Social Councils were never realised. In addition the latter two cases have been regarded merely as a programmatic exercise of the unions. But these cases are also very instructive in assessing West German trade union strategies up to the present as will be shown in the last section which discusses some developments in recent years.

FOUNDATIONS OF AN INSTITUTIONAL STRATEGY

Trade Unions, State Incomes Policy and Concerted Action (CA)

1. State incomes policy as pursued from 1966/67 onwards originally met the main objectives of the unions (here we only refer to the unions of the DGB, the German Trade Union Federation). Central to the "economic policy principles" of the 1963 Grundsatzprogramm was the maintenance of full employ-

ment through continuous economic growth. This was to be achieved through scientifically-based, co-ordinated and planned policies, which were also intended to facilitate a fairer distribution of income and wealth. The unions were prepared to accept national budget guidelines, worked out jointly with them, as "orientation data for our own free decisions".

This offer was taken up under the "new economic policy" of the Grand Coalition formed by Christian and Social Democrats from 1966 to 1969, a policy, which was inspired by the SPD. The Stability and Growth Act of 1967, as a "procedural 'Basic Law' of the market economy" (Schlecht), complemented the "global steering" of the economy through monetary and fiscal policies with the instrument of an incomes policy. The government has to deliver an annual economic report, which, among other things, has to concretise its economic and finance policy objectives for the year in progress. In the event of the macro-economic balance becoming endangered, the government has "to make available orientation data for the mutually co-ordinated behaviour (concerted action) of the bodies of the public sector, trade unions and associations of enterprises" (paragraph three). The national budget in the DGB programme had thus become an annual government report; the objectives to be decided jointly had become orientation data from the government. The CA, not described in any greater detail in legislation, received the character of a "permanent dialogue between the institutions of the state and the autonomous groups" (Schlecht 1968: 17). The unions, without whose co-operation the "new economic policy" would have been unsuccessful, nevertheless saw a new chance to introduce and implement political objectives, especially as many remarks made by K. Schiller (Social Democratic Minister of Economic Affairs) were, or could be, interpreted as meaning that the trade unions were to be conceded "an active participation in the formulation of government's economic policy" (Seitenzahl 1974: 63).

The government's policy concept was "in large measure" identical with the unions' own basic programme (Markmann 1967). Although freedom of collective bargaining was not suspended, it was nevertheless modified since participation in "any planning" of macro-economic data implied a "prior decision" over wages policy. In exchange for the trade unions' prior contributions in the field of wages policy to overcoming the recession of 1966/67, "social symmetry" had to be achieved by means of social policy: through a "policy of redistribution of wealth heavily promoted by the state", through a better education policy and an "expansion of factory, and implementation of supra-factory, co-determination", which enabled the trade unions to "participate in the formulation of the objectives of economic and social policy". The continuous participation of unions in such framework planning demanded a firmly institutionalised CA (Markmann 1967; cf. also Henschel 1967).

2. When the trade unions tried to realise these objectives after the recession (from autumn 1967 onwards), they were opposed by the employers. For the latter did not accept that such issues belonged to the macro-economic management tasks of the CA (cf. Bretschneider 1969). Thus, after the general election of 1969, broad domestic policy topics no longer appeared on the agenda of the CA. In addition, the trade unions now discovered that their participation in the development of orientation data in the framework of the CA "is neither anticipated, nor are there preliminary ideas for such a development" (Henschel 1969). This combined with the restriction of union wage policy through orientation data which were confined to wages rather than extending to all incomes (against which the unions continually protested - cf. Seitenzahl 1974: 110 ff.) to prevent the realisation of trade union ideas. The hopes "of the majority of leading unionists of a co-operative relationship, based on equal rights, with the SPD" (Seitenzahl 1976: 22) had thus been disappointed.

Leading trade unionists and DGB academics and, in particular, functionaries and activists from the middle and lower levels more and more criticised the disadvantages of the CA. At the congresses of the IG Metall trade union in 1969 and 1971 and of the DGB in 1969, the leadership had to react to the criticism from active members and try to legitimate trade union involvement in the CA. Although they initially defended "their participation more aggressively, by emphasising the alleged scope for moulding policy through the CA, they later operated defensively by playing down the significance of the Concerted Action as a non-binding discussion forum." In particular, the leadership denied that collective bargaining policy had been constrained by orientation data and the practice of the CA (Bergmann 1975: 82). This line of argument certainly contradicted statements in many trade union publications, but it was nonetheless "necessary" to refute criticism of past and future participation in the CA. The executive boards of the trade unions obviously saw no possibility of a withdrawal.

3. The experience with the CA did not provoke any

discussion over alternative strategies. The unions remained participants although no side any longer had "any interest in this meeting" (Adam 1972: 93). On the one hand, the unions played down the CA; on the other, union leaders justified further participation with the arguments that the CA provided an opportunity to represent trade union positions and that the field of public discussion should not be abandoned to the entrepreneurs. In 1977, the DGB stayed away from the CA in protest against the employers' appeal over the co-determination law to the Federal Constitutional Court. This was in no way intended to indicate a final breakdown of the CA, but rather as a clear warning to the employers. At the 1977 congress, E. Loderer warned the IG Metall against going it alone and leaving the CA. Instead he recommended consultations with other unions. And as congress demanded the setting up of economic and social councils, it could not therefore pursue a "policy of the empty chair" (Protokoll 1977: 249 ff. and 335). While Loderer indicated willingness to participate further in the CA, the chairman of the IG Chemie, K. Hauenschild, expected that the DGB would soon return to the CA (cf. Frankfurter Rundschau 30 January 1978 and 3 March 1979). The 1978 DGB congress also kept the question open by rejecting a motion which wanted in principle to exclude any further participation in the CA. But it announced its preparedness to discuss with the government measures aimed at realising the objectives laid down in the Stability and Growth Act.

So it was in 1979 that a government press spokesman could argue that, following the collapse of the CA, the government had "carried out" the "prescribed economic policy 'harmonisation' with the parties to collective bargaining" in bilateral talks (Frankfurter Rundschau 3 March 1979). After the co-determination judgment of the Federal Constitutional Court, the DGB signalled its readiness to talk with the employers as well "in order to re-establish the old foundation for reciprocal relations" (Frankfurter Rundschau 8 May 1979). Although the Economics Minister was trying to set up a new version of the CA, this proved contentious. It was in the interest of the trade unions to have a "more efficient form" of the CA, as it was "certainly dispensable in its form up until now" (Loderer 1979) and had made it more difficult to safeguard the interests of wage- and salary-earners' (Kluncker, cf. Frankfurter Rundschau 18 December 1980). These assessments validated intra-trade-union criticism after the event. The Economic Minister succeeded only once (in January 1980) in bringing about a round of talks with trade unionists and employers together.

4. The fact that the CA remained "dispensable", is possibly due to the development of a "secret institution" (Piel 1979): the "Kanzlerrunde". This "discreet circle" (ibid.) with a few representatives from the trade unions and employers was called together at irregular intervals during the life of the CA. Its proceedings were strictly confidential and were said to be efficient and successful. Its "decisive purpose" was to create a climate favouring a consensus in, among other fields, distribution policy. This circle can be interpreted as a "substitute" for the CA; it appears to have taken over some of its functions. For H. O. Vetter (then chairman of the DGB) felt that it was a perfect model for a "really effective discussion", because the participants managed to "speak with one another in a way which we did not have in the old Concerted Action" (TV interview, printed in: Der Arbeitgeber, no. 20/31, 1979: 1072).

Thus experiences with the CA have not caused much change in trade unions' fundamental preparedness to co-operate with the state and entrepreneurs in economic and social policy. More than this, they participated at the highest executive board level in a deliberative circle, which was described as Helmut Schmidt's own "form of Concerted Action in politics". This form advanced "co-determination as a technique of government" but only "for the smallest possible group". Together with the international economic pressure for a domestic political consensus, this had accelerated tendencies "which one can in fact call corporatism" (Hofmann 1980).

The Commission for Economic and Social Change

1. The "commission" was formed in 1971 and dissolved, with the publication of its concluding report, in 1977. It was a successor of the "working group on automation", which had been set up in 1969 within the framework of the CA. Both bodies originated on the suggestion, and as a result of the pressure, of the trade unions. The IG Metall, which, under the impact of technical and structural changes in the 1960s, had held several conferences on automation, first demanded a "co-ordinated action of trade unions, employers, science and the state" in 1965. "All ministerial, scientific and private activities" should be co-ordinated in "permanent institutions" in order to guarantee an effective structural and growth policy. This demand was repeated several times and spelled out most precisely by O. Brenner (then chairman of the IG

Metall). He suggested a quadripartite "German Commission for Technical and Structural Change", among whose tasks should be the systematic promotion of new technologies and research into the social and economic effects of technological developments (cf. Brenner 1967: 23 ff.). After discussions in the CA, the "working group on automation" was agreed to. It was a relatively informal body with no specific tasks nor any statutory-organisational anchoring. Nevertheless, the employers proved to be "very co-operative and sensible" (Geschaeftsbericht der IG Metall 1968-70, p. 90). In contrast, the unions criticised the representatives of the state, who sought to hinder any discussions aimed at reaching settlements between the groups. Therefore, a commission "independent of the government", with a "legislative basis" and "similar to the Council of Economic Experts" was demanded (Protokoll of the IG Metall 1968, p. 221). In 1971, the Social Democratic-Liberal government gave in to the "pressure of the trade unions" (Lecher 1977: 172) and transformed the "working group on automation" into the "Commission for Economic and Social Change".

2. The "Commission", with five representatives each from the trade unions and the employers and with seven academics, all nominated *ad hominem* by the government, was to draw up a "report on the problems associated with technical, economic and social change, with a view to the further development of social policy (Gesellschaftspolitik)" (Gutachten 1977: 4). This body's scope for action and conflict was limited by its formal assignment and its statute, which was predetermined by the state. The commission was to "illuminate the possibilities in economic and social policy of promoting technical and social change in the German economy, *within the framework of a market economy*, and to shape it in the interests of the population" (ibid., p. 4; our italics). This meant that a "systemic limit" was set from the start: the use of power for private economic purposes was made taboo. Moreover, a conflict-regulating mechanism was built into the commission: it "makes public statements only in the form of the final report. It can publish the results of the investigations carried out under its commission, but may not take a public stance on them before the final report" (ibid., p. 5). This created a pressure towards consensus and taking joint responsibility for majority decisions; differing opinions could only be expressed in the concluding report.

3. For the unions these restrictions did not diminish the high status of this body. In the DGB working group on

"Economic and Social Change", which comprised 40 persons, a comprehensive, scientifically-orientated "back-up service" was installed to support the representatives in the Commission. The strategy of the unions was to prove the superiority of their standpoint quasi-scientifically. Almost all the work of the trade union members in the commission was taken over by this working group (cf. Lecher 1977).

The employers, who managed without such documents, behaved co-operatively when it came to determining the main topics and awarding research contracts, but obstructed all discussions on political questions (for example, extension of co-determination). They could usually find support in the interpretations of the academics, who, as representatives of the "general interest", oriented themselves towards the status quo (ibid., p. 181). Thus, it was obvious that trade union demands were pruned down considerably, despite numerous minority votes, while the employers' basic line was adopted (see Bispinck and Wilhelm 1977: 148).

4. The state's pre-determination of the framework sufficed to achieve the political goal: to facilitate the formation of a wide consensus and to make it effective within the body. The concluding report of 1977 lays

> its principal emphasis not on the proving of theoretically possible alternatives for action (...), but on those upon which, in the area of conflict between the different standpoints represented in the commission, it proved possible to reach a consensus, or with which a consensus seemed attainable in an earlier stage of discussion (Gutachten, p. 6).

Generally, the commission assumes

> that a fundamental consensus exists over medium- and long-term economic policy objectives between all societally relevant groups in the Federal Republic. The relatively great stability of our social system is the most important underlying pre-condition for the further development and modernisation of our economy. The work of this commission bears testimony to the existence of a fundamental consensus (ibid., p. 43).

The union representatives shared this assessment. G. Friedrichs found the adaptation process within the commission "noteworthy" and useful. He did not even mention the curtailment of responsibilities, but almost euphorically stressed the "unusually high status of the commission", its unique assignment" and its "unique composition". "For the first time the unions had the chance to participate jointly in developing the long-term planning of governmental tasks" (Gewerkschaftlich kommentierter Kurzbericht, p. 12).

This statement certainly illustrates the ideas of the trade unions - but not the work of the commission. In no way did the government expect it to present concrete reform proposals for social policy. For the form of integration (ad hominem appointments, "global" final report with advisory status only) was too non-binding. Rather, on the side of the state, the crucial thing was the very process of clarifying opinions, the attempt to establish a further foundation and a further area of activity for the social-partnership approach. The report is not significant because of its contents, but - as a journalist accurately perceived - "its strength lies elsewhere. Because of the composition of the commission, it is an integral part of the process by which the foundations of the social consensus are held intact in the Federal Republic" (Herlt, cited in Bispinck and Wilhelm 1977: 148).

Trade Unions Demands for Economic and Social Councils (ESC)

1. Trade union ideas about ESCs were closely related for a time to the discussion about the CA and the Commission for Economic and Social Change. ESCs were to eradicate the deficiencies and disadvantages of the existing forms of supra-factory co-determination and to be centre-pieces of a "broad system" for exercising trade union influence. "Processes such as the 'Concerted Action' and committees for investigating special issues of technical change and vocational training, to name only a few examples, could be drawn into these bodies or connected to it" (Leminsky 1971: 609). ESCs are a traditional demand of the DGB, although they are not mentioned explicitly in a basic programme until 1981. They took a major role in the "DGB's proposal for a law on a new order for the West German Economy" in 1950. (cf. Gesetzesvorschlag des DGB zur Neuordnung der deutschen Wirtschaft 1950 and Otto 1971: 111 ff.). The ESC theme was confirmed again in 1956 but soon afterwards it no longer seemed to be an issue, as the balance of forces hardly gave grounds for expecting that it could be realised. From 1966-67 onwards, when the party majorities had changed and the instruments of economic policy were generally discussed (cf. 2.1 and 2.2.), the DGB saw a new opportunity for establishing ESCs. In 1969, when the Social Democrats and the Liberals formed their first coalition, the DGB again demanded co-determination in the macro-econ-

omic area as well. With confidence in the promise contained in the government programme that the question was being examined thoroughly, and in the general "reform euphoria" of that time, the DGB continued to work on a plan for supra-factory co-determination. In 1971 its federal committee adopted detailed demands for bipartite ESCs on the national, federal state, and economic region levels (cf. Mitbestimmung 1971).

2. ESCs are intended to help realise the main objectives of the DGB: "Macro-economic co-determination ought to ensure that the interests of wage- and salary-earners become part of an anticipatory and planned economic policy". It was not possible to exercise influence in the sense that the unions could enjoy a "direct co-decision-making right" and an "obligation for co-responsibility", of course, as "the overall responsibility of government and Parliament might be prejudiced". Nevertheless the "information, advisory and consultation rights" of the ESCs were broadly defined: the Federal ESC was "responsible for general economic and social policy, including finance, tax and transport policies, in so far as the interests of wage- and salary-earners are affected by them." It would be entitled to give opinions and have evidence submitted to it, to conduct enquiries, to summon ministers and heads of public authorities, to comment on draft laws and to take initiatives on legislation itself. These rights would belong to just one-third of the bipartite body! The efficiency of the ESC's work was to be ensured by "permanent offices" and permanent committees. The plenary assembly and committees were to meet, in principle, in public. Corresponding regulations were to apply for the ESCs in the Federal States (Laender) and the economic regions. The state ESCs were responsible "in particular for structural, transport, labour market, energy and housing market policies, as well as vocational training". The regional councils had similar tasks; above all, they were to take over the legal functions of the chambers of industry and commerce and of the chambers of craft enterprises, which, as the DGB had often demanded, would then lose their public status (all quotations: Mitbestimmung 1971).

3. Trade union justifications of ESCs (cf. Gewerkschaftliche Monatshefte, nos. 9 and 10, 1971, no. 10, 1973) mostly refer to the increasing steering of socio-economic processes by the state, to the dependence of wage- and salary-earners on the decisions of entrepreneurs, to continuing economic concentration and to centralisation of economic policy decisions.

The arguments, however, followed different lines.

A power-analytic argument can be found, for example, in articles by W. Kaltenborn (1971, 1973). The fundamental structure of society has not really changed since capitalist industrialisation. Wage- and salary-earners and trade unions are still systematically and structurally disadvantaged. ESCs could be essential steps towards strengthening their position in society. In particular the principle that council proceedings be open to the public would prevent the continuing dominance of business standpoints in public opinion. The entrepreneurs' advantage in relations with the state and their informal intercourse with the administration would, for example, be made more difficult. The principle of parity would no longer make the unions appear to be just one of many interest groups. Kaltenbach even argued that ESCs could spur on "a change in the system" (1971).

B. Otto (1971), too, observes unequal structures of influence and deficiencies in implementing trade union objectives. For him, however, ESCs are not instruments of an oppositional force (Gegenmacht), but a means whereby trade unions and businessmen can be committed in the same way to the "general interest of the state" (p. 167)! He developed a normative argument in favour of an Ordnungspolitik which is a clear example of neo-corporatist thought:

> A federal economic and social council opens the way to an institution oriented towards the general interest, bound by a responsibility for the economy as a whole, and adapted to the needs of interest-representation based on equal rights. Instead of an 'optional' exertion of influence, the legally binding inclusion of wage- and salary-earners' organisations as well as of employers' associations in the process of economic policy formation would be realised (p. 198).
>
> The take-over of sovereign functions (...) demands the subordination of associations' interests to a general will formulated at the peak of the economy and the preparedness of the participants to implement the decisions, once they are made, on the middle level of their own organisations (p. 203).
>
> The unions are then no longer an independent organisation of struggle (Kampfverbund) for the implementation of wage- and salary-earners' interests, but instead take over the role of a 'bearer of sovereignty', which aggregates and represents the 'partial' interests of a

> certain population group. The unions become 'keepers of order' (Ordnungsfaktoren) (ibid.).
> The assumption of sovereign functions has the consequence that the unions or the wage- and salary-earners sent by them into the councils are subject to direct state supervision and control (p. 204).
> The realisation of supra-factory co-determination will influence profoundly the position and function of the unions in our society (p. 205).

All this without any trace of critical concern!

4. We have found no debate between these two lines in the published trade union discussion. The latter is generally rather "sterile":

(a) The need for economic and social councils is derived almost automatically in three logical steps; the disadvantaged position of the trade unions requires forms of supra-factory co-determination; the existing forms have been deficient; therefore the trade unions must demand ESCs, which permit a comprehensive influence and facilitate the implementation of trade union objectives.

(b) Just as this "automatism" is unquestioned, so too are the implications of ESCs for inner-organisational development and union policy. For Otto, these are rather desirable limitations; but Kaltenborn also fails to qualify his argument. For example, he argues that the ESCs' "publicity principle" gives a chance for the trade unions to mobilise social pressure, but does not mention the danger of an additional public and state pressure on the trade unions. That an institutional strategy potentially works against a mobilisation strategy goes unnoticed.

(c) No absolutely essential basic guidelines were set for establishing the ESCs. Thus experiences with Concerted Action were not applied in a positive manner. Generally, the question as to how ESCs are to be politically implemented is still unanswered. When, in 1977, the SPD disappointed trade union hopes for ESCs again, this did not lead to an open, critical debate.

Institutional Strategies for Trade Union Participation:

PARTICIPATION OR AN INCORPORATION OF TRADE UNIONS?

The Dominance of an Institutional Strategy

The three cases discussed above confirm that West German trade unions certainly cannot be regarded as mere "objects" of integration. It is not the institutional strategy as such, which is noteworthy, as it is a feature of supra-factory co-determination; noteworthy is rather its dominance in the thought and action of the unions (for a more detailed account of the three cases cf. Kastendiek et al. 1981). The institutional strategy has almost become an end in itself: for example, in 1977, E. Loderer did not want to rule out further participation in Concerted Action because the demand for economic and social councils would otherwise be discredited. The institutional strategy is to be realised by means of an institutional policy, although the former was justified by the shortcomings of the latter. Inadequate implementation of union objectives is never considered as a possible consequence of the institutional strategy; but it serves again and again as a justification for this form of politics (cf. the above-mentioned "automatism" of the demands). To criticise institutional strategies in general and as such would be foolish: "To set to work, using institutional means, where power is exercised; power from which wage- and salary-earners are dependent" is certainly necessary (Mitbestimmung 1971: 570). The problem is how to define premisses on which this principle is, or ought to be, implemented and the priority it assumes in the overall strategy. Even approaches which regard the unions as an "oppositional force" (Gegenmacht), do not see institutions of supra-factory co-determination as the products of the mobilisation of social pressure, but as a pre-condition for such mobilisation.

After 1966 the unions evidently believed that social pressure was not even necessary for the implementation of their objectives: the entry of the SPD into the government finally seemed to open the door into institutions "where power is exercised". Two lines can be observed in union discussions here: one stated its confidence in the party and expected the SPD to take over and implement trade union ideas. The other manifested attitudes ranging from scepticism to rejection and feared negative effects of the emerging politics of compromise of the CDU-CSU-SPD government from 1966 to 1969 (cf. Hella Kastendiek 1978: 40 ff.). Different political opinions resulted from these two lines: on the one hand, general support of the coalition's policy, above all of those elements which were formulated and represented essentially by the SPD (i. e. the "new economic policy") and, on the other hand, an emphasis on the limits of politics for wage- and salary-earners in and through an SPD which had become a "people's party". The latter line gave rise to demands which even extended to calling for a wage- and salary-earners' wing in the SPD. Both lines embody institutional strategies: the first relies on the governmental policy of the SPD; the second on the possibility of realising union ideas by exercising influence within the party.

When Concerted Action in particular proved that confidence in the SPD had been "misplaced" and scepticism justified, discussion within the unions moved for a time in the direction of the second 'line'. This was a "precarious" situation:

- Criticism of the policies of the SPD in government endangered the established form of party-trade union relationship (although its general existence was not challenged).
- Social Democratic trade unionists - especially at the middle and lower levels - introduced this criticism into the party where it became a "factor of disturbance".
- Criticism in individual unions was also directed against their executive boards and the support they gave for Concerted Action, which profoundly affected internal power relationships.
- Diverging discussions in the individual unions over governmental policy and union participation in Concerted Action threatened the structures for compromise in the DGB.

In this situation, rejection of the Concerted Action and the form of Social Democratic economic policy which it represented would have had a demonstrative effect and incalculable consequences for the party, the unions, and the relationship between them. For the unions, it would have meant above all an open confession of the failure of their institutional strategy - which would have led inevitably to the discussion of union strategy as a whole. Therefore, criticism "had to be" repressed. On the one hand, the significance of the Concerted Action and the orientation data was played down, in order to counter the criticism; and on the other hand, this criticism was parried with demands for more efficient institutions of trade union participation. Thus, the concept of institutional strategy was "saved". The demands for economic and social councils, which were renewed parallel to the experience with the Concerted Action and which intensified between 1969 and 1971, are thus related to the intra-union discussions just described. Even the boycott of Concerted Action since 1977 was justified in the same way: a better form of the body was necessary. The cessation of union participation only really became possible when the entrepreneurs' appealed the Co-determination Act to the Federal Constitutional Court. This enabled unions to withdraw without their withdrawal being interpreted as a protest against Social Democratic policy.

The SPD was "spared" again when it became clear that the demands for economic and social councils lacked any chance of being put into practice. Some unions - just as after the experiences with the Concerted Action - spoke about the need for relying on "our own power". This was not to be achieved by means of a non-institutional political strategy, however, but by means of improved co-ordination of trade union politics at various levels - that is, by making the trade unions more effective as institutions. The general institutional strategy was not modified, let alone abandoned; some of the demands emanating from it were simply deferred for the time being.

Partial Corporatism in the West German Trade Unions

The patterns of trade union thought and behaviour originating from the unions' fixation with an institutional strategy lead us to the theses of a partial incorporation of the West German trade unions and of a partial corporatism in their politics. We do not speak of total incorporation or a comprehensive corporatism of union politics because both can only develop within the framework of general co-operation between the state, capital and the trade unions. The unions have offered this co-operation, but it has been refused by the state as well as the entrepreneurs. The unions try to use such co-operation as has been conceded to them (which is only partial, limited to specific issues, and determined by the economic conjuncture) as a route to attaining general co-operation.

This gradualist approach to co-operation proved to be a mechanism whereby the unions put forward concessions but did not receive the reciprocal concessions they expected. Thus their political reasoning seems to correspond only superficially to the exchange thesis in the theoretical discussions of "bargained corporatism" supposedly based on consensual co-operation and inevitably bringing advantages for all participants. The institutional strategy of the West German unions certainly contains the theory of exchange: rights to participate in the formulation of socio-economic objectives and policy decisions in exchange for the willingness to give joint backing and support to economic and social policy and wage-bargaining policy in the light of macro-economic-data; wage restraint in exchange for social improvements; joint formulation of assessments and perspectives for economic and social change in exchange for regard for a political consensus. But this logic of exchange has three central weak points. In the parlance of "trade"; first there is bargaining with different goods - participation versus explicit recognition of its framework. Second, there is a non-simultaneous exchange - the offer of co-operation already embodies this recognition; the price is paid before the reciprocal concession has been delivered. Third, the unions have no means of obtaining reciprocal concessions because their institutional strategy excludes the mobilisation of social pressure as a political instrument. Threatening gestures are useless, since the state and management know that attempts to mobilise this pressure will actually occur rarely. Why, then, should they return concessions?

Comprehensive and comprehensively organised and institutionalised tripartite co-operation is not in the interest of

- the state bureaucracy, which has confidence in its established rights and instruments of steering and intervention;
- the bourgeois parties, which put their faith in other strategies for regulating industrial relations (cf. Alemann and Heinze 1979 and Hans Kastendiek 1980: 98-103);
- the entrepreneurs, who reject the idea of a "secondary economic constitution", especially as the "necessary talks between the parties involved in economic life" can "also be held without institutionalisation" - as had regularly happened since 1948 (Triesch 1971: 542 and 537; Muehlbradt and Lutz 1969);
- the SPD, whose commitment to moderation of social developments and conflicts by the state depends on continuing flexibility in its co-operation with the social groups (cf. Hans Kastendiek 1980: 101 f.).

It is in the interests of these actors, however, to meet the trade unions' wishes far enough for them either to realise their institutional strategy partially or to present it as realisable. Thus, while they are not conceded any rights of co-decision-making, they are conceded information and advisory rights, in particular when the economic policy problems make partial consideration of union demands for participation advisable.

Thus, although only a "lame partnership" (Leminsky's description of the Concerted Action [1971: 606]) has developed, the unions fulfil their offer, just as if the reciprocal concessions had been yielded or essential steps taken towards them. Bargaining over institutional participation takes place with and in the existing institutions. As the unions' "bargaining power" does not derive from a policy of mobilisation, it can then be derived only from the readiness of its members and wage- and salary-earners to follow them. Securing this readiness within the unions becomes the pre-condition for the success of the institutional strategy. It is no accident, then, that, since the end of the 1960s (that is, since the discussion of the experience with Concerted Action and after the 1969 strikes), tendencies towards centralisation and disciplining of dissident members in intra-trade-union politics have increased. The logic of a gradualist approach to co-operation dictates that the unions' ability to engage in co-operation must be continually re-affirmed; politics becomes a dependent variable of the institutional strategy, instead of vice versa. The difficulty of securing this co-operation when union demands are not fulfilled becomes an argument in the bargaining process: the state and entrepreneurs should see that their unco-operative behaviour might endanger the "social peace". The expansion of union participation becomes a pre-condition for the stability of the present order, which is thus confirmed and propagated as a framework for political orientation.

In this way, the unions are endowed with functions of intermediation between the leadership and mass levels of societal organisation which complement "classical" forms of representation and domination. The partial corporatism found in the politics of the West German trade unions has made them "intermediary organisations" between the central institutions of economic and social policy-making and wage- and salary-earners.

ECONOMIC CRISIS AND POLITICAL CHANGE: WITHDRAWAL OF INSTITUTIONAL STRATEGIES?

Union policies might be expected to undergo considerable reorientation in response to the current social political and economic situation. The situation is characterised in particular by the following features: persisting economic crisis, the effects of a continuing high level of unemployment, growing conflicts over social distribution, experience of being unable to control the technological revolution and its consequences, and shifts in political majorities. But we are confronted with a seemingly paradoxical situation, in which, although the institutional strategy of the unions has been seen to fail, this strategy is nevertheless still being pursued and reaffirmed.

The Foundering of the Institutional Strategy

The loss of hegemony of the SPD meant that even before the government changeover in the autumn of 1982, the unions had in effect already lost their most sympathetic audience at state level in the fields they had been active in for years, namely economic, financial and employment policies. The traditional policy of representation of union interests via the SPD was subjected to considerable stress within the unions when the SPD introduced its market-oriented policy of modernisation and economy in the mid-seventies (Hoffmann, 1982) in response to the changed economic situation. Since 1980, the relationship between the SPD and the unions had been increasingly subjected to stress by measures which reversed previously achieved social reforms and by the budgetary measures of the Social Democratic-Liberal coalition.

For the first time union protest was openly voiced against the government, and particularly against the SPD (DGB demonstration in Baden-Wuerttemberg in 1981). And yet the unions continued to strive for changes in economic and employment policies by conducting talks with the government, Bundestag fractions and management. The employment programme published at the beginning of 1982 was proclaimed as a "common initiative", but it fell far short of the demands of the unions. Initially it eased the pressure from the middle and lower levels of the unions, i. e. it seemed to be a device to secure the unions' general consent to the 'governmental functions' of the Social Democrats and to their concept of societal formation (Zeuner, 1983). But this strategy was pushed to its limits when in the 1983 budget discussions, the confrontation course of the FDP (Free Democratic Party) completely removed the SPD's narrow remaining margin for economic and socio-political manoeuvre. As part of the governing coalition, the SPD no longer thought the country could continue to afford an employment programme, and increasingly questioned the wiseness of this method of overcoming the crisis. Meanwhile the FDP in government had completely dismissed any policy which incorporated class compromise, and explicitly rejected any influential role of the unions. Only then, when the SPD had lost all bargaining power within the coalition and with the unions, and the party itself had become embroiled in a severe identity crisis, did the unions distance themselves from the SPD. They did not want to get drawn into the downward spiral of the SPD and put further stress on the ability of their own organisations to integrate. So in autumn 1982, the unions called for demonstrations against the policies of the Social Democratic-Liberal coalition government.

For almost 16 years the SPD had been able to incorporate the unions into their government policies by setting up negotiating structures, and had subjugated them to the specifically Social Democratic concept of a policy of state-moderated "modernisation of the economy". But as the economic crisis worsened, relations between the unions and the SPD were put to a severe test. The SPD found it had increasingly less room for economic manoeuvre, and was thus increasingly less willing to grant concessions to the unions or to allow them a chance of partial influence in policy formulation. On the one hand the SPD intensified its formal and informal negotiating structures with the unions, but, on the other hand, the material content of these negotiating structures became less and less substantial. The SPD was unable to offer sociopolitical improvements or a role in policy decisions. Apparently the SPD tried to instrumentalise the unions by binding them into negotiating structures without a material exchange (as decisions to be executed had already been laid down in precise detail).

Thus the role of the unions has changed from that of an actor with partial participation in the decision making process, to that of a mere guarantor for decisions taken outside their jurisdiction, in the course of social democratic government policy making. This has exacerbated not only the differences in and among the unions of the DGB, but also inner-party controversy. Conflicts within the party and between the party and the unions began to be more important than conflicts between capital and labour. A majority expressed the view that the two organisations are still following the same line, and some parts of the unions were even prepared, in the absence of any alternative, to take on the political role they were offered. However, a minority view was also heard, emphasising the vast distance between the party in government and the true party base, and urging the unions to grasp "their own power" again. This minority did not fundamentally call into question the institutional strategy as the dominant means of policy control by the unions on a national level. But it was also apparent that attempts were being made to define the content of restrictions on co-operation more precisely.

Although the institutional strategy of the unions actually failed, and even the SPD's policy of involving the unions met its match with the stress of trying to overcome the economic crisis, this policy had nevertheless made an important contribution towards socio-political restabilisation. In particular it had considerable long-term effects. The Social Democratic party in government in Western Germany is, unlike any other party in government, fundamentally obliged to incorporate union interests in its policies because of the complex organisational and personal links with the unions. Had the unions not provided their support as a mass organisation, the massive increases in the numbers of unemployed, far-reaching dismantling of social service structures, and an incomes policy advocating redistribution in the face of a fall in real wages could not possibly have been borne politically by the government without growing class conflict and a crisis of state legitimacy. But the increasing discrepancy between (a) the concept of a worker-oriented policy and (b) a government policy which was effectively an austerity policy overwhelmed the ability of the party and the unions to integrate their various demands. This led to increased inner-party conflict and to a partial loss of unity in and among the unions. They separated into government-siding and government-distancing organisations, and there were also fractions within the organisations. Intra-organisational consensus was no longer guaranteed.

A policy of institutional strategy characterised by the dominance of an Ordnungspolitik inevitably disorientates and weakens the solidarity of its members in the longer term. The loss of hegemony of union and political labour organisations has been considerably aided by a number of features: acceptance of the conditions laid down by capitalist society as a prerequisite to any participation in bargaining, abandonment of the theory that the economic crisis and mass unemployment are immanent features of the capitalist policy of restructuring, and surrender of the policy of developing collective strategies and social alternatives.

Institutional Strategies for Trade Union Participation:

Reaffirmation of the Institutional Strategy

Although the return of the SPD to the opposition meant that the institutional strategy of the unions had in fact failed, the change of government in this conjuncture did contribute to the fact that no broader internal debate ensued among the unions on possible changes in their policies. The anti-union stance of the new government, and the re-orientation of the SPD towards the unions masked the failures of earlier policy strategies and gave union leadership more room for manoeuvre when faced with criticism from within its own ranks. It also took some of the pressure off relationships between the various unions within the DGB. The DGB's structures for accommodating compromise had already been severely taxed and were partly in danger of collapsing completely as a result of the varying degrees of support extended to the government during the final years of the SPD-FDP coalition. The end of the SPD as a party in government, where the unions had been on the receiving end of policies, meant the end of the unions' specific function as mediator between state policy and the labour force. Even before this, although there had been some criticism within and among the unions, the institutional strategy had never been fundamentally challenged as a dominant political factor. Thus the fact that the SPD was no longer responsible for government meant that union strategies could continue.

The first sign of this continuity was the unions' willingness to enter negotiations with the new conservative-liberal coalition, whilst outwardly expressing protest at the government's economic and financial policies. They hardly had any choice since they had oriented themselves for so long towards the government wing of the SPD and thus had been incorporated relatively successfully into state policies during the 16 years of the SPD-FDP coalition (Zeuner, 1976 and 1983). However, although the unions declared themselves willing to negotiate, and presented themselves as guarantors of the social consensus, the new government rejected any form of participation. This course of confrontation with the unions gained strength from the increasing disorientation and loss of solidarity in the current crisis. In turn populist politics were employed to try and win union members over to government policies as "individuals" rather than as class-conscious workers. The position of the unions was by now so weak that the CDU/CSU-FDP coalition did not need to associate itself with corporative policy patterns: it was now possible to create and stabilise social consensus by direct contact with the masses and to by-pass the unions. Neo-conservative strategies operate on various levels (legislation, wage policies, industrial law, etc.) to bring about decisive shifts in social power to the benefit of management. The government intervenes directly in wage disputes on behalf of the employer; it also takes steps to bring critical unions into disrepute and to isolate them. It appears that the unions have largely relinquished their function as an "intermediary organisation" at state level.

But the new coalition's rejection of a role for the unions certainly does not mean the end of the institutional strategy. From its position as a party in opposition, the SPD drew up a new plan for union integration, and re-established communications with the unions. Thereby they hoped to open up the prospect of a new form of common, institutionally anchored policy in preparation for a government of the future. Even the mass demonstration in the autumn of 1982, actually planned as a protest against the SPD-FDP coalition, allowed the unions and the SPD to stand shoulder to shoulder (Schulterschluss) again. Both the party and the unions took advantage of the solidarity produced both within and around the party by the passage of the SPD into the opposition; and they both joined in criticism of the conservative-liberal coalition government.

The strategies of the SPD in opposition aim to reintegrate the majority behind the defeated social democratic-liberal coalition. They attach particular importance to re-establishing the links between the party and the unions. The programmes for economic, employment and technological policies (cf. Hella Kastendiek, 1984) drawn up since then make use of the strategies and negotiating perspectives of the earlier Social Democratic concept of a "people's party". Likewise the 1983 election programme reformulated the concept of a state-sponsored structural policy for modernising the national economy and a "solidarity pact against unemployment". The objective is a new type of link with the unions when the SPD returns to government. Thus the SPD is the only party which offers the unions a role in state policies and gives open political recognition to its contribution to "social peace".

This development helps to explain why there has so far been no broader discussion of the possible re-orientation of union policies. Lothar Zimmermann, a leading functionary in the DGB, nonetheless claims that the DGB is considering a fundamental re-orientation of the means of union struggle. If the "strategy of argument" practised for decades no longer brings results, the DGB must elaborate "strategies of mobilisation". The unions must now "under certain circumstances" relinquish their traditional role of partner and participant in societal transformation - including legislation on co-determination and wage agreements (Frankfurter Rundschau, 15. 12. 83). But it must be assumed that negotiating patterns will mainly follow the old "strategy of argument", even if the unions are temporarily excluded from socio-political decision-making. After the government change-over, both the unions and the SPD called for new "initiatives on co-determination". They stressed the importance of comprehensive development of co-determination rights for employees at all social levels if the economic crisis and the expected consequences of the technological revolution are to be managed in a manner acceptable to society. Both the unions and the SPD see co-determination as the key to socially acceptable handling of the technological revolution. But so far there are no concrete concepts beyond these general postulates.

The arguments to date nonetheless indicate contrasting views on the strategic value of co-determination for the purpose of social steering of technological development. Once again we find both the Ordnungspolitik and power-analytic arguments noted in the context of economic and social councils. The notion of Ordnungspolitik particularly stresses the <u>process</u> of social steering and locates it within the framework of changed demands for national and international adaptation and restructuring. The extension of co-determination is again seen as a stabilising factor in the present social order, since it can help guarantee the social consensus necessary for continued development. The power-analytic version argues for furthering and protecting the interests of those employees who are affected by technological innovations.

As in the past, however, there is no open discussion between the two sides on the position of co-determination. All groups are demanding extension of co-determination, and this could actually prove to be the factor which holds them all together. For this demand would considerably restrict controversy within the SPD and within the unions and contribute in particular towards stabilising the closer co-operation (Schulterschluss) between the two bodies. This is particularly feasible because there is little likelihood again that these demands can actually be pushed through. This new co-determination may not heed previous experience concerning the feasibility of enacting these traditional demands, but then neither does it discuss the old strategy of socio-political representation of interests. Thus the new co-determination concept not only diverts attention from the examination of earlier - failed - strategies, it also reinforces the traditional domination of the institutional strategy of recognition of interests on a macro-economic level. Demands which are offered as alternatives or which exceed the demands of co-determination (e.g. socialisation, direct control of investment) are blocked off by stressing the union's concept of a socially controlled development of technology through a comprehensive extension of the rights of co-determination. Only a small, but nevertheless firmly rooted, minority in the unions sees a "chance for a successful union policy for 'socially tolerable technological development' .... by organising resistance in the factories and 'making it a publicly effective movement'" (Frankfurter Rundschau, 11.2.84, quoting S. Bleicher, member of the General Council of the DGB).

So far, however, there has been no stocktaking or general reflection on union policy, and no discussion of new strategies and concepts for furthering union interests. The "mature" internal organisational structures and power situations and the ties of the unions to the SPD remain untouched. It remains to be seen whether the unions can simply stand idly by until their proposals for national socio-economic policies can be met by a new SPD government, or whether the anti-union policies of the current government will in fact provoke a reaction before that time. But then it might transpire that unions have lost much of their internal legitimation and ability to mobilise in these fields - in contrast to the situation with wages policy. If this happens, it will presumably only serve once more to "confirm" the institutional strategy.

REFERENCES*)

Adam, H. 1972: Die Konzertierte Aktion (...), Koeln

Alemann, U. v. and R.G. Heinze, (eds.), 1979: Verbaende und Staat, Opladen

Bergmann, J., O. Jacobi and W. Mueller-Jentsch 1975: Gewerkschaften in der Bundesrepublik, Frankfurt - Koeln

Bispinck, R. and K. Wilhelm 1977: Krise der Sozialpartnerschaft. Die "Kommission fuer wirtschaftlichen und sozialen Wandel" (...), in: Blaetter fuer deutsche und internationale Politik, 2/77, pp. 141-149

Brenner, O. 1967: Kooperation aus gewerkschaftlicher Sicht,

Bad Godesberg (Rationalisierungskongress des RKW)
Bretschneider, J. 1969: Lohnpolitik und Konzertierte Aktion-der Standpunkt der Arbeitgeberverbaende, in: GM 6/69, pp. 329-337
Crouch, C. 1983: Pluralism and the New Corporatism: A Rejoinder, in: Political Studies, vol. 31 no. 3, pp. 452-462
Esser, J. 1982: Gewerkschaften in der Krise, Frankfurt
Esser, J. and W. Fach 1979: Dann waere das "Modell Deutschland" ernsthaft in Frage gestellt, in: Frankfurter Rundschau, 14.12.1979, p. 10
Gewerkschaftlich kommentierter Kurzbericht: Wirtschaftlicher und sozialer Wandel in der Bundesrepublik Deutschland. Gewerkschaftlich kommentierte Kurzfassung des Berichts der "Kommission fuer wirtschaftlichen und sozialen Wandel", Schriftenreihe der IG Metall Nr. 73
Gutachten 1977: Wirtschaftlicher und sozialer Wandel in der Bundesrepublik Deutschland, Goettingen
Henschel, R. 1967: Konzertierte Aktion - Autonomie und Planung, in: GM 4/67, pp. 200-206
Henschel, R. 1969: Gewerkschaften am Scheideweg, in: GM 4/69, pp. 215-220
Hoffmann, J. 1982: "Das Ende der Fahnenstange" - Sozialdemokratie und keynesianischer Klassenkompromiss in der Bundesrepublik, in: Prokla 49, pp. 9-30
Hofmann, G. 1980: Die Handschrift des Kanzlers. Helmut Schmidt sucht den Rueckhalt von Unternehmern und Gewerkschaftern, in: Die Zeit, 8.8.1980, p. 3
Kaltenborn, W. 1971: Ueber die Notwendigkeit gesamtwirtschaftlicher Mitbestimmung, in: GM 9/71, pp. 521-535
Kaltenborn, W. 1973: Probleme gesamtwirtschaftlicher Mitbestimmung, in: GM 10/73, pp. 634-643
Kastendiek, Hans 1980: Neokorporativismus? in: Prokla 38, pp. 81-106
Kastendiek, Hans 1981: Die Selbstblockierung der Korporatismus-Diskussion, in: U. v. Alemann, (ed.), Neokorporatismus, Frankfurt - New York, pp. 92-116
Kastendiek, Hans, Hella Kastendiek and H. Reister 1981: Inkorporierung der Gewerkschaften? in: Alternative Wirtschaftspolitik 3, Argument-Sonderband 68, Berlin, pp. 144-177

*) GM = Gewerkschaftliche Monatshefte (periodical of the German Trade Union Federation)

Institutional Strategies for Trade Union Participation:

Kastendiek, Hella 1978: Arbeitnehmer in der SPD. Herausbildung und Funktion der Arbeitsgemeinschaft fuer Arbeitnehmerfragen (AfA), Berlin

Kastendiek, Hella 1984: Struktur- und Organisationsprobleme einer staatstragenden Arbeitnehmerpartei. Zum Verhaeltnis von SPD und Gewerkschaften seit 1966, in: R. Ebbighausen and F. Tiemann, (eds.), Das Ende der Arbeiterbewegung in Deutschland? Opladen, pp. 407-442

Lecher, W. 1977: Die Gewerkschaften und die Kommission fuer wirtschaftlichen und sozialen Wandel - ein Lehrstueck? in: WSI-Mitteilungen 3/77

Leminksy, G. 1971: Aufgaben ueberbetrieblicher Mitbestimmung, in: GM 10/71, pp. 602-611

Leminsky, G. 1977: Grundfragen ueberbetrieblicher Mitbestimmung, in: GM 12/77, pp. 716-725

Loderer, E. 1979: Die konzertierte Aktion in ihrer bisherigen Form ist entbehrlich, in: Der Gewerkschafter 5/79

Markmann, H. 1967: Gewerkschaften und Wirtschaftsplanung, in: Gewerkschaftl. Umschau 9/67, pp. 185-187

Mitbestimmung 1971: Beschluss "Mitbestimmung im gesamtwirtschaftlichen Bereich" des DGB-Bundesausschusses, in: GM 9/71, pp. 569-575

Muehlbradt, W. and E. Lutz 1969: Der Zwang zur Sozialpartnerschaft, Neuwied - Berlin

Mueller-Jentsch, W. 1976: Zum Verhaeltnis von Staat und Gewerkschaften, in: C. Pozzoli, (ed.), Rahmenbedingungen und Schranken staatlichen Handelns, Frankfurt, pp. 150-155

Otto, B. 1971: Gewerkschaftliche Konzeptionen ueberbetrieblicher Mitbestimmung, Koeln

Piel, D. 1979: Des Kanzlers diskrete Runde, in: Die Zeit, 23.11.1979, p. 27

Schlecht, O. 1968: Konzertierte Aktion als Instrument der Wirtschaftspolitik, Tuebingen

Schmidt, E. 1976: Grenzen staatlicher Intervention in den Prozess der Klassenauseinandersetzungen, in: C. Pozzoli, (ed.), Rahmenbedingungen und Schranken staatlichen Handelns, Frankfurt, pp. 143-149

Seitenzahl, R. 1974: Einkommenspolitik durch Konzertierte Aktion und Orientierungsdaten, Koeln

Seitenzahl, R. 1976: Gewerkschaften zwischen Kooperation und Konflikt, Frankfurt - Koeln

Triesch, G. 1971: Keine wirtschaftsdemokratische Sekundaerverfassung, in: GM 9/71, pp. 535-542

Zeuner, B. 1976: "Solidaritaet" mit der SPD oder Solidaritaet der Klasse? Zur SPD-Bindung der DGB-Gewerkschaften, in: Prokla 26, pp. 3-32

Zeuner, B. 1983: SPD-Bindung der Gewerkschaften - krisenfest? in: B. Zeuner, (ed.), Genossen, was nun? Bilanz und Perspektiven sozialdemokratischer Politik, Hamburg, pp. 91-115

NOTES ON CONTRIBUTORS

Elmar Altvater is Professor of Political Economy in the Political Science Faculty of the Free University of Berlin. Has published books and articles on marxist state theory, crisis theory, the world market, and trade unions. Currently working on international monetary and credit relations and on the relation between real and monetary accumulation.

Mimmo Carrieri is a research fellow of the CRS Institute in Rome. He has published articles on industrial relations and neo-corporatism in various readers and journals, including *Stato e Mercato*, *Democrazia e Diritto*, and *Problemi del Socialismo*.

Gian Primo Cella is Professor of Theory of Trade Unions and Social Conflict and Director of the Institute of Political Science at the University of Trieste. He is the author of *Divisione del lavoro e iniziativa operaia* (1976) and has edited *Il movimento degli scioperi nel XX secolo* (1979) and (with T. Treu) *Relazioni industriali* (1984).

Colin Crouch is Reader in Sociology at the London School of Economics. He has written extensively on industrial relations, trade unions, and corporatism. His publications include *Class Conflict and the Industrial Relations Crisis* (1977), *The Politics of Industrial Relations* (1982), *Trade Unions: the Logic of Collective Action* (1982), and (with Alessandro Pizzorno) *The Resurgence of Class Conflict in Western Europe* (1978).

Mario Dal Co is a senior research fellow of IRES-CGIL in Rome. He has published in political economy journals and national newspapers as well as contributing to readers on economic policy and labour market issues.

Carlo Donolo teaches political sociology at the University of Salerno. He is the author of *Mutamento o transizione?*

(1977) and is co-editor (with F. Fichera) of Il governo debole (1981).

Kurt Huebner is an economist who works as Editor of the social science journal PROKLA. Has published on crisis theory, unions, and alternative economic strategies. Currently working on long-term economic developmental tendencies and problems of the international monetary and credit systems.

Richard Hyman is Reader in Industrial Relations at the University of Warwick. He works in the Industrial Relations Research Unit and has completed many studies of strikes, industrial relations, and shop stewards. His books include Industrial Relations (1975), Strikes (1977), and (with Ian Brough) Social Values and Industrial Relations (1975).

Otto Jacobi is a Research Officer at the Institute for Social Research in Frankfurt. His research on economic development and economic policy focuses on the theory and politics of trade unions and the functions of industrial relations systems.

Bob Jessop lectures in politics at the University of Essex. His research interests include state theory, corporatism, postwar British political economy, and Thatcherism. His publications include The Capitalist State (1982) and Nicos Poulantzas (1985). His current research concerns the Thatcher and Kohl governments in Britain and West Germany.

Hans Kastendiek lectured at the Free University of Berlin until 1982 and has since been a Research Officer at the Institute for Social Research in Frankfurt. He has worked on the development of political science in West Germany, on state theory, and on corporatism.

Hella Kastendiek is a Research Officer at the Central Institute for social science research at the Free University of Berlin. She is working on the development of the SDP in West Germany and its relations with trade unions.

Ulrich Mueckenberger is Professor of Labour Law at the University of Bremen. His principal research interests comprise labour and welfare law, industrial relations, and social policy.

Paolo Perulli is a Research Fellow at the University of Venice and Director of the IRES-CGIL in Rome. He has edited (with B. Trentin) Il sindacato nella recessione (1983), co-authored (with M. Cacciari) Piano economico e composizione di classe (1975), and has written various articles on industrial relations.

Hugo Reister is a Research Officer at the Central Institute for social science research at the Free University of Berlin. His principal research interest is trade unionism.

Marino Regini teaches sociology at the University of Milan and comparative politics at Johns Hopkins University in Bologna. He edits the journal *Stato e mercato*. He has published *I dilemmi del sindacato* (1981) and has contributed to several books in Italian and English.

Michael Stanger is a research officer in the political science Faculty of the Free University at Berlin. He has worked on state theory, labour market theory, and alternative economic policies. His current research concerns technological development and long-term developmental tendencies in the economy.

Tiziano Treu is Professor of Labour Law in the University of Pavia and President of the Italian Industrial Relations Association (AISRI). His books include: *L'Uso politico dello Statuto dei lavoratori* (1975), *I sindacati in Italia dal '45 a oggi* (1981), and (co-edited with G. Cella) *Relazioni industriali* (1984).

LIST OF TRANSLATORS

Author:	Translated by:
Elmar Altvater, Kurt Huebner, Michael Stanger	Hans-Juergen Meinderink
Marino Regini	Martin Slater
Otto Jacobi	Doug Webber and Hans-Juergen Meinderink
Mario Dal Co, Paolo Perulli	Susan Fisher
Gian Primo Cella, Tiziano Treu	Susan Fisher
Mimmo Carrieri, Carlo Donolo	Susan Fisher
Otto Jacobi	Doug Webber and Hans-Juergen Meinderink
Ulrich Mueckenberger	Isobel M. Barnden
Hans Kastendiek, Hella Kastendiek, Hugo Reister	Doug Webber, Isobel M. Barnden

INDEX

For Product Safety Concerns and Information please contact our EU representative GPSR@taylorandfrancis.com
Taylor & Francis Verlag GmbH, Kaufingerstraße 24, 80331 München, Germany

www.ingramcontent.com/pod-product-compliance
Lightning Source LLC
LaVergne TN
LVHW010619300926
849162LV00001B/5
* 9 7 8 1 0 3 2 3 9 3 2 1 6 *